A Discourse

upon the
Exposicion & Understandinge of Statutes
With Sir Thomas Egerton's Additions

Edited from Manuscripts in the Huntington Library
by
SAMUEL E. THORNE
Northwestern University School of Law

THE LAWBOOK EXCHANGE, LTD.
Clark, New Jersey

ISBN 978-1-58477-355-9

Lawbook Exchange edition 2003, 2017

The quality of this reprint is equivalent to the quality of the original work.

THE LAWBOOK EXCHANGE, LTD.
33 Terminal Avenue
Clark, New Jersey 07066-1321

*Please see our website for a selection of our other publications
and fine facsimile reprints of classic works of legal history:*
www.lawbookexchange.com

Library of Congress Cataloging-in-Publication Data

A discourse upon the exposicion & understandinge of statutes: with Sir
Thomas Egerton's additions: edited from manuscripts in the Huntington
Library / by Samuel E. Thorne
     p. cm.
   Originally published: San Marino, Calif. : Huntington Library, 1942.
   Includes bibliographical references and index.
   ISBN 1-58477-355-3 (cloth: alk. paper)
    1. Law—England—Interpretation and construction. 2. Statutes—
England. I. Title: Discourse upon the exposicion and understandinge of
statutes. II. Thome, Samuel Edmund, 1907- III. Egerton, Thomas, Sir,
1540?-1617. IV. Henry E. Huntington Library
   and Art Gallery

KD691.D57 2003
348.42'022—dc21   2003047457

Printed in the United States of America on acid-free paper

A Discourse

upon the
Exposicion & Understandinge of Statutes
With Sir Thomas Egerton's Additions

Edited from Manuscripts in the Huntington Library
by
SAMUEL E. THORNE
Northwestern University School of Law

San Marino, California
HUNTINGTON LIBRARY
1942

Anderson & Ritchie: The Ward Ritchie Press
Los Angeles, California, U.S.A.

PREFACE

To LAWYERS and historians, alike, the earliest treatise yet brought to light on the interpretation of statutes in England cannot fail to be of interest. No extended apology need be made, therefore, for printing the *Discourse upon the Exposicion & Understandinge of Statutes* from two copies—both written early in Elizabeth's reign—among the Ellesmere manuscripts in the Huntington Library. In an attempt to place the *Discourse* in perspective, however, I have prefaced it by an introduction for which a word of justification is necessary. To write a detailed account of statutory interpretation in England from the fourteenth to the seventeenth century is obviously impossible in the space an editor may properly claim, and the reader will discover that I have sketched that history only in bold outline. He will find himself provided with nothing more than a rough contour map which marks the plain and the mountain range but leaves the approaches relatively unexplored. In addition, since the subject occupies the borderland between legal and constitutional history—a terrain that presents the difficulties characteristic of each—it is well to add that the climber in such territory cannot help but be conscious that possibilities of dangerous error and chances for fatal misjudgments have increased at least twofold.

The present volume represents the first fruits of an extended examination of Lord Ellesmere's manuscripts, made possible by the generosity of the Trustees of the Huntington Library. Much of the work was done while I was an Associate Member of the Research Staff there during the summers of 1937-39. I have had the advantage of discussing many of the problems raised by the *Discourse* with Professor Charles H. McIlwain, whose interest has at all times been most helpful.

[v]

Professor Theodore F. T. Plucknett, to whom it is usual for me to appeal for aid which is always forthcoming, read an early transcript of the text and saved it some errors. Mr. H. G. Richardson, Professor Harold C. Havighurst, and the late Professor Hermann Kantorowicz kindly answered questions that I put to them. I am deeply indebted as well to Captain R. B. Haselden and Mr. Herbert C. Schulz for a painstaking reading of my final text against the manuscripts. Professors Edwin F. Gay and Godfrey Davies examined with care and offered valuable comments on the introduction, as did Mr. Homer D. Crotty. To Dr. Max Farrand, Director of Research at the Huntington Library, I am very grateful for constant friendship and generous assistance in numberless ways. Miss Dorothy Scarborough, of Northwestern University Law School, bore the many retypings of the book with remarkable and admirable equanimity. Finally, it is very pleasant to acknowledge the courtesy and kindness of the Huntington Library staff.

S. E. T.

Chicago, Illinois
May, 1941

CONTENTS

[vii]

Introduction

INTRODUCTION

THOUGH much has been written on the interpretation of statutes in the Year Books, in a very real sense the history of statutory interpretation begins in the sixteenth century, after the Year Books had come to a close and the great outburst of legislation that marks the reign of Henry VIII had been concluded. It was only then that statutes began to occupy a position roughly comparable to that which they hold today and that judges first became conscious that in restricting the words of an act, in the interests of justice, or in extending them to include equally deserving but unmentioned cases, they were performing something more than an incidental, routine function of judicial administration. Long custom condones the use of the word 'interpretation' to describe the actions with respect to legislation of fourteenth- and sixteenth-century judges alike, and the history of statutory interpretation distinguishes them only in so far as they vary in scope, but the increased necessity for reconciling the words of acts of Parliament and the simple administration of justice between party and party that faced the judges of the later period sets their practice off sharply from that which had preceded it. The juridical and constitutional questions latent in the application of statute law, though not yet acute, were becoming sufficiently manifest to change the courts' treatment of legislation into a practice to which the term 'interpretation' is properly applicable, and it is in no sense accidental that the word is first commonly used in the sixteenth century to describe the judicial handling of statutes. But the elements which thus complicated the function of judges in Elizabeth's reign by compelling them to preserve a progressively difficult balance between justice in individual cases and the dictates of an

3

authoritative Parliament had not troubled to an equal degree
their predecessors on the bench. It is, consequently, almost
completely in the reflected light of the sixteenth and later
centuries that the acts of Year Book judges in connection with
legislation have taken on the appearance of a like process
carried on under essentially similar circumstances. Or, to view
the matter from another side, that the rules of statutory interpretation formulated in the sixteenth century in response
to an emerging sovereignty were, like all new developments
in the common law, drawn from the old books, must not be
taken as proof that they had always been necessary and always
in existence.

There are, of course, many cases in the Year Books in which
courts held the general words of an act inapplicable to a
situation that clearly fell within them and, under opposite
conditions, extended the operation of a narrowly phrased rule
to include analogous cases not expressly provided for by the
statute. If a developed sanction behind acts of Parliament
during this period is posited, the norm of judicial action with
respect to legislation must naturally have been one of strict
adherence to its precise terms, and all variations in the courts
from the words of statutory enactments then can only appear
as illustrations of a power wielded by judges which permitted
them to depart, to a greater or lesser degree, from legislative
dictates. Under such a view it is immediately clear that the
judicial interpretation of statutes begins with the earliest Year
Books in the reign of Edward I, and this is, in fact, the currently received theory, though it is not usual to find the
assumption that lies back of it so explicitly stated.[1] There is,
however, little evidence to support the presumption. Indeed,

[1] T. F. T. Plucknett, *Statutes and Their Interpretation in the First Half
of the Fourteenth Century* (Cambridge, 1922); *idem, A Concise History
of the Common Law* (3d ed.; London, 1940), pp. 292-97; J. M. Landis,

the treatment of enactments in the courts, itself an accurate indication of the contemporary definition of a statute, suggests with some force that any rigorous sanction behind parliamentary acts, comparable to that which appears in rudimentary form in the sixteenth century, is lacking for the period that preceded it. In the absence of a compulsion to follow acts of Parliament regardless of their effect and of a sanction that makes any effort to apply a statute to situations not expressly within its words an infringement of the legislature's prerogative, the need for attributing wide powers to judges in order to explain departures from or extensions of the terms of enactments disappears. Such powers have, in fact, only been imputed to Year Book judges in the light of an assumed necessity that reflects the political thought not of their own but of a later age, and this view is given added support by the Year Books themselves, which contain no recognition of the existence of judicial powers with respect to legislation and do not distinguish sharply between the legislative and judicial elements in the administration of justice.

It is needless to pretend that under these circumstances the definition of a statute may be easily formulated, though some of its attributes will become patent in the course of this discussion. The concept quite evidently does not have the firmness of outline that will characterize it at a later period, but this lack of precision is to be expected and it permits a satisfactory disposition of the difficulties that beset the oversimplified history of statutory interpretation. For example, toward the middle of the fourteenth century a growing unwillingness on the part of judges to extend enactments to

'Statutes and the Sources of Law,' in *Harvard Legal Essays* (Cambridge, Mass., 1934), pp. 214-18; S. B. Chrimes, *English Constitutional Ideas in the Fifteenth Century* (Cambridge, 1936), pp. 289-99.

cases not expressly provided for in them is clearly noticeable
in the Year Books.[2] Since current historical writing presumes
a developed sanction back of parliamentary acts, an explanation for the limits set to the activities of judges must be sought
elsewhere, and it has been found in the growing separation
of the courts from the king's immediate personal sphere which
forced judges, no longer able to draw upon the vast reserve
of power at the disposal of the king's personal entourage, to
resign themselves to a simple application of the words of
statutory enactments.[3] But it is doubtful whether the plea
rolls or the Year Books of the first three Edwards show that
judges were helped by drawing upon any reserve of royal
power, and without further proof this solution remains a
troublesome one. It is likely, however, that there is no need
to go so far afield or to look beyond contemporary constitutional changes to account for the more rigorous treatment of
legislation in the courts. The middle years of the fourteenth
century witnessed the growth of the conception of Parliament
as consisting not of the king and the Council on the one
hand, Lords and Commons on the other, but of the king and
the Commons and the Lords, and they saw as well a further

[2]Plucknett, *Statutes*, pp. 86-90, 121, 168. It will be noted that though he
speaks generally of the advent of 'strict interpretation' by the middle of
the fourteenth century (so, more recently: *Concise History*, pp. 296-97,
and elsewhere: *infra*, p. 43, n. 87) the cases are all refusals to extend an
act beyond its words and the maxims quoted make only that point:
'*Privilegia statuti sunt stricti juris*'; 'Nous ne poms prendre lestatut plus avant
qe les paroules en ycele ne parlent.' If, on the other hand, the plain words
of an act led to what were considered improper results there was no hesi-
tation in restricting them or in disregarding them completely: *idem, Statutes*,
pp. 57-71; S. E. Thorne, 'The Equity of a Statute and Heydon's Case,'
Illinois Law Rev., XXXI, 205. Two cases may be urged against this: Y.B. 15
Edw. III (Rolls Ser.), pp. 50-52 (Plucknett, *Statutes*, p. 125), and H. 30 E.
3, 5, [pl. 20]. But these were harsh decisions that may be paralleled in the
earlier period—at the conclusion of the second the reporter noted 'Et multi
dixerunt quod male &c.': *infra*, p. 120, n. 43.

[3]Plucknett, *Statutes*, pp. 167-69; *idem, Concise History*, pp. 296-97.

and sharper separation of undifferentiated legislative power into that possessed by the king and that exercised by Parliament, the beginnings of legislation based upon a petition of the commune, and the appearance of the principle of the inviolability of a statute.[4] The consequent hardening in the definition of the nature of a statute—a recognizable stage in the slow evolution of the concept toward its modern form—was accurately reflected in a parallel development in the reciprocal judicial function with relation to it.[5] The curtailment in the middle fourteenth century of the freedom with which enactments had been boldly supplemented by reading into them provisions wholly judicial in origin is, indeed, no more surprising than that the last appeal by the courts to the Council for an exposition of the meaning of a statute should come from the same period.[6] Both were equally the result of an institutional development that was ultimately to make an act of Parliament the only valid form of legislation and 'the highest authority that this kingdom acknowledges upon earth.'

The accepted history of statutory interpretation presents other difficulties that have proven awkward. If departures from the words of enactments reflect only an authority in judges to interpret statutes—an authority possessed by them because of their closeness to the monarch and the discretion at his command—with the separation of the courts from the *curia* in the middle fourteenth century and their very complete differentiation in the years following, the strict application

[4]H. G. Richardson and G. O. Sayles, 'The Early Statutes,' *Law Quarterly Rev.*, L, 554-55, 560, 562, 569; B. Wilkinson, *Studies in the Constitutional History of the Thirteenth and Fourteenth Centuries* (Manchester, 1937), pp. 247-72; G. Barraclough, 'Law and Legislation in Medieval England,' *Law Quart. Rev.*, LVI, 76-92, and the literature there cited.

[5]*Infra*, pp. 42-45.

[6]*Infra*, p. 152, n. 145.

of acts of Parliament may be confidently expected.[7] Nevertheless, in the latter part of the fourteenth century and until well into the sixteenth, the treatment the courts accorded legislation, though modified in some important respects from that customary in an earlier period, did not differ essentially from it. Similarly, when the courts may no longer expect outside aid from the king, or the king in Parliament, they must themselves definitely assume the task of interpretation, and the early appearance of rules for that purpose can then be reasonably anticipated.[8] But the science of interpretation developed in the later Year Books is disappointing, and not until the sixteenth century is the technical equipment of judges vigorously supplemented and extended in that direction. These contradictions exist only if the development of Parliament (and the concurrently evolving concept of legislation and its binding force) is not made a variable in the equation. When that is done it becomes evident at once that only to the extent to which the modern idea of a statute had been realized in the middle years of the fourteenth century can either the present emergence of rules of statutory interpretation or the appearance of a rigidity in the application of legislation be expected. Since at that time many of its modern attributes and characteristics were lacking, we cannot expect to find these developments as early as the fourteenth century; in fact, the vague beginnings of both date not from the years of Edward III but from the conclusion of the momentous legal activity that marks the reign of Henry VIII.

During the Year Book period the task of a judge was complicated to no comparable degree by the compulsion that will often force judges of a later day, secure in the belief that the

[7]Plucknett, *Statutes,* p. 169; *idem, Concise History,* p. 297; Chrimes, *op. cit.,* p. 290.

[8]Plucknett, *Statutes,* p. 56.

responsibility is not theirs, to follow an act into anomaly or, in the converse situation, to refuse an extension of its words to *casus omissi* on the ground that to do so would be an act of legislation completely outside their proper function. Acts of Parliament could easily be extended to analogous cases, and, in the opposite situation, if the application of a broadly-phrased statute to a particular complex of facts led to injustice, a judge was under no constraint to follow its words but could disregard them. Contrary to modern practice under similar circumstances, he need make no apology for this, nor was it necessary that he in some way attempt to reconcile his action with the statutory provision, though such justification was upon occasion made. Statutes were regarded in the courts as essentially isolated rulings, supplementing or modifying common law, enacted to aid the judiciary in deciding the questions of *meum et tuum* that pressed for solution, and, of more importance in the present connection, as subsisting, like the rules of the common law itself, wholly within a private-law scheme.[9] Later, when the sanction back of statutes

[9]The distinction between statutes and common-law rules was not sharply marked: that Yelverton in M. 8 E. 4, 12, pl. 9, can regard his decision that notice was necessary to bind the defendant as laying down 'vn positiue ley' illustrates the lack of any clear distinction between the ultimate results of adjudication and legislation (*infra*, n. 1), and to regard it (Chrimes, *op. cit.*, p. 198) as a frank 'admission of judicial legislation [that] is very striking' is to read the Year Book, as the author's note indicates, in the light of §1 of the Swiss Civil Code and the recent theories of M. Duguit; it is similarly anachronistic to regard Bereford's treatment of *De donis* as 'judicial legislation': C. K. Allen, *Law in the Making* (3d ed.; Oxford, 1939), p. 375, n. 2. *Novel ley* could be made equally well in the courts and in Parliament (Plucknett, *Statutes*, pp. 30-31; Chrimes, *op. cit.*, pp. 252-54). Though Dr. Chrimes (p. 211) finds the Student guilty of confusion, St. Germain (*The Dialoges in Englishe betwene a Docter of Diuinity, and a Student in the lawes of England* [London, 1580], fol. 16ᵛ) is simply making the point that legal rules, or, in his terminology, 'maximes' (*infra*, p. 78, n. 164), are of the same strength and effect in the law as statutes. It is a commonplace to note that Parliament was not sharply set off from the other courts of the king (*infra*, p. 14, n. 16) nor were statutes regarded as quite different from

is stressed, they will form a cognate group, but in the Year Book period, when the content of enactments was of paramount importance, despite the fact that they were separately collected, a statute was felt to be more closely allied with the particular subject with which it dealt than with other parliamentary acts. Thus, neither Fitzherbert, writing at the close of the fifteenth century, nor his predecessor dealt separately in their abridgments with the abstract problem of statutes and statutory interpretation. In the late sixteenth century, however, a separate title was devoted to the subject in Sir Robert Brooke's *Graunde Abridgement*, and this illustration of a more general attitude toward statutes was followed shortly by another—the *Treatise concerning Statutes* that bears Sir Christopher Hatton's name on its title-page.[10] But before either of these, an unknown author of independent mind, quite willing upon occasion to differ from rules supported by the authority of the readers at the Inns of Court, had brought together the scattered remarks of judges and serjeants to form, so far as is yet known, the first distinct account of statutory interpretation in England. Written prior

---

the judgments, records, and fines customary there: Plucknett, 'The Lancastrian Constitution,' in *Tudor Studies* (London, 1924), p. 164; T. 3 E. 4, 7, pl. 1: 'Littleton: . . . car tiel record & act de Parliament est pluis hault en le ley, & est de tiel nature come recordes ou fines en courts le Roy, car hors d'un act de Parliament home poit auer *Habere facias seisinam* & *scire facias* auxy a auer execution per force de cel record, ou a entre per force de cel, sicome il ferra sur vn recouery ou fine.' Fortescue found the essential difference between common law and statutes to lie merely in the sharper penalty that may accompany the latter: Chrimes, *op. cit.*, pp. 201-3.

[10]*A Treatise concerning Statutes, or Acts of Parliament, and the Exposition thereof, written by Sir Christopher Hatton, late Lord Chancellour of England* (London, 1677). Its evident dependence upon Plowden's *Commentaries* indicates a date subsequent to 1571, and the reference (unless it be an interpolation) to 'Sir Edward Saunders, late chief Baron, of worthy memory,' points to a year after 1576. Hatton died in 1591 but there is some evidence that his treatise, if it is his, was 'modernized' before it was sent to the printer.

to 1571, and probably prior to 1567, the *Discourse*, now printed for the first time, takes its place as in all probability the first in the stream of volumes on that subject which has been flowing ever since.

This short tract, reproduced from two manuscripts in the Ellesmere papers in the Huntington Library,[11] thus represents perhaps the earliest attempt to deal with a difficulty that was then presenting itself only vaguely but was to become increasingly sharper and more troublesome—the preservation of a balance between parliamentary authority and the administration of justice. As such it enables more to be known of the growth of the sovereignty of Parliament and the functions of the judicature with respect to legislation in sixteenth-century England than has yet appeared. It provides both a point at which the far-reaching but gradual changes in political thought that characterize the period may be halted and assessed, and a touchstone for the reappraisal of statutory interpretation in legal history. The concept of Parliament and of the actual binding force of its acts that was held in a particular period, and the reciprocal treatment that during the same period the courts accorded legislation, are, of course, inseparably intertwined, and this introduction therefore ventures into territory which, if not terra incognita, lies within the treacherous borderland between law and political theory. It endeavors to trace the slow transition from a state in which law or justice is supreme to one in which the will of Parliament is pre-eminent, as revealed by the impact of this change upon judicial practice with respect to legislation. The growth of a necessity for statutory interpretation and of a technique in the application of enactments that becomes more and more cautious and complex, reflects the advances toward parliamentary sovereignty that were being made and supplies, at the

[11]For a detailed description of the manuscripts see *infra*, pp. 92-100.

same time, an accurate measure of their extent.[12] Viewed from the strictly legal side, the rules set forth in the *Discourse*, which represent an early attempt to formulate principles that have been sought by lawyers from that day to this, are themselves of importance to the historian of Anglo-American law, and an effort has been made to set out the sources from which they were drawn. Taken from the old books, they illustrate most strikingly how cases acquire new color in the light of the needs of a later age and how law grows through the reinterpretation of earlier experience.[13] Though the ju-

[12]The Year Books contain, of course, many attempts to ascertain the meaning of acts of Parliament and of particular words used in them: arguments based upon both grammar and logic had made their appearance but they were not crucial since they were useful only in relation to 'things indifferent' (A. P. D'Entrèves, *The Mediaeval Contribution to Political Thought* [Oxford, 1939], p. 124) when any one of a number of meanings could be reasonably adopted. As long as the words of statutes may be extended, restricted, or, upon occasion, disregarded *in toto*, and it is unnecessary to accommodate the attainment of justice with the commands of a sovereign will, there is little need for interpretation and it does not appear. Thus remarks such as those collected *infra*, p. 125, n. 55, p. 140, n. 113, etc., do not become usual until the sixteenth century. Prof. Plucknett (*Statutes*, p. 56) in a sense recognizes this, for it is implicit in his statement that interpretation cannot be expected until 'the courts have to accept statutes as the commands of an authority external to themselves whose will is known to them only as expressed in the written word.' Emphasis must be placed, however, not only on the word 'external,' as the rudimentary science of interpretation that emerges during the fifteenth century makes clear beyond doubt, but strongly upon the words 'commands,' 'authority,' and 'will.' His admirable and useful *Statutes*, for example, would have seemed pedantic, perhaps even unintelligible, prior to the sixteenth century: certainly Hengham and Bereford would have seen in it an exaggerated emphasis upon acts incidental to the simple administration of law or justice.

[13]The same process may be seen to advantage in the present-day use of Heydon's case (3 Rep. 7) and other sixteenth-century decisions to permit recourse to data extrinsic to the statute for purposes of interpreting it: *infra*, p. 68, n. 143; the literature is collected in Allen, *op. cit.*, pp. 421-30; F. J. de Sloovère, 'Extrinsic Aids in the Interpretation of Statutes,' *University of Pennsylvania Law Rev.*, LXXXVIII, 527. It has become usual in writings on statutory interpretation tacitly to assume a continuity in the concept of a statute and to ignore the growth of the doctrine of legislative sovereignty. If this is done, the strict application of enactments which

dicial practice with respect to statutes recorded in the Year Books differs fundamentally from that disclosed in a post-sixteenth-century law report, the use of Year Book cases in a modern work on statutory interpretation is not uncommon and does not strike even a careful reader as incongruous. The bridging of this gap represents another of the triumphs of the common law that never cease to perplex and astonish the historian.

I

That all were bound by statute is one aspect of the sanction that is presumed to lie back of legislation during the Year Book period. If that assumption can be established, then the fact that some acts of Parliament were held in the courts not to bind tenants on the ancient demesne of the crown, citizens of London and residents of Ireland must be regarded as illustrating a judicial power which permitted judges to exempt a particular area or a definite class of persons from the operation of a statute. But if, on the other hand, the assumption fails through lack of proof, the assertion that the exemption of these persons is the result of judicial interpretation must fall with it. Therefore, this portion of the introduction is devoted

---

characterizes the Augustan Age can be regarded simply as a lapse or a judicial self-abnegation of power, and it then becomes the duty of judges to vitiate the error of their predecessors by a return to older and easier methods of statutory application: see the papers noted in Thorne, in *Ill. Law Rev.*, XXXI, 202. Similarly, if the institutional development is neglected and the cases are read as if the definition of a statute had always been that understood today, support may be found in them for almost every form of statutory application, and current treatises on the subject are in fact repositories from which broad or narrow rules (depending upon the century from which they are taken) may be chosen to fit the exigencies of the occasion: see the use of Plowden in Cox *v.* Hakes, (1890) 15 App. Cas. 517, and in Landis, in *Harvard Legal Essays*, p. 213; for a realistic view of statutory interpretation along these lines see J. Willis, 'Statute Interpretation in a Nutshell,' in *Canadian Bar Rev.*, XVI, 1.

to an examination of the foundations upon which the sanction rests.

In the early fourteenth century men knew quite well that the source and authority for all legislation, of whatever kind and extent, was the royal will, presumed to be functioning with the advice of the Council;[14] but that was not equally true in the centuries following, when Parliament had established itself as a rival in legislation.[15] In their infrequent attempts to account for the binding force of parliamentary enactment, the lawyers in the later Year Books did not turn to the royal authority, but instead, characteristically in an age that stressed the similarities between Parliament and other courts rather than the differences that distinguished them,[16] to the drawing of still another parallel between the two institutions. Thus, an act of Parliament was compared to the record of the familiar courts at Westminster: a judgment there admittedly bound only parties to it and their privies, but since Parliament was the highest court of the realm its judgment was the highest record in the law, to which,

[14]Richardson and Sayles, in *Law Quart. Rev.*, L, 544, 548-53; Wilkinson, *op. cit.*, pp. 248-49; Sayles, *Select Cases in the Court of King's Bench under Edward I* (Selden Soc.), III, xiv, xxxviii.

[15]Sayles, *op. cit.*, pp. xxxviii, xli; Barraclough, in *Law Quart. Rev.*, LVI, 80-85. In the Year Books it is common to find the powers of king and Parliament contrasted—one example (despite its confusion of rule of court and statute) will suffice: H. 8 H. 6, 21, pl. 6: 'Martin: . . . il y ad vn *Statut* qui est appelle *Dies communes in Banco* . . . & *non obstante* le grant le Roy del conusance, vncore il ne peut granter que trop petit jour sera contrary al *Statut*, que est vn *Ley*, *sans ceo* que il est auctorise per Parliament . . .'

[16]C. H. McIlwain, *The High Court of Parliament* (New Haven, 1910); W. S. Holdsworth, *A History of English Law*, II (1923), 434, n. 4; IV (1924), 182-86; XI (1938), 123; K. Pickthorn, *Early Tudor Government: Henry VII* (Cambridge, 1934), pp. 134-35; Chrimes, *op. cit.*, pp. 70-75; F. D. Wormuth, *The Royal Prerogative, 1603-1649* (Ithaca, 1939), p. 61.

in a sense, all men were party and privy.[17] Dissociated from
their surroundings, such expressions may be taken to support
the conclusion that all were bound by statute; and that
acts of Parliament, by the middle fifteenth century, did
in fact bind all the king's domains and all persons in those
territories, has recently been inferred from these and similar
expressions in the Year Books.[18] But the phrase 'chescun home
est priue & partie al act de parlement' must be taken neither
in its literal sense nor as an incontrovertible statement of fact,
for, at that time and during the century following, every
statute did not bind all the king's subjects—for example, the
tenants on the ancient demesne of the crown—nor can the
undoubted exemption of this class of persons be attributed,
in the absence of evidence, simply to a judicial interpretation
of the statutes in question, though that does become the
explanation for the result toward the close of the sixteenth
century.

It is clear that the king's courts had jurisdiction over tenants

[17]T. 3 E. 4, 2, pl. 1: 'Laicon: . . . le defendant ad plede vn act de parliament enuers le pleintife quel est le pluis hault recorde en le ley: car per
tiel recorde chescun home est lie, car chescun home est partie a ceo, issint
que le pleintife est partie & priuie a cest record, quel luy liera auxibien
come si ieo vst plede vn recouere de mesme cel terre . . .'; H. 21 H. 7,
1, pl. 1: 'Butler: . . . car [Act de Parlement] est vn des plus haut records
que est en le Ley, & tiel record a quel chescun in Angleterre est priue, &
sera lye per ceo.' Other grounds may be stressed: *infra*, p. 20, n. 37; H.
21 H. 7, 4, pl. 1: 'Vauisor: . . . car si on ad rent charge hors de certain terre,
& cel terre par *Act de Parlement* fuit done a vn autre person, &c. jeo ne
cure: car jeo di que par cel *Act de Parlement* sa rent est alle a toujours,
pur ceo que cestuy que auoit l'rent fuit party a cel *Act*, car chescun de
Angleterre est party al *Act de Parlement;* issint nul encontre son act demesne
ne puit claime rent ou annuitie . . .'; Chrimes, *op. cit.*, pp. 78-80.

[18]Chrimes, *op. cit.*, pp. 79, 266-69; reliance is also placed upon R. L.
Schuyler, *Parliament and the British Empire* (New York, 1929), pp. 1-39,
but these indicate merely that some acts of Parliament bound the dominions.

in ancient demesne for personal actions,[19] but suits touching land there could not be brought before the justices.[20] Thus, ancient demesne was a good plea to jurisdiction in novel disseisin,[21] *replegiare*,[22] and account,[23] and, similarly, in actions given by statute, if they concerned land, such as elegit,[24] redisseisin,[25] and waste.[26] On the other hand, essentially personal actions such as trespass, which looked primarily toward damages, were proper,[27] and, by the same token, ancient demesne was not a valid plea to jurisdiction when suits were

[19]M. 2 E. 3, 15, pl. 10: 'Aldeburg: Cest court ne doet pas prendre le conisans si le plee touchast le soile de auncient demesne . . . mes pur riens que est vncore dit, ceo plee poit este termine tout en le personaltie, de que le conisans appent proprement a cest court.'; Y.B. 17-18 Edw. III (Rolls Ser.), p. 143: 'Shardelowe: Et, si vous ne preistes pas, donqes est le plee tut personele, de quei ceste Court conustra . . .' Many of the cases cited in the following notes contain the plea of counsel, 'C'est vn action personel, & nous ne demandons nul terre par le briefe.' It may also be noted that cases which could not be regarded (in some sense) as concerned with personalty did not come before the justices.

[20]Fleta 4 §4; Britton (ed. F. M. Nichols; Oxford, 1865), II, 13; *Registrum Breuium Originalium*, fol. 9; *Vieux Natura Breuium* (London, 1584), fol. 11v; P. Vinogradoff, *Villainage in England* (Oxford, 1892), pp. 94, 96; F. Pollock and F. W. Maitland, *History of English Law* (2d ed.; Cambridge, 1923), I, 385.

[21]Y.B. 8 Edw. II, 1 (Selden Soc.), pp. 42-46; P. 7 H. 6, 35, pl. 39.

[22]Y.B. 5 Edw. II, 2 (Selden Soc.), pp. 76-77, 78; H. 46 E. 3, 2, pl. 2; *infra*, p. 17, n. 30.

[23]H. 21 E. 3, 10, pl. 30; H. 46 E. 3, 2, pl. 2; P. 21 E. 4, 3, pl. 3; H. 8 H. 6, 34, pl. 36; M. 14 H. 8, 5, pl. 5.

[24]Westminster 2, ca. 18: Y.B. 8 Edw. II, *cit. supra*; Y.B. 20 Edw. III, 2 (Rolls Ser.), p. 521; Plucknett, *Statutes*, p. 64, n. 3; Brooke, *Parlement & Statutes*, 81; Dyer 373, pl. 13.

[25]Merton, ca. 3: Fitzherbert, *Nouvelle Natura Breuium*, 189G.

[26]Westminster 2, ca. 14: P. 7 H. 6, 35, pl. 39; H. 8 H. 6, 34, pl. 36; H. 32 H. 6, 25, pl. 12; Brooke, *Parlement & Statutes*, 17.

[27]Britton, II, 13; Y.B. 17-18 Edw. III (Rolls Ser.), p. 143; H. 46 E. 3, 1, pl. 2: *infra*, p. 17, n. 30; P. 7 H. 6, 35, pl. 39, Cokain.

brought upon statutes having similar aims.[28] Hence remedies, whether supplied by common law or statute, were refused or permitted with equal ease, depending upon whether realty or personalty was involved[29]—a dichotomy which was in turn a direct reflection both of the tenants' privilege to have disputes touching the soil decided within the manor and of the established rule that once the ownership or possession of land in ancient demesne had been decided outside the manorial court the nature of the tenancy was changed and the land transformed into frank fee.[30] Accordingly, if the suit in-

[28] 5 R. 2, st. 1, ca. 7: P. 21 E. 4, 3, pl. 3; T. 2 H. 7, 17, pl. 1; Hob. 47.

[29] There were exceptions: *quare impedit* lay for an advowson appendant to a manor in ancient demesne 'pur ceo que ceux en Ancient demesne n'ont pouuer a garder brief al Euesque,' as provided in Marlebridge, ca. 12: P. 7 H. 6, 35, pl. 39; *Vieux Natura Breuium,* fol. 4ᵛ; Hob. 48; similarly: M. 11 H. 6, 3, pl. 8, Danby; Jenk. 34. Occasionally, the specific requirements of some statutory provision seem to form the only stumbling block to its enforcement in ancient demesne: H. 32 H. 6, 25, pl. 12; *Abridgement of the booke of Assises* (London, 1555), fol. 147; Brooke, *Parlement & Statutes,* 81; 4 Rep. 65-65ᵛ; 4 Inst. 270.

[30] Vinogradoff, *op. cit.,* p. 96; *Rolls of the Justices in Eyre . . . for Lincolnshire, 1218-19, and Worcestershire, 1221* (Selden Soc.), p. 497; Y.B. 8 Edw. II, 1 (Selden Soc.), p. 43: 'Herle: Estre ceo nous ne clamoms rien en ceux tenementz si noun gage pur nostre dette tanqe &c. par quey la nature de la tenaunce ne pust en nule manere estre chaungee par nostre plee.'; p. 44: 'Cest assise est done par statut a recouerir lestat dount il fut ouste le quel ne chaunge mie la tenaunce qil ne cleime forqe vn chatel taunqe a vn temps.'; H. 46 E. 3, 1-2, pl. 2: 'Persay: Si vn port *Replegiare,* & luy pleint de ses auers a tort pris, il est bon respons adire, que le lieu ou il suppose le prisel estre fait est auncient demesne, il est clere ley que le brefe abatera; auxy en brefe d'Accompt port vers baille de manor en auncient demesne; issint moy semble icy. Finchden: En le cas ou vous mittes de *Replegiare,* il nest pas merveile, car la poit le franktenement viendra en debate, & issue poit este pris solement sur le franktenement . . . mes en le case ou nous sumous a ore [trespass], coment que vous dites que le lieu ou il suppose le prisel estre fait est votre commen, il couient que vous dites, & issint [?vncore] nous fesomus sans tort faire, issint coment que vous parles de le commen que touche franktenement, le point del issue serra sur le personaltie, issint cest matter nient semblable . . .'; P. 3 H. 4, 14, pl. 3: 'Markham a Norton: Jeo vous dirra le cause pur que le parol serra remaunde car si nous tiendromus le plee cyens per force de cest cause,

volved land the plea to jurisdiction was sustained and the case transferred to the court of ancient demesne, where action must be pursued by little writ of right close. This could be made to serve the purposes of some real actions by protestation, but, since these included only common-law actions, litigants to whom the royal courts were closed were denied both the remedy given by statute and the more effective statutory process.[31]

Thus, some general statutes bound ancient demesne; others, that did not expressly except it, if they infringed or led to

---

ceo court dauncient demesne serra ouste de lour jurisdiction, & les tenements serront deuenus frank fee a touts jours, & ceo ne serra pas reason . . .'; H. 8 H. 6, 34, pl. 36: 'Cottesmore: Jeo scay bien que vous ne demandez nul terre par le brief; mes vncore vous auez Jugement de recouerer le lieu wast, en quel cas per cel Jugement la terre issint recouer sera deuenu franc fee. En brief *d'Amesurement de pasture* la party ne demande nul terre; vncore pur ceo que la pasture sera amesure par cest *Court;* en quel cas il serra deuenu frank fee par cest amesurement, c'est la cause que la *Court* n'aura my la conusance.' For the corresponding privilege of the tenant, which requires actions touching realty to be decided in the manorial court by customary law, see: Pollock and Maitland, *op. cit.*, I, 385, n. 1; P. 7 H. 6, 35, pl. 39, Newton: *infra*, p. 19, n. 32; *Vieux Natura Breuium*, fol. 11; 5 Rep. 105ᵛ.

[31] H. 14 H. 4, 20, pl. 24: 'Hankford: Action de trespas fuit al common ley, mes issint ne fuit my cest accion. Et auxy en la Citie de *Londres* ont per Chartre de tener touts plees &c. Et vn bil de Conspiracie ad estre sue la, &c. Et puis ad estre reuerse per brief d'error, pur ceo que cest action est done per le statute de puis le temps que fuit lour franchise graunte, & issint est *decies tantum.*'; H. 32 H. 6, 25, pl. 12: 'Et de laisser le proces done per le *Statut* & prendre le proces per le *Comen Ley* &c. cestasauoir distres infini tanque il appiert & donques trier per *Pais,* &c.'; M. 22 E. 4, 23, pl. 2; T. 6 H. 7, 5, pl. 4; P. 11 H. 7, 22, pl. 11; Brooke, *Parlement & Statutes*, 81: '. . . & auxi videtur michi quod alia racio est que ils [de auncien demesne] ne poient auer ceo [elegit] la, que est pur ceo que touts lour accions sont per [petit] brefe de droit, & serra protestacion de quel action que luy pleast [for these see A. E. Levett, *Studies in Manorial History* (Oxford, 1938), pp. 152-53], mes ceo serra tantum daccion done al comen ley, & le Elegit, & assise pur tenant per Elegit, est per statute, quel ceux que ount conusance de plee deuaunt lestatute, ne vicount en son tourne, Senescal in Leet nec huiusmodi ne mellera, nisi lestatute eux donent auctoritie per expresse parollz . . .'; Hob. 47: *infra*, p. 31, n. 57.

the forfeiture of customary rights, did not. So formulated, the rule would have met with the approval of contemporaries, but there were occasional efforts to take a larger view. For example, that the action of waste, supplied by act of Parliament, was not available in ancient demesne, was accounted for on the ground that tenants there were not parties to the making of the statute.[32] But, though this was clearly true, ancient demesne undoubtedly was bound by some acts, in particular those touching personalty,[33] and, on the other hand, if indeed the tenants had been parties, there was no certainty, as the example of London indicates, that every act would have automatically bound it. This theory is plainly inadequate, and its minor place in the report shows that its author was using an obvious distinguishing characteristic of ancient demesne in doubtful support of a well-established rule, based in fact upon considerations of private law, rather than propounding a doctrine of political representation.[34] Another hypothesis was put forward some years later: special customs and privileges, such as those of London and ancient demesne, are not destroyed by general statutes, but must be expressly

[32]P. 7 H. 6, 35, pl. 39: 'Newton: Homes en *Ancien demene* ne poient estre enpledes per actions dones per le *statut* [Westminster 2, ca. 14] car ils ne sont parties al fesance del *statut*, ne al election des Cheualiers, des Burgeses, ne ils ne serront contributories a lour expences; issint que cest briefe de *Wast* ne peut courrir sur leur terre, eins chescun aura remedy vers autre solonque les customes de ancien temps enter eux vses. En *Londres* on n'aura briefe de *Wast* la nient plus que en *Ancien demene*, &c.' This is comparable to Portyngton's remark in M. 20 H. 6, 8, pl. 17 (18), *Select Cases in the Exchequer Chamber* (Selden Soc.), p. 83: 'Et auxi quaunt a ceo que Fortescu ad dit que si vne x ou xv soit graunte en le parlement icy que ceo ne liera ceux dirlande ieo voille bien pur ceo quils nount commaundement ouesque nous de venir al parlement par briefe &c.'

[33]*Supra*, n. 28. Similarly, though Ireland is not represented in the English Parliament, it was bound by some acts: *infra*, p. 32, n. 59.

[34]This is the meaning given to Newton's words in Dyer 373ᵛ (M. 22/23 Eliz.), as evidenced by their confusion with those of Fortescue in the Rector of Edington's case (P. 19 H. 6, 64), *cit. infra*, n. 35.

superseded.[35] This was but slightly more satisfactory, for, had the act contained express words, doubt must remain concerning whether the consequent forfeiture of rights would have been accepted as a matter of course by the justices and serjeants of the fifteenth century.[36] A third position might be taken which, like its fellows, was also a simple recognition of the fact that statutes which destroyed private rights in ancient demesne did not affect it: acts of Parliament bind all to whom they extend,[37] but they extend only to those at

[35]P. 19 H. 6, 64, pl. 1: 'Markham: . . . mesque le Rector fuit party a cest general grant de *xv*, vncore cest special grant que fuit fait a luy n'est oste par ceo, si non per special parolls fait, s. *nient obstant aucun special grant grante adeuant &c.* Fortescue: . . . Car le *Statut* de *Westminster second de donis conditionalibus* que done vn *Formedon* a reconter terre taile en qui est nul, &c. vncore ceo ne lie ceux d'*Londres*, mes la en tiel cas ils auront brief de *Droit*, & feront proces [protestacion]: & l'cause est, pur ceo que tiel general chose ne exclura aucun especial de que expres mention [ne] soit fait: mes tiel general *Statut* liera chaqun que est al *Common Ley*, mes ne peut defeter aucun special priuilege, eins que ceo serra vse come fuit adeuant: issint icy. Vampage: La cause que chaqun est excepte de tiel general grant est, pource que le grant se fist per tiel parolls, *modo solito*, & n'ad vse a estre leue la. Fortescue: Non, Sir, ceo n'est la cause, mes l'cause est pur ceo que chaqun est priuilege & exempte de tiel general grant, & ne serra lie sinon specialment: & [est] pruue bien per le Cas que j'ay mis, car en le *Statut de Westminster* n'est aucuns parolls semble a ceux parols [*modo solito*], & vncore ceo ne liera ceux de Londres.'; M. 20 H. 6, 13, pl. 25 (*Select Cases in the Exchequer Chamber*, p. 85): 'Ayscogh: . . . quar si le graunt vst este generalle en le conuocacioun donques a ma entent ne vst este questioun mes que le priour doit auer auaille de soun patent aore.'

[36]See Ascoghe's remarks, and those of the Chancellor, in M. 20 H. 6, 12, pl. 25 (*Select Cases in the Exchequer Chamber*, pp. 85-87); also M. 21 E. 4, 45, pl. 6, Catesby; M. 8 H. 6, 18-21, pl. 6, and the cases cited *infra*, pp. 71-74, nn. 154, 156, 158. For a careful examination of the cases cited in this and the preceding note, see Plucknett, in *Tudor Studies*, pp. 161-81. It will be noted that almost a century later the *Discourse* still considers the maxim *qui tacet consentire videtur*, and the private-law doctrine of estoppel it contemplates, useful in deciding what was rapidly becoming a question of public law: *infra*, p. 165.

[37]M. 21 E. 4, 45, pl. 6: 'Catesby: . . . par chescun act de parlement chescun a que act extend serra lie, pur ceo que chescun home est priue &

common law. Thus it may be said that tenants in ancient demesne were not at common law, though that analysis was useful only in connection with statutes that concerned realty, for clearly they did not enjoy this extraordinary status when the act in question involved merely personalty.[38]

But such abstract thinking about statutes did not play an important role in the cases, for in most instances discussion was restricted simply to the specific content of the enactment in question, and its effect upon the customary rights of those in ancient demesne, without reference to any general theory of statutes and their application. That the privileges of the tenant would be infringed, or the lord disinherited, was itself sufficient reason for holding an action unavailable in ancient demesne, and the problem presented by a statutory remedy was not sharply distinguished by contemporaries from that raised when a common-law action that affected the privileges of ancient demesne adversely was held to be inapplicable. The efforts made to formulate a broader view may be taken to indicate that in some minds the difficulties involved were vaguely apprehended, but no greater weight than this may be given them. The infrequent appearance of theories such as those just examined makes it impossible to regard them as

---

partie al parlement, car les Commens ont vn ou ij pur chescun commune pur lier ou deslier tout le commune . . .'

[38]Pollock and Maitland, *op. cit.*, I, 391; Holdsworth, *op. cit.*, III (1923), 264, n. 1; Y.B. 8 Edw. II, 1 (Selden Soc.), p. 44, Bereford; P. 19 H. 6, 64, pl. 1, Fortescue: *supra*, n. 35; Plucknett, in *Tudor Studies*, p. 167. If a fine had been levied, the land in ancient demesne became frank fee, its privileges were lost, and the tenements were then 'al common ley': it might then be urged (M. 18 H. 6, 28, pl. 11, Markham) that a plea touching such lands 'est merement personel, car cest record ne touche le tenancie en aucun maniere, mes seulement en sa nature n'est autre forsque vn mene per quel l'original que fuit deins *Ancien demene* serra remue hors de cest *Court* deuant vous, pur ceo que les tenements en demande sont al *Common Ley*, come vn des pleintifes que or apparust ad mire par vn fine al *Court*, que proue que est personel.'

anything more than occasional, *ad hoc* explanations for results
that could be secured without their aid, and their inadequacy
reflects little save that private-law considerations of *meum*
and *tuum* were actually controlling. They were, in fact,
supererogatory, occupying a subordinate place in discussion
and responsible in no substantial degree for the decisions
reached, since the attention of judges was directed primarily
to the simple administration of justice between party and
party. If a statute led to a legally reasonable result it extended
to ancient demesne; if it infringed rights or produced injustice there, it did not. Under such circumstances, the
difficulties involved in denying the application of a statute
which included no exemption of ancient demesne did not
arise. That tenants there were not bound by some general
statutes did not disturb the lawyers of the fifteenth century,
whose thoughts moved wholly within the frame of private
law, and they thus felt themselves under no obligation to
provide an adequate solution of problems that still lay in the
future. The general theories found in the Year Books not
only offer no support for the doctrine that all the king's
subjects were bound by statute, but indicate its opposite, and
the decisions themselves exhibit no effort to regard the cases
as 'exceptions out' of statutes made by judges, to draw a
distinction between the words of an act and the intention
of its makers, or to reconcile in other ways the fact that
ancient demesne was unaffected by some statutes and the
maxim 'chescun sera lye per act de Parliament.'

With the appearance of a more modern attitude toward
statutes in the sixteenth century, a qualified recognition of
problems that had previously been latent took place, and
corresponding modifications may be detected in the judicial
approach to legislation. But during this transitional period,
in which both old and new ideas of Parliament existed side

by side, a theory phrased to meet the demands of a completely developed parliamentary sovereignty was not yet needed and was not formulated. The *Discourse* reproduces the statement that ancient demesne was not bound by statute, 'for they come not to the Parlyament,'[39] but that statement is qualified almost immediately by another, that had not been used earlier in this connection—a general statute, 'suche an estatut as makethe a lawe,' binds ancient demesne. Brooke's *Abridgement* presents an equally confused analysis: some general statutes do not bind ancient demesne, but whether that is due to the reasonable meaning of the statute or to the fact that ancient demesne is not represented in Parliament is not made clear.[40] In Elme's case, tried a few years later,

[39]P. 110: this despite the earlier remark: 'The moost auncient court & of greatest authoritye ys the kynges hyghe court of Parlyament, the authorytie of which ys absolute & byndethe all maner of persons bycause that all men are pryvie & parties thereunto.'

[40]*Parlement & Statutes*, 99: 'Elegit est done per lestatute Westminster 2, ca. 18 . . . quell statute est general, & vncore ne lia auncient demesne, & sic vide plusors statutes que sont generall & ne except auncien demein, ne counte pallentine, ne le v. ports, & vncore per le resonable intendment de statute ceux ne extendra a eux, & ratio auxi est que homes de ceux lieux ne veigne al parliament come Cheualiers & Burgesses . . .'; *Parlement & Statutes*, 101: 'Nota quod sepissime inuenitur que Galis ne les counties palentines que ne veigne al parliament ne sera lies per le parliament dengliter, quar auncient demesne est bon plee in accion de wast done per estatute, & vncore auncien demesne nest excepte; & est enacte 2 [& 3] E. 6, cap. 28, que fines oue proclamacion serra in Chester, quar les former statutes nextendront a ceo; & est enacte que fine oue proclamacion serra similiter in Lancaster, 37 H. 8, cap. 19; & proclamacion destre sur exigents est done per statute en Chester & en Gales, 1 E. 6, cap. 10, & autiel acte pur Lancaster, 5 & 6 E. 6, cap. 26; & lestatut de iustices de peace ne extendra al Galis ne countie palentine, & ideo acte est ent fait pur Chester & Galis, 27 H. 6, cap. 5; mes vide tit. *County palentine*, 17 & 20 que ascuns actes extendra al countie palentine.'; *Auncien demesne*, 20; *Parlement & Statutes*, 17: 'Vide 8 H. 6. 35. Accion de Wast sur lestatute ne gist in auncien demesne, & si ceo fuit port al comon ley auncien demesne est bon plee, car ceux ne sont lie per lestatute, vide quare tit. *Auncien demesne* 20. & sic vide que auncien demesne nest excepte in lestatute, & vncore ne sont lies per lestatute.'

though the argument that 'lands in ancient demesne, like those of London which are customary, are not bound by statute since tenants there do not contribute to the fees of knights of parliament' again appears, it receives less attention,[41] counsel on both sides arguing, instead, to the question whether general statutes do or do not bind ancient demesne. Fleetwood, for the tenant, took the position that 'the statute *De donis* does not touch ancient demesne because no general statute binds it or defeats special custom,' and supported it by a number of examples.[42] In reply the argument was made that the cases put forward did not prove the tenant's contention,[43] and that the words of the statute 'are general, including no exception of ancient demesne,' and therefore 'land in ancient

[41]It receives passing mention in Dyer 373ᵛ, but does not appear in 1 And. 71 (M. 22/23 Eliz.).

[42]I cite only one: 'Et mit le Case *38* [*28*] *lib. Assis.* [pl. 24] & en diuers auters lieus, *scilicet* que Citizen de *London* poit deuiser son terres la en mortmain, le statute de mortmain nient obstant . . .'

[43]'Sur que ceux Cases per le contrary party fuerunt respondus & dit que nuls de ceux Cases proue le matter in question; car le reason que Citizens poient deuiser in mortmain nient obstant le statute nest pur ceo que le dit statute ne tolle lour custome, mes pur ceo que les customes sont per statutes pur cest purpose faits reuiues, come le statute de 14 E. 3, cap. 1, per que est ordein que ils aueront lour franchises & vsages queux ils ont reasonablement vses & eu &c., & diuers auters statutes sont a mesme le Fine, queux statutes sont vsualment plede quant le dit custome est allege, pur que ceo ne proue le matter intend . . .' Thus in a manner reminiscent of the fifteenth century (Plucknett, in *Tudor Studies*, p. 171), statutes are considered grants of equal validity, and no attempt is made to define their relations to one another: Plowd. 36ᵛ (4 E. 6): 'Mes vncore nyent obstant que ceo extend a touts auters gaolers cy pleinment, sicome il vst este expresse per playne parolx: vncore ceux de Loundres vsont de lesser tiels daler alarge oue baston en chescun lyeu deins lour iurisdiction, et ceo ne serra adiudge eschape en eux . . . et le reason de ceo nest pur ceo que lestatute ne lequitie de ceo nextende a eux, mes le reason de ceo est lour prescription in ceo point, & toutes lour customes et prescriptions sont confirme per les estatutes . . .'; 8 Rep. 126, 129: *infra*, p. 165, n. 191.

demesne is bound just as other lands are.'[44] Since, clearly, if the act were applied 'the donor would have that which was intended, the issue likewise, there would be no injury or tort to anyone and the land would in no way be altered or changed,' the court was inclined 'to believe the law to be that this statute extends to ancient demesne, notwithstanding the fact that it is a general statute.' Nevertheless, the demandant was forced to admit that some general acts did not bind ancient demesne, though he attributed this to the particular requirements they contained.[45] Unfortunately, the tenant died before judgment, so that no conclusion was reached.

Behind this sixteenth-century treatment of the problem lies the same unwillingness to prejudice the customary privileges of ancient demesne that had prevailed earlier, though these were now protected, as in Elme's case, by a distinction between general and specific acts. Both sides admitted that express words in a statute can bind ancient demesne,[46] but that

[44] '. . . & in auncient demesne *Formedon in discender* ad estre vse & allow quel ne serra si le statute ne fait ceo; . . . en breue de entry sur le statute de *Anno 8 H. 6.* ou *5 R. 2.* auncient demesne nest Plee & ceux Actions sont dones per les estatutes . . . *Marlebridge, cap. 17.* done breue de account vers gardein en socage, si breue soit port vers gardein en socage des terres in auncient demesne est bone Plee pur ceo que en breue de account al commen ley fuit bone Plee & le Action voile giser en auncient demesne vers gardein en socage come est tenus [H.] *21 E. 3, fol. 8* [*10, pl. 30*], quel proue que le gardein pur le terre en auncient demesne est lie; & experience allow que le statute de *Westminster 3.* lia auncient demesne . . .'

[45] '. . . & vncore il fuit confesse que ascuns statutes generals ne lieront auncient demesne, come le statute de Redisseisin & wast. Le reason del primer est apparant pur ceo que Assize ne poit estre port per le ley si le tenant voile de ceo prender aduantage de les terres en auncient demesne a le commen ley. Et des terres en auncient demesne Wast ne gist pur ceo que sil respondera al commen ley il ferra le terre frank-fee quel fuit inconuenient & nient intend per le statute . . .'

[46]*Infra*, p. 111 and n. 21. The same distinction is applied to the king: *infra*, p. 110 and n. 15; and to Ireland: *infra*, p. 33, n. 60.

all acts of Parliament bound it was not yet understood, for whether a general statute might have that same effect remained doubtful. The distinction, which stressed not the content of the enactment but the form in which it was expressed, marks an unmistakable departure from the approach customary in the Year Books. It clearly served a useful purpose in avoiding the inadvertent destruction of rights by acts that did not include an exemption of ancient demesne, but it was open to direct attack. Against its validity the view that general statutes extend to all, reflected in the *Discourse*'s statement that 'suche an estatut as makethe a lawe' binds ancient demesne and in Brooke's comment that Westminster 2, ca. 18, is general but *nevertheless* does not bind ancient demesne, could already be forcefully urged,[47] and likewise immediately evident was the fact that some general statutes (in particular, those that touched only personalty) had always been held to bind it. A more tenable position, with which the Year Book cases agreed in result,[48] was advanced in the *Discourse:* 'by generall wordes in a statute, pryvate mens interestes be not taken awaie, notwithstandinge that which is commenlye sayde, that everye man ys partie & privie to an acte of Parlemente.'[49] Thus, an act phrased in general terms

[47]For this there was verbal authority in the Year Books: Chrimes, *op. cit.*, pp. 262-63, 269, n. 2; but his conclusion that by 1474 'a general statute admittedly extended to every man' is premature.

[48]The view taken by Fortescue (*supra*, n. 35), though similar in form, places its emphasis upon rights and is quite clearly within the framework of private law; that in the *Discourse* is closer to the modern point of view: it reflects the growing strength of the principle that acts of Parliament bind all the king's domains and all persons within those territories but does not accept it fully—this may be seen as well in the fact that its author still felt free to use the private-law doctrine of estoppel in this connection: *supra*, n. 36.

[49]*Infra*, p. 164. Plowd. 59 (4 Edw. 6): 'Et, sir, en le case del Rector del Edyngton 19 H. 6, ou le roy auoyt graunt al Rector, et ses confreres, que a quel heure que disme fuit graunt a luy per le clergy, que ils serront

will not destroy private rights in ancient demesne, but the language used leaves doubt concerning whether ancient demesne was bound by the act and excepted from its operation or whether the statute did not extend to it despite the fact that tenants there, just as all men, were 'partie & privie' to the act. To contemporaries such a distinction, if not unintelligible, was unnecessary, and was not made,[50] but the inclusion of the rule within a chapter entitled 'Construction de statute conter les parollz' indicates the change that was taking place. To deny that all statutes, regardless of their effect or the form in which they were drawn, bound ancient demesne, was becoming increasingly difficult,[51] and it thus became

---

discharge, et puis vn disme fuit graunt per le clergy per lour conuocation, et la est tenus per le meliour opinion que le Rectour serra discharge per le dit graunt del roy, nyent obstant que il soyt adiudge per le ley vn del conuocation, & issint vn del grauntors, car le common ley dit, que nul serra dempnifie per tiel generall graunt fayt per parlyament. Et pur ceo le briefe de droit patent en Loundres ne fuit tolle per lestatute de Westminster 2, capitulo 1. De donis conditionalibus, mes ceo remaine a ore, et le demaundant faira son protestation de suer en nature de Formedon en discender, come il faira en auters actions realles la. Issint que acts de parlyament ne voile preiudicer ascun.'

[50]3 Rep. 8. (P. 26 Eliz.): 'Et en cest case fuit debate al large, en queux cases les generall parols des Actes de parliament extender al copiholds, ou customarie estates, & en queux nemy; & pur ceo, cest rule fuit prise & agree per tout le court, que quant vn Acte de parliament alter le seruice, tenure, interest del terre, ou auter chose en preiudice del Seignior, ou del custome del mannor, ou en preiudice del tenant, la les generall parols de tiel acte de parliament ne extendra a coppiholds. Mes quant Act est generalment fait pur le bien publique, & nul preiudice poit accruer per reason de alteration dascun interest, seruice, tenure, ou custome del mannor, la souent foits coppiholde & customarie estates sont deins le general puruiew de tiels actes.'

[51]The statement is not expressly made, however, until the seventeenth century: 4 Inst. 270: '. . . and regularly all generall statutes extend to ancient demesne.' Then, of course, it is necessary to take the view (2 Inst. 112) that 'statutes must be so construed, as no collaterall preiudice grow thereby.'; Jenk. 87: 'general statutes ne sont destre construe a destroyer custome de antient demesne.'; infra, p. 84, n. 176.

correspondingly evident that 'pryvate mens interestes' were protected there, not because acts touching realty or general statutes did not extend to ancient demesne, nor yet because tenants in ancient demesne were not at common law or were unrepresented in Parliament, but solely through judicial 'exceptions out' of statutes.

Whether courts may exempt a particular area or a definite class of persons from the operation of an act of Parliament was a question that had not arisen in the Year Books, nor had discussions concerned with it appeared. No judge or serjeant had regarded the nonextension of an act to ancient demesne as an 'exception out' of the statute, accomplished through an exercise of judicial discretion, for to say that ancient demesne was bound by an enactment but saved from its operation is a refinement (superfluous in a private-law scheme) for which no contemporary support can be found—indeed, as has been pointed out, explanations were sought in other quarters. But, as the necessity arises of reconciling the attainment of a just result in a particular instance with political and juridical principles that foreshadow the emergence of a developed public law, that distinction is adopted. Though Year Book judges had not looked to an 'exposition' or 'construction' of the act, made in the light of reason or general convenience, to account for the fact that some statutory provisions were not available against tenants on the ancient demesne of the crown, yet, as the sanction behind parliamentary enactments is stressed and the doctrine that 'chescun sera lye per act de Parliament' makes its way, that approach becomes common.[52] These analyses, the product of a more

[52]The phrase 'exception out of the statute' does not appear during the Year Book period: see Plucknett, *Statutes*, p. 57. The slow growth of the theory that a statute extends to all, and that its nonapplication is an illustration of judicial discretion, can be seen in a dispute in 1590 as to whether an act that does not in fact bind everyone can be a general statute

complex legal structure and valid only for a later stage of development, were nevertheless applied to the earlier period as well, revealing the Year Book cases as illustrations of that 'liberty and authority that judges have over laws, especially statute laws, according to reason and best convenience to mould them to the truest and best use.'[53] Certainly, one legitimate inference from the old books, as they were reread in an age of transformed ideas about Parliament and the effective scope of its acts, was that fifteenth-century judges had wielded a vigorous and wide-sweeping discretion that allowed them to narrow the words of statutes by excepting situations out of their operation. But with the increasing importance of Parliament a rule which stressed the powers of judges was not likely to meet with marked success, and the decisions,

---

within the rule that such acts need not, though particular statutes must, be pleaded specially 'ou auterment le court ne duist prender conusans de ceo': 1 And. 251: '. . . mes si ceo [i.e., that everyone must be bound by it] serra le cause de fair vn statute general, il ensuera que le statute de 4 H. 7. concernants Fynes oue Proclamations n'est general Ley, ne le statute de 1 R. 3. cap. 1. touchant vses, & diuers auters statutes general, come cestuy que plede Record in Assise & faile de ceo a le jour serra disseisor [Westminster 2, ca. 25]; per queux, enfants ne femmes couerts, lunaticks, & semble persons [ne] sont lies, & vncore sont general statutes come sont communement terme, & sont tiels d'ont le Court doient prender notice sans pleder ou monstre de eux, come per les pledings, liures, & experience appere, & vncore ceux statutes ne liount touts persons ne eux touchont, car en ascun de eux les persons deuant mencyons sont express-ment ou per intendment mencyons [?excludes].'

[53]Hob. 346 (13 Jac.); Egerton: *infra*, p. 140, n. 112; O. Gierke, *Johannes Althusius und die Entwicklung der naturrechtlichen Staatstheorien* (Breslau, 1880), p. 278: 'Und diese dem Naturrechtsgedanken immanente Unterscheidung zwischen formellem und materiallem Recht war nichts weniger als ein blosses Theorem. Sie entfaltete vielmehr, von allem mittelbaren Einfluss auf die Gesetzgebung abgesehen, schon dadurch eine unmittelbare praktische Wirksamkeit grössten Umfanges, dass sämmtliche zur Rechtsanwendung berufenen Behörden Befugniss und Pflicht empfiengen, durch die Mittel der damals so ausserordentlich weit gefassten "Interpretation" jedem Akt des Souveräns in möglichsten Einklang mit dem materiellen Recht zu setzen.'

neutral themselves, were susceptible as well to other interpretations, more in accord with contemporary legal theory.
They also appear as authority (1) for the doctrine that Parliament can do no wrong and must be presumed not to intend
harsh or harmful results, and (2) for the statement that affirmative statutes do not destroy common law or common custom,
and (3) as evidence for the validity of a distinction between
the 'sense' or 'the meaning of the act' or 'the intention of the
makers of the act,' and its words. These methods for avoiding
the injustice to which a statute may lead in a particular instance if literally applied will be examined at greater length
below.[54] It is important here only to note that since their
emergence is in response to the growth of the doctrine that
all the king's subjects are bound by acts of Parliament the
appearance of that principle must be postponed until the Year
Book period has come to a close and much of the sixteenth
century has passed.

   Brooke in one place does regard the exemption of ancient
demesne from Westminster 2, ca. 4, as 'a construction of
the meaning of the statute, and nevertheless the statute is
general and makes no exception of ancient demesne.'[55] From

---

[54]For the view that Parliament can do no wrong and does not intend
harsh or harmful results see *supra*, n. 49, and *infra*, p. 82, n. 172; in the
late sixteenth century the privileges of ancient demesne and London are
saved by a distinction between affirmative and negative acts: R. Crompton,
L'Avthoritie et Ivrisdiction des Covrts (London, 1594), fols. 13ᵛ-14:
'Ceux de Londres poient bargainer & vender lour terre la a cel iour,
come poient auant lestatut de inrolments, & issint poient in auters Burroughs
& Cities, & fuit lopinion de Justices dambideux benches que les terres in
cities &c. sont ou common ley exempt del act, & vide que terre deuisables
auant *32. H. 8. ca. 1.* sont deuisable a ceo iour nient obstant lestatut auantdit,
Dyer 155. & issint, estatut in affirmatiue ne alter comen ley, ne comon
custome dun ville que trench al inheritance.'; 3 Rep. 35: *infra*, p. 164,
n. 190; Co. Litt. 115; for the concepts of 'reason' and 'lentent del feasors'
see *infra*, p. 81, n. 170; for the distinction between 'les parols & lentention
del act' see *infra*, p. 77, n. 162.

[55]*Auncien demesne*, 20.

this it might be inferred that the nonextension of an act was being explained as a judicial construction of it, and thus that the doctrine 'chescun sera lye per act de Parliament' had already achieved complete acceptance, but that was not yet clear to the men of the sixteenth century. Though it was becoming difficult to deny that Parliament 'representeth and hath the power of the whole realm . . . For everie Englishman is entended to bee there present either in person or by procuration and attornies . . . And the consent of the Parliament is taken to be everie mans consent,'[56] the implications of that position were not yet fully comprehended. In the *Discourse* weight is still given to the fact that ancient demesne is not bound 'for they come not to the Parlyament,' and, similarly, in Brooke's *Abridgement* and Dyer's report of Elme's case, that was still a useful if minor argument which apparently did not impress contemporaries as completely anachronistic. It gradually loses its importance but is not squarely challenged until 1613.[57] As the fact gradually became clear that all par-

[56]Sir Thomas Smith, *De Republica Anglorum*, ed. L. Alston (Cambridge, 1906), p. 49—which is contemporary with the *Discourse*. This bears only a formal resemblance to Catesby's remark (*supra*, n. 37) made a century earlier, and the two can be joined only with difficulty: cf. J. G. Edwards, 'The *Plena Potestas* of English Parliamentary Representatives,' in *Oxford Essays in Medieval History* (Oxford, 1934), pp. 153-54. Similarly, Hody's remark in 1441 (M. 19 H. 6, 2, pl. 2; Brooke, *Parlement & Statutes*, 69; Crompton, *op. cit.*, fols. 17ᵛ, 138ᵛ) must be taken with caution: *supra*, n. 40; cf. Chrimes, *op. cit.*, p. 267. Cf. E. T. Lampson, in *Am. Pol. Sci. Rev.*, XXXV, 952-60.

[57]Hob. 47 (10 Jac.): 'Another point considerable is this: that if a new action be given by Statute which lyeth in the Kings Court and will not lye in ancient demesne, yet if that action meddle directly with the possession, you shall rather lose your action then have it in the Kings Court to the prejudice of the priviledge of ancient demesne. And that is the case of an action of waste, 7 H. 6, 35. & 8 H. 6, 34. But the reason is given in bookes, that the tenant in ancient demesne should not be subject to statute lawes, because they do not contribute to fees of Knights of Parliament, and so may seeme to have no voice there. I hold that conceipt veyne, for that is but an ease granted them in favour of their labours of the earth, as many others have freedome from serving in Juries,

liamentary enactments bound ancient demesne there was a corresponding alteration in the distinction between general and express statutes. First stated objectively—ancient demesne is not bound by general statutes—it was then modified in the light of growing parliamentary sovereignty into the narrower, transitional rule that general words in an act do not destroy private rights, and finally assumed its modern form, in the phrasing of which the completed change in emphasis is apparent: statutes which incroach upon private rights must be cautiously regarded by judges, and general words therein strictly construed.[58]

The emergence of the idea that acts of Parliament bound all the king's domains, and all persons in those territories, may likewise be seen in the cases relating to Ireland, though the parallel remains a partial one. During the Year Book period there was certainty only that, depending upon content, some statutes bound Ireland, others did not.[59] In Elizabeth's reign,

---

Pontage, Murage, and many such, and *F.N.B. 128:* the Villains of Lords of Parliament are free from contribution to the fees of Knights as well as they, and we see that they are subject to all other statutes not concerning their freehold as well as others.'

[58]P. B. Maxwell, *On the Interpretation of Statutes* (7th ed.; London, 1929), p. 245. Anticipations of this rule appear in Coke: *infra*, p. 84, n. 176; Jenk. 87: *supra*, n. 51. The objective distinction between general and express acts as applied to the king similarly breaks down in the later sixteenth century: Plowd. 236v-237; *infra*, n. 15. So, too, the application of the rule in the situation contemplated in the *Discourse, infra*, p. 149, n. 140, §8: see Plowd. 127; 4 Rep. 4-4v.

[59]M. 2 R. 3, 11-12, pl. 26: Ireland is not bound by acts of the English Parliament 'quia non hic habent milites parliamenti, sed hoc intelligitur de terris et rebus illis tantum efficiendo, sed personae illae sunt subiecti regis . . .'; M. 1 H. 7, 2-3, pl. 2, since it held the act, which did not touch realty, applicable to Ireland, is in accord, though it has been understood as overruling the earlier case: Holdsworth, *op. cit.*, IV, 28, n. 2; Pickthorn, *op. cit.*, p. 147. But the remark of Hussey, C.J. ('que les Statuts faits en *Angleterre* liera ceux d'*Ireland*'), is comparable to the general explanations put forward in connection with ancient demesne

when the doctrine that ancient demesne may be bound if
expressly named was first advanced, it was applied as well to
Ireland,[60] and the old and the new views continued to exist

and must not be taken at full face value: *infra*, p. 110: 'But thoughe those
of Irelande be not bounden by our Parliament because they have a Parliament of theire owne, yet notwithstandinge when they are in Englande,
as they are subiecte to the kynge, so are they subiecte unto his lawes.';
Brooke, *Parlement & Statutes*, 98: 'Nota que le parliament dengliterre ne
lia Ireland quoad terras suas, quar ils ount parliament la, mes ils poient
eux lier quant al choses transitory, come eskipper de lans ou marchandice,
al intent de ceo carrier al auter liew vltra mare que a Calice [2 H. 6, ca. 4],
& huiusmodi, quar ils sunt subiects le roy.'; Crompton, *op. cit.*, fol. 22ᵛ
(misnumbered 21): 'Nota, ceux de Ireland sont lies per estatute Dengliterre
pur lour biens, si estatut done forfeture de biens, pur feisans de chose
counter lestatute, mes nemy pur terres, ne touchant lour terre la, 2 R. 3,
fol. 12, & vncore ceux Direland ne mettont ascun Seignior ne chiualer,
ne burges al parliament Dengliterre, car ount parliament la, quant pleist al
Roigne.'; 7 Rep. 22ᵛ: *infra*, p. 34, n. 60; Jenk. 164: 'Statutes de Angleterre ne lie terres ne biens de eux de Ireland, mes lie lour persons, come
lestatute de H. 6. que nul transportera ascun Merchandise perde la mes
a Calice lie touts les subjects de Ireland et auters . . .'; see also Horace
(later Mr. Justice) Gray's notes to Quincy (Mass.) 514-15. The same point
may be made in the case of Wales: Plowd. 121ᵛ (T. 2 Mar.): 'Car fuit dit
que Gales, coment que il fuit de long temps south le regiment del roies
del Engleterre, vncore il ne fuit pas parcel de Engleterre ne les gentes
de ceo ne fueront lyes al leyes de Engleterre, ne rule per eux, ne vyendront
al Parliamentes de Engleterre tanque lestatute fuit fait en anno 27 Henrici
8 . . .'; 128ᵛ-129; Crompton, *op. cit.*, fol. 137ᵛ; [Thomas Egerton], *The
Speech of the Lord Chancellor . . . touching the Post-nati* (London, 1609),
pp. 80-81; McIlwain, *The American Revolution* (New York, 1924), pp. 93-94.

[60] 1 And. 263 (T. 33 Eliz.): 'Et fuit pluis dit que les Statutes faits en le
Parlement en Angleterre ne lieront ceux de Ireland, car ilz ont Parlement enter eux quel serra vain si le Parlement de Angleterre eux
lie . . . ne ils ne mit Cheualiers, Burgesses, &c. a ceo Parlement, quel nient
obstant fuit agre per touts les Juges, que il serra trye icy pur diuers
reasons, especialment de ceo que les Statutes de Angleterre lie cybien
ceux de Ireland come Angleterre quant ils parlent de ambideux . . .'; 2
And. 116 (T. 40 Eliz.): 'Et apres diuers choces moues touchant ceo point,
fuit tenus per les dits Attendants que le Statute de 27 H. 8, de vses, & le
Statute de Wills ne lieront le dit Isle [de Mann] ne l'enheritans de ceo
ne ascun auter Statute fait en Angliterre sans especiall & expresse Ordinance pur ceo; & est en mesme case come Ireland, ou le people est rule
per les Leys & Acts de Parlement de lour terre, & nemy per ascun Ley
de ceo terre sinon per Act de Parlement que ordean Ley expressment

side by side into the next century.[61] Later the rule based upon feudal theory and that which incorporated the distinction between general and express statutes both disappeared, and the opinion was held that all acts of Parliament bind Ireland, and have always bound it, though there appeared as well the contrary view that no acts of the English Parliament bind it.[62] The advocates of each position adduced

pur eux de Ireland & Wales.'; Calvin's case, 7 Rep. 22ᵛ: 'And 2. R. 3. 12. *Hibernia habet parliamentum, & faciunt leges, & nostra statuta non ligant eos, quia non mittunt milites ad parliamentum* (which is to be vnderstood, vnlesse they be especially named) *sed personae eorum sunt subiecti regis* . . .'; 4 Inst. 201, 287, 351; Jenk. 164: 'Statuts de Angleterre que expressement nosme *Ireland*, lie eux & lour terres & biens come lestatut de *York* fait 12. E. 2. & 13. E. 1. de mercatoribus & outers.'; Quincy (Mass.) 516, n. 9. Coke's parenthetical remark has been regarded as an 'unwarranted gloss' (Schuyler, *Parliament and the British Empire*, p. 65), but it is clearly an accurate reflection of existing law.

[61]The lack of any unifying theory in the late sixteenth century is apparent in Brooke (cf. *Parlement & Statutes*, 98: supra, n. 59; and 90 (2): 'Vide Tit. Accion sur lestatute in *Fitz*. 6 par loppinion del cheif Justice que les statuts Dengliterre liera ceux de Irelande, que fuit in maner agree par les auters Justices, & vncore il fuit deny le darren iour deuant, tamen nota que Ireland est vn realme de luy mesme, & ad parliament in luy mesme.'), as well as in Crompton's remarks: after the statement quoted supra, n. 59, he adds: '*Vide* action sur lestatute *Fitz*. 1 [6] & 11 H. 6 [M. 1 H. 7, 2-3, pl. 2] ou Hussey chiefe Justice dist que estatut Dengliterre lie ceux de Ireland, que ne fuit mult dedit per auters iustices a cel temps, coment que le darren terme ascun fuerunt in contrarie opinions. *Vide 20 H. 6. 9* [Select Cases in the Exchequer Chamber, p. 83] que ils ne sont lies per lestatut Dengliterre, come si dismes soient grant per parliament Dengliterre, ceux Direland ne sont lies, pur ceo que ne sont sommons al Parliament icy, per Fortescue & Portingeton.' Coke's report of Calvin's case (6 Jac.) includes both rules: supra, n. 60; similarly, Jenkins: supra, nn. 59 and 60.

[62]The arguments put forward in the Anglo-Irish controversy are carefully reviewed and restated in McIlwain, *American Revolution*, and Schuyler, *op. cit.* Darcy and others writing on the Irish side were aware that some statutes passed by the Parliament in England had been in force in Ireland, and they therefore regarded them as merely declaratory, adopting a distinction between declaratory and introductory acts. Mayart and his supporters, on the other hand, ignored statements such as those in n. 59, supra.

precedents from the time of Henry II to that of the Long
Parliament, but neither position could be found in the sources,
for neither was based upon unambiguous historical authority.
As in the case of ancient demesne, the theories advanced were
superimposed upon the facts rather than drawn from them.
There is need here only to note that the introduction of
public-law ideas in connection with the problem of the validity of English statutes in Ireland was coincident with their
use in discussions concerned with the binding of ancient
demesne by statute, and that the doctrine 'chescun sera lye
per act de Parliament' in a form broad enough to include
both Ireland and ancient demesne did not definitely appear
until the seventeenth century. With respect to the latter,
however, the nonextension of a statute to ancient demesne
was in some quarters already being regarded by Elizabeth's
reign as a 'construction conter les parollz,' thus indicating
an earlier recognition of the principle in that connection.

II

After the reign of Henry VIII statutes were seen to form
a cognate group, and rules for their general application first
became necessary. The distinction between general and express statutes, as applied in the cases of ancient demesne and
Ireland, was an attempt to deal satisfactorily with legislation
on this new level, and as such it took the place of the private-
law considerations that had been controlling during the Year
Book period. Though Year Book cases might be and were
cited in its support, it was, as has been indicated, the product
of the Elizabethan rather than the Lancastrian age, and,
though it could be buttressed by precedent not precisely in
point, it was only brought into prominence in the sixteenth
century and then first applied to situations that had not
required its use earlier. To this characteristic example of the

common-law technique, aptly summed up in Coke's well-known words 'out of the old fields must come the new corne,' the development of the distinction between affirmative and negative statutes offers a close parallel. Not until the sixteenth century were the few chance remarks the Year Books contained upon acts in the negative and affirmative seized on and adapted to the solution of problems of statutory interpretation then first becoming troublesome. In the canon law and the theological literature that centered about the Decalogue and its interpretation, the distinction was a familiar one (and thus the extract from Lambert Daneau's *Ethices Christianae* that Egerton wrote into the margin of his commonplace book was merely a simple paraphrase of a rule recognized three hundred years before),[63] but in English law, though it had appeared in rudimentary form in the reign of Edward III,[64] and thereafter at irregular and widely-spaced intervals

[63]St. Thomas Aquinas, *Commentarium in Epistolam ad Romanos*, c. XIII, lect. 2: 'Praecepta negativa sunt magis universaliora et quantum ad tempora et quantum ad personas. Quantum ad tempora quidem, quia praecepta negativa obligant semper et ad semper. Nullo enim tempore est furandum et adulterandum; praecepta affirmativa obligant quidem semper, at non ad semper, sed pro loco et tempore: non enim tenetur homo ut omni tempore honoret parentes, sed pro loco et tempore. Quantum ad personas autem, quia nulli homini est nocendum. Non autem sufficientes sumus, ut unus homo possit omnibus servire.'; Pecock, *The Repressor of Over Much Blaming of the Clergy* (Rolls Ser.), II, 505-6: 'Forwhi summe comaundementis of God ben negatyues, that is to seie, weernyngis or forbodis . . .; and these bynden to alwey, and to whom euere eny of these comaundementis is oonys a comaundement, to him thilk same comaundement is euermore perpetueli a comaundement. Summe othere comaundementis ben affirmatyue comaundementis, that is to seie, biddingis that certein deedis be doon . . . and these comaundementis binden not to alwey, and to whom these ben comaundementis for oon while, they mowen ceese to be comaundementis as for an other while.'; A. van Hove, *Commentarium Lovaniense in Codicem Iuris Canonici*, I, 2 (Mechelen, 1930), p. 148. The extract from Daneau is printed *infra*, n. 35.

[64]43 Liber Assisarum, pl. 22 (Brooke, *Pannel & array*, 9; *Parlement & Statutes*, 70; Crompton, *op. cit.*, fol. 16); perhaps 30 Liber Assisarum, pl. 5, Shardelowe.

in the Year Books, prior to the sixteenth century it had filled
no necessary function and consequently had occupied only
a subordinate place.

The rule as understood in the handful of cases in which
it appears in the Year Books is simply that an express negative provision permits no departure from its words, or, as
counsel advised the justices, 'it is mandatory upon you.'[65]
That statutes phrased in the negative should be singled out
as especially binding is itself an interesting commentary upon
the contemporary view of legislation and, as such, worthy
of remark. Clearly, when only 'things indifferent' are involved—whether assizes should be taken outside the county
despite the statutory prohibition, whether a lord should be
fined contrary to the statute or merely amerced, whether a
plea smaller in amount than that set by the act may be re-

[65]P. 22 E. 4, 11, pl. 3, Pigot: *infra*, n. 43, but note the cases on the same
statute in which it was disregarded. In M. 38 H. 6, 18, pl. 36, and apparently
in M. 39 H. 6, 19, pl. 28 (both *infra*, n. 44), the bench refused to take
cognizance of an assize of mortdancestor since Magna Carta forbade it
in negative words, though if the statute had read 'assisae capiantur' a
contrary result would probably have been reached. But see *infra*, n. 46;
P. 5 E. 4, Long Quinto, 33-34, Choke: *infra*, Appendix II; P. 10 E. 4, 7,
pl. 18 (Y.B. 10 Edw. IV [Selden Soc.], pp. 63-66; Chrimes, *op. cit.*, pp.
261-62): in this case (using Plowden's [fol. 66v] summary), 'en action
de trespas per le lessee pur ans dauers prise, le defendant dit que le lessor
tient de luy per seruices &c. & pur tant areres il prist les auers, & le
pleintif dit ryen arere &c. & sur ceo fueront al issue, & fuit troue pur le
pleintif, & lopinion de touts les justices la fuit, que nient obstant que le
defendant ad accept le brief bone, que vncore le pleintif nauera iudgment,
mes le court abatera le brief.' This was due to the fact that Marlebridge,
ca. 3, 'est en le negatiff' and expressly forbids the lord to be fined. The
court compared the case to an appeal brought by a woman on the death
of her father—however much the defendant affirms the writ still the court
must abate it, for Magna Carta, ca. 34, is 'en le negatif' and provides that
'nullus capiatur vel imprisonetur propter appellum femine de morte
alterius quam viri sui.'; H. 14 H. 8, 15, pl. 2: 'Fitzherbert: Vn n'auera
onques *Accedas ad Curiam* . . . sinon que les damages passent xl. s. car
le statut de Gloucester est en le negatif . . . [this was opposed] Mes
Fitzherbert tint son opinion vt supra enconter luy, & il dit s'il fuit issint donq
nous auons touts les ples que sont in le County, ou le *Statut* est prohibition.'

moved from the county court to that at Westminster—a rule so phrased might be adhered to without difficulty, though even under such circumstances it was often disregarded. But if a negatively phrased enactment led to anomalous results—the crucial case in which the rule's strength can be properly assessed—judges were under no compulsion to follow it and thus, like the general theories of statutory application put forward during the Year Book period in connection with ancient demesne, the fluidity of the principle reflects a scheme in which neither rules nor the precise words of an act but considerations of justice were actually controlling. For this reason, arguments based upon the negative phrasing of a statute were not often urged upon courts, and the distinction makes only occasional and isolated appearances when counsel possessed nothing more persuasive to present. Thus, in Edward IV's reign the distinction was once applied in a dictum to the frequently discussed question of parallel common-law and statutory remedies: it was Choke's opinion that 'where a statute that gives a process is in the affirmative, the party may have this process or the common law process, but it is different where the statute is in the negative, that is to say, he must then have this process and no other.'[66] But much earlier it had been settled that a new statutory remedy did not necessarily abolish the earlier common-law process, and that the litigant could at his election have the old procedure or the new.[67] Whether the common-law process was still available had never turned on the affirmative or negative

[66]P. 10 E. 4, 7, pl. 18: *cit. supra*, n. 65. Choke had used the distinction earlier in P. 5 E. 4, Long Quinto, 33-34; T. 4 H. 7, 11, pl. 6, Vavisor: *infra*, n. 35.

[67]Plucknett, *Statutes*, pp. 128-34; P. 46 E. 3, 12, pl. 12; M. 47 E. 3, 10, pl. 7; M. 47 E. 3, 14, pl. 15; M. 50 E. 3, 24, pl. 5; P. 7 H. 4, 12, pl. 8; M. 11 H. 4, 23, pl. 46, Culpeper; M. 3 E. 4, 27, pl. 24, Genney; T. 5 E. 4, Long Quinto, 41.

phrasing of the act that provided the new remedy, but on practical, legal considerations raised by the facts of the particular case before the court; and after Choke's remark that continued to be true. His dictum does not appear again in the Year Books, though debates on parallel remedies continued to arise.[68] Thus, during the Year Book period, as the few examples show, the distinction enjoyed only a limited vogue and played an inconsequential part. In the sixteenth century, however, it became widespread, prominent, and frequently cited.[69]

The extent to which, by the early years of Elizabeth's reign, the simple and seldom-urged principle of the Year Books had been amplified and logically extended may be seen to advantage in the fourth chapter of the *Discourse*. Its author quite clearly explained the old cases in the light of the new learning, though the distinction between affirmative and negative statutes had been far from the thoughts of the justices who had decided them,[70] and the same may be said of Brooke,[71] Crompton,[72] and Coke.[73] That an act was in the

[68]T. 17 E. 4, 4, pl. 3; M. 2 R. 3, 18, pl. 45; H. 3 H. 7, 1, pl. 1; M. 14 H. 7, 10, pl. 20, Tremaile; M. 15 H. 7, 15, pl. 7; H. 21 H. 7, 19, pl. 31. Here an analogy may be drawn to the cases of ancient demesne that, after Newton's and Fortescue's attempts to frame general theories, continued to turn on whether the statute led to the forfeiture of rights.

[69]The discussion in Chrimes, *op. cit.*, pp. 258-62, based as it is upon Coke and Viner, represents the seventeenth century more adequately than it does the fifteenth.

[70]P. 117, n. 35: the cases H. 3 H. 7, 1, pl. 1, P. 46 E. 3, 12, pl. 12, and M. 50 E. 3, 24, pl. 5, make no mention of the distinction; p. 118, n. 37: M. 13 E. 2, *Mesne*, 68, P. 7 H. 4, 12, pl. 8, and T. 17 E. 4, 4, pl. 3, are similarly not in point; p. 118, n. 38: the two Liber Assisarum cases are vague; the others there cited agree only in result.

[71]*Parlement & Statutes*, 29, 75: *infra*, p. 159, n. 173 (cf. the case abstracted: P. 5 H. 7, 17, pl. 10, with Brooke's remarks upon it); 108; Chrimes, *op. cit.*, p. 260, n. 5.

[72]*Op. cit.*, fol. 12 (misnumbered 13); fols. 13ᵛ-14, citing Dyer 155[ᵛ];

affirmative quickly became the standard reason brought forward to explain why every act (despite the enhancement of
the law-making power of Parliament to such a degree that
it was coming to be 'so transcendent and absolute that it cannot be confined within bounds')[74] did not always supersede
the prior common law[75] or earlier statutes,[76] or destroy every
inconsistent custom.[77] Here a useful purpose was served,
since, like the distinction between general and express acts
in connection with ancient demesne, it prevented the inadvertent destruction of rights and remedies by statutes whose
authors, as Coke noted, had not fully considered the effects
of their words.[78] But clearly the distinction had not been

---

fol. 15: cf. the reasons given in the case: H. 14 H. 7, 17, pl. 7, and in
Brooke, *Parlement & Statutes*, 21; *Parnor de profits*, 10. Plowd. 113 is the
first appearance of the view adopted by Crompton; fols. 15ᵛ-16, citing M.
39 H. 6, 3, pl. 5; fol. 19, citing Dyer 50.

[73]11 Rep. 64. It should be noted that of the sixteen cases cited by Coke
in support of the statement, 'Come in briefe de mesne le proces al common
ley fuit distres infinit, & coment que lestatute de Westminster 2, ca. 9,
done pluis speedie proces & in le fine foriudger, vncore le pleintif poet
prender quel proces il voet, ou al common ley, ou sur le dit Statute, quia
ambideux en laffirmatiue,' but one, and that from the sixteenth century
(Plowd. 207), uses the reason he alleges. Coke in effect subsumes the
results of the cases under a new major premise.

[74]4 Inst. 36; A. F. Pollard, *Parliament in the Wars of the Roses* (Glas-
gow, 1936), pp. 28-29.

[75]Plowd. 112, 113ᵛ; Brooke, *Parlement & Statutes*, 70: *Repleder & Ieofaile*,
36; 1 Rep. 25; 6 Rep. 19ᵛ; 9 Rep. 23ᵛ; 10 Rep. 82; 11 Rep. 59, 61,
62ᵛ, 64ᵛ; Co. Litt. 115; 2 Inst. 200, 313, 448 (9), 472 (11); Hob. 173; Jenk.
210, 212, 238, 287.

[76]This had been a troublesome question: *supra*, n. 43; Plucknett, *Statutes*,
pp. 91 *et seq.*

[77]*Supra*, n. 54.

[78]6 Rep. 40ᵛ: 'Per que appiert, que plusorz mischiefes surdont sur le
chaunge dun maxime & rule del common ley, que ceux queux ceo alteront
ne poyent veier quant ils font le change; car *Rerum progressus ostendunt
multa quae in initio praecaueri seu praevideri non possunt.*'

used for such purposes earlier. That rights would have been infringed or unjust results would have ensued upon the application of a statute had previously been sufficient to hold it ineffective, and there had been no more need to advance the fact that the statute was in the affirmative to avoid these consequences than there had been to plead the rule that general acts do not extend to ancient demesne in order to prevent them. Both principles appear simultaneously in the sixteenth century, though in relation to different situations, and reflect an attitude toward and a method of dealing with statutes that mark a complete departure from those customary in the Year Books.

Shortly after its appearance the distinction, mechanical in the sense that it was based solely upon the form in which an act was expressed,[79] was hedged about by exceptions and modifications.[80] As the *Discourse* points out, there already were 'divers cases wherein this grounde ys broken,' which permitted its arbitrary character to be avoided.[81] Similarly, some of the rules laid down in the *Discourse* do not appear subsequently,[82] and the procedure soon became usual, as Egerton's supplementary note indicates, to imply negatives in affirmatives and to distinguish negative acts introductory of new law from negative statutes declaratory of the common law.[83] The distinction rapidly proved to be an inadequate one

[79]R. Pound, 'Common Law and Legislation,' *Harvard Law Rev.*, XXI, 397-400; Chrimes, *op. cit.*, pp. 258-60.

[80]Similarly, the distinction between general and express statutes, *supra*, pp. 31-32, and that between penal and beneficial acts, *infra*, pp. 52-54.

[81]*Abridgement of the booke of Assises*, fol. 20: 'Home auera assise en banke le roy, car il nest en case destatut s. communia placita &c., car il nad commen iour eyns die lune &c.'; Crompton, *op. cit.*, fols. 68ᵛ, 69 (misnumbered 75); Hatton, *Treatise concerning Statutes*, p. 84: *infra*, n. 48.

[82]*Infra*, n. 40.

[83]*Infra*, n. 48; Pound, in *Harvard Law Rev.*, XXI, 398.

42   A DISCOURSE

but, like its companions, it bears on its face the period from which it stems and must not be regarded as the product of many years of careful thought devoted to the development of a satisfactory rule nor as the final fruit of judicial experiment in case after case since the middle fourteenth century. It was in fact a first and therefore halting attempt to deal with the sixteenth century's new and pressing problem of statutory interpretation.

III

The freedom with which legislation was handled by Hengham and Bereford, and their companions, in the early fourteenth century has been examined in detail,[84] though it must not be attributed to extraordinary powers in their possession, for there is no indication of the existence of these, but rather to the fact that no particular sanction attached to the words of statutes, which were merely suggestions of policy to be treated with an easy unconcern as to their precise content. An enactment might be radically supplemented by reading into it provisions that were wholly judicial in origin, yet for such actions judges did not feel it necessary to offer apologies, nor do explanations of any sort appear.[85] Alterations of this kind were not regarded as interferences with legislative power, and thus *ultra vires* acts to be explained only in the light of a broad judicial discretion, but instead as an integral and in no way exceptional part of the judge's task, which had for its objects the reaching of legally sound results and the proper administration of justice between litigants.

[84]Plucknett, *Statutes; idem, Concise History*, pp. 292-97.

[85]Bereford's treatment of *De donis* is an obvious example: Y.B. 5 Edw. II, 1 (Selden Soc.), p. 177; Y.B. 5 Edw. II, 2 (Selden Soc.), p. 226; Plucknett, *Statutes*, pp. 51-52; *idem, Concise History*, p. 295. Prof. Plucknett places too great an emphasis upon Bereford's casual remark, 'Celuy qe fit lestatut il supposa . . .': Holdsworth, *op. cit.*, III, 114-15; *infra*, p. 59, n. 125.

In the middle fourteenth century, however, the constitutional changes to which attention has already been called led to the formulation of what was in many respects a new definition of a statute.[86] As the still rudimentary concept of legislation took form the exact function of judges with relation to it became increasingly uncertain, and the slow development of these doubts is closely paralleled by a corresponding movement in the courts toward the adoption of a policy—which takes definite form by 1340—denying the extension of statutes beyond their words.[87] The appearance of this strict rule and the more severe approach to legislation it entails must not, however, be taken as proof of the present emergence of the modern concept of a statute or as an indication that a fully developed sanction back of acts of Parliament had come into existence.

In the early fourteenth century, if the words of an act supplied a remedy for one complex of facts but did not provide for a comparable situation that deserved equal treatment, no difficulty was experienced in achieving justice by permitting the same result in the analogous case. To a modern mind such an extension, though it would today be regarded as judicial legislation on an excessively broad scale, is less drastic than others that were contemporaneously made, since it is interstitial in character and therefore more limited

[86]*Supra*, pp. 6-7.

[87]*Supra*, n. 2. For evidence of the continuance of the policy in the later fourteenth century see the statute of 36 E. 3, st. 1, ca. 9, and the comments upon it by Plucknett: 'Some Proposed Legislation of Henry VIII,' in *Transactions of the Royal Historical Society*, 4th Ser., XIX, 131; *idem*, 'L'Interpretation des lois,' in *Recueil d'études en l'honneur d'Edouard Lambert* (Paris, 1938), I, 440; J. E. A. Jolliffe, *The Constitutional History of Medieval England* (London, 1937), pp. 378-79; Thorne, in *Ill. Law Rev.*, XXXI, 205. But this rigidity was at most temporary and in England as in Italy was modified within a generation: Thorne, '*Statuti* in the Post-Glossators,' *Speculum*, XI, 454, 459; W. Engelmann, *Die Wiedergeburt der Rechtskultur in Italien* (Leipzig, 1938), pp. 162-71.

in scope. But a distinction of this kind, dependent as it is upon a more sophisticated concept of legislation, is not visible in the undifferentiated practice of the early fourteenth century, for at that time all extensions, whether circumscribed by the words of the statute or not, were equally proper or, with the advent of a stricter approach toward legislation, correspondingly improper. After the third quarter of the century, however, judicial action with respect to statutes is distinguished into that which is equivalent to legislation and that which falls short of it—a separation reflected in the emergence of the doctrine of 'lequity de lestatut.'[88] If the words of an act remedied a particular hardship, for example, by giving an action *de bonis asportatis* to executors, the equity of the statute allowed administrators the same action, since, though they were not mentioned in the act, they were 'in the same mischief.' The appearance of that doctrine reflects the fact that a definition of legislation had been formulated, during the middle years of the fourteenth century, which now made it possible, not only to distinguish in some degree between statutes and ordinances,[89] but also, and to an equivalent extent, between judicial action that was completely legislative in character and that which did not overstep the proper function of courts. Though the making of *novel ley* was not actually outside their province, judges no longer attempted to supplement the words of an act to the extent that a wholly new rule was provided, as had been done by Hengham and

[88]The earliest cases are M. 48 E. 3, 28, pl. 14; M. 50 E. 3, 24, pl. 5. The instance noted by Dr. Sayles (*Select Cases in the Court of King's Bench*, III, xxxvii) is an example of *aequitas*: Pollock and Maitland, *op. cit.*, I, 189; *infra*, p. 78, n. 163. The early Year Book cases cited by Dean Landis (in *Harvard Legal Essays*, p. 216, nn. 6 and 8) precede any appearance of the doctrine.

[89]Richardson and Sayles, in *Law Quart. Rev.*, L, 556-62; Barraclough, *ibid.*, LVI, 81-83.

Bereford, but less drastic action on their part was clearly permissible. Put more precisely, the terms in which an act was phrased had gained greater importance than they had possessed earlier and could not be easily augmented without parliamentary action,[90] but, on the other hand, a statute was not yet thought to provide solely for the one set of circumstances it mentioned, and thus its words had not acquired the sanction that was later to force courts to take the position that a case similar to that dealt with in a statute, but entirely unprovided for by it, must remain so.[91]

The bold supplementation of statutes, recognized after the middle fourteenth century to be legislative action, was no longer within the province of judges, but, just as analogous cases were within a common-law rule, so situations unmentioned in an act but in the same mischief as that toward which it was directed were aided by 'lequity de lestatut.' Though the doctrine is framed in terms that do not suggest a judicial authority to extend a statute beyond its words, but rather a vague penumbra of essentially similar cases surrounding the precise words of an act to which it must in justice apply, later usage has come to regard it as an example of a power exercised by judges which enabled them to bring within reach of a statute situations that admittedly lay outside its express provisions.[92] But to describe the process in terms of conflicting legislative and judicial authority or, in other

[90]Or action by the king: Richardson and Sayles, in *Law Quart. Rev.*, L, 549-55, 562.

[91]Even at the end of the sixteenth century, when Coke (5 Rep. 37ᵛ) quotes the maxim *casus omissus & obliuioni datus dispositioni juris communis relinquitur*, it was still far from being used in its modern sense: *infra*, p. 67, n. 143.

[92]W. H. Loyd, 'The Equity of a Statute,' *Univ. of Penn. Law Rev.*, LVIII, 76-86; Landis, in *Harvard Legal Essays*, pp. 214-18; Chrimes, *op. cit.*, pp. 295-99; Thorne, in *Ill. Law Rev.*, XXXI, 205.

words, to visualize it as an illustration of the power of the judiciary to supplement legislative fiat, is to conceive it in modern and therefore anachronistic form. It was simply a facet of the administration of justice, and thus the doctrine of 'lequity de lestatut' reflects nothing more than the familiar medieval definition of equity,[93] and rests wholly upon the maxim *de similibus idem est iudicium*.[94] The extension of an act to an analogous case was clearly not looked upon as an infringement of parliamentary authority, for the Year Books are completely silent on that aspect of the matter and objections directed against extension were never based upon an

[93]H. Fitting, *Juristische Schriften des früheren Mittelalters* (Halle, 1876), p. 146; Bracton, *De Legibus et Consuetudinibus Angliae*, fol. 3: 'Aequitas autem est rerum convenientia quae in paribus causis paria desiderat iura et omnia bene coaequiparat.'; C. Güterbock, *Bracton and His Relation to the Roman Law* (Philadelphia, 1866), p. 80; Maitland, *Bracton and Azo* (Selden Soc.), pp. 27-28; *infra*, p. 78, n. 163.

[94]Just as does the comparable doctrine of extension by analogy found in medieval Roman and canon law: Engelmann, *op. cit.*, pp. 157-58: 'Dagegen ergibt sich die Rechtsanwendung von Bestimmungen auf von der sinnerklärenden Auslegung nicht mitumfasste Fälle oder Tatbestände nicht schon durch Auslegung, sondern erst durch ein Werturteil über die rechtliche Gleichartigkeit oder Ähnlichkeit des zu beurteilenden Falles mit dem durch Gesetz oder Rechtsbrauch geregelten Falle nach dem römischen Grundsatze gleicher Rechtsgeltung bei ähnlicher Sachlage aus gleichem Geltungsgrunde (*"ratio aequitatis"*), dem Grundsatze analoger Rechtsanwendung, nach welchem sich die Tragweite (*"vis et potestas"*) geregelter Rechtsgeltung weit über die Grenzen der Bewussten und erkennbaren Regelung hinaus erstreckt.'; Van Hove, *op. cit.*, I, 2, p. 326: 'Fundatur analogia in exigentia ipsius iuris, in eius *aequabilitate* nempe, quae postulat ut, deficiente regula positiva, res quae eiusdem sunt rationis eodem iure regantur: "In similibus idem est iudicium;" "Ubi eadem est ratio, ibi idem ius." '; C. Lefebvre, *Les Pouvoirs du juge en droit canonique* (Paris, 1938), pp. 109, 119: 'La conaissance du fondement ultime de l'analogie dépend de la nature même du processus employé. Il consiste, on l'a vu, à étendre une disposition à un autre cas non prévu, à égaliser deux situations semblables ou même identiques. L'analogie repose donc essentiellement sur la nature du droit qui est équitable, "*aequum.*" Tous, tant canonistes que juristes, mettent en relief ce caractère qui fournit la base la plus solide à la légitimité de l'opération analogique.'

insistence that the words of the act, since they were the expression of the legislative will, must be taken precisely as they stand. Nor do the Year Books give any indication that the juridical and constitutional questions that would be stirred by like action today were discussed or raised. For that reason, judges did not consider it necessary to assume a reserve of discretion at the disposal of the judiciary—'a liberty and authority over laws, especially statute laws'—that would permit the extension of statutes to similar cases, to explain their actions as 'interpretations' of statutes, or to justify them as applications of the intention of the makers of the act.[95] These explanations will be needed in the sixteenth century, when the words of parliamentary acts begin to take on the appearance of sovereign commands, and they will then emerge, but during the Year Book period enactments did not yet possess the rigidity that was later to make any departure from their terms *ipso facto* an act of judicial will. Whatever liberties judges may seem to be taking with statutes, and whatever powers would be needed to justify their actions today, they were themselves conscious of performing nothing more than an ordinary, routine step in the administration of justice between party and party.[96]

[95]What 'lentent del fesors del statut' had been is not discussed in connection with the doctrine of 'lequity de lestatut' in the Year Books. Similarly in canon law: Van Hove, *op. cit.*, p. 326: 'Non fundatur [analogia] in voluntate legislatoris, ne interpretativa quidem.' The same is true of the medieval Roman law: Engelmann, *op. cit.*, p. 159: 'Die analoge Rechtsanwendung setzt voraus, dass der Geltungsgrund (ratio) der anzuwendenden Rechtssatzes ersichtlich ist und dass gegen de gleiche Rechtsgeltung im ähnlichen Falle kein Grund der Gerechtigkeit und Billigkeit spricht . . . Nach allgemeinen Grundsätzen sind Gesetze und Gewohnheitsrecht, die einen erkennbaren Geltungsgrund (ratio aequitatis) haben, der entsprechenden Anwendung auf ähnliche Fälle fähig, für deren Gleichbehandlung die gleiche ratio aequitatis spricht.'

[96]They were, in fact, applying the ordinary procedure of the common law: Bracton, fol. 1ᵛ: 'Si autem aliqua nova et inconsueta emerserint et

Under such circumstances, definite principles indicative of
the factors that must be present for a situation to be remedied
by 'lequity de lestatut' did not evolve: if a useful result could
be reached, or if no remedy was otherwise available, a case
might be brought within an act that had not dealt with it
in express terms.⁹⁷ A rudimentary rule does appear in Henry
IV's reign, though it was by no means always observed in
practice: analogous cases are not to be taken by the equity
of penal statutes.⁹⁸ Later in the Year Book period, statutes
in derogation of common right,⁹⁹ and those that restrained

---

quae prius usitata non fuerint in regno, si tamen similia evenerint, per simile
iudicentur, cum bona sit occasio a similibus procedere ad similia.'; see the
use of the words 'per lequitie de le common ley' in H. 11 H. 4, 40, pl. 2.
Similarly in medieval Roman law: Engelmann, *op. cit.*, p. 158: 'Die gemeinrechtliche Geltung des Grundsatzes analoger Rechtsanwendung bedarf
keiner Belege. Die Voraussetzung seiner Geltung war schon bestimmend
für Art und Inhalt der Kodifikation Justinians. Er beherrscht auch die Arbeit
der Glossatoren und ist mitbestimmend für den Inhalt und die Bedeutung
des Glossenwerks des Accursius und für die Art des Rechtsunterrichts
der späteren italienischen Rechtslehrer. Ausdrücklich wird die analoge Rechtsanwendung dem Richter vorgeschrieben in 1. 12 D. de
legibus 1, 3: "*ad similia procedere atque ita jus dicere debet,*" für kaiser-
liche Entscheidungen in 1. 11 C. de leg. 1, 14: "*omnes . . . judices . . .
sciant hanc esse legem non solum illi causae, pro qua producta est, sed et
omnibus similibus,*" . . . Gewöhnlich wird der Fall analoger Anwendung
in der Lehre genauer als "*extensio ad alium casum,*" "*ad casum non com-
prehensum,*" "*ad casum non expressum,*" gekennzeichnet.'

⁹⁷*Infra*, pp. 143-47, nn. 120, 121, 128, 135; Landis, in *Harvard Legal Essays*,
p. 215.

⁹⁸The available Year Book cases are collected *infra*, p. 154, n. 152. Similarly in canon law: Lefebvre, *op. cit.*, p. 120: 'Cette équité, qui sert de base
à l'analogie, fournit en même temps la mesure de son utilisation: elle ne
pourra être employée pour étendre des dispositions contraires à l'équité.
C'est ainsi que l'ancien droit interdit l'analogie quand il s'agit de lois cor-
rectives, exorbitantes, ou penales . . .'; Engelmann, *op. cit.*, p.159: 'Bei
odiosen Bestimmungen nach der Regel des kanonischen Rechts reg. 15:
"*odia restringi et favores convenit ampliari.*" Das gilt für Strafbestimmun-
gen, die Strafen verschärfen.' This must not be confused with the maxim
nulla poena sine lege which is much later in origin: see *infra*, p. 67, n. 143.

⁹⁹H. 14 H. 7, 18, pl. 7, Vavisor: *infra*, p. 160, n. 176. Similarly in the
medieval Roman law: Engelmann, *op. cit.*, p. 159; *idem*, 'Der geistige

or abridged the common law,[100] are said to fall within that rule,[101] and the argument was made that 'when a statute abridges the common law nothing will be taken by equity of it but it must be read *stricte*.'[102] The answer to this contention was a denial that the act abridged common law or the counterassertions that it enlarged the law, that it was beneficial, that if the act were not extended to the case before the court 'great mischief would ensue,' or, more rarely, that the act did not restrain but was an affirmance of the common law. Such reasoning, however, must not be given undue prom-

Urheber des Verbrechens nach dem italienischen Recht des Mittelalters,' in *Festschrift für Karl Binding* (Leipzig, 1911), II, 582-84, and especially the words of Baldus there quoted: '. . . item statuta, quae sunt contra rationem, non extenduntur . . . ubi deficit ratio, quae debet esse bona et aequa, non potest fieri extensio, quia a ratione iniquitatis non fit extensio, sed a pari ratione aequitatis.'

[100]The Year Book cases in which this argument is used are noted *infra*, p. 160, n. 175. The same idea lies back of the theory that the common law is the inheritance of the subject: M. 18 H. 6, 19, pl. 2 (*Select Cases in the Exchequer Chamber*, p. 74): 'Dauers: Chescun liege homme del Roy est enherite en ley sicome il est en terre . . . cest suerte est encountre le ley et chescun est enherite dauer le ley &c.'; M. 2 E. 4, 19, pl. 13, Billings; Plowd. 236ᵛ; P. Birdsall, 'Non Obstante,' in *Essays in History and Political Theory in Honor of Charles Howard McIlwain* (Cambridge, Mass., 1936), pp. 37-76. The parallel to medieval Roman law may be pointed again: Thorne, in *Speculum*, XI, 456; Engelmann, *Die Wiedergeburt der Rechtskultur*, p. 153: 'Statuten, die dem gemeinen Recht widersprechen, sind im Zweifel so auszulegen, dass sie dem gemeinen Recht weniger Abdruch tun. Daher sind dem gemeinen Recht widerstreitende Bestimmungen der Statuten, wenn sie keine ratio aequitatis erkennen lassen, nach Sprachgebrauch der Statuten in genauem Wortsinne, im Zweifel in einschränkendem Sinne auszulegen.'; pp. 159, 165: 'Streng auszulegende Statuten "*contra jus commune*," die geltendem gemeinem Recht widerstreiten, sind nach der zunächst verherrschenden Lehre nicht analog anzuwenden, auch wenn ihre ratio erkennbar ist . . .'

[101]The word 'penal' continues to include all three: it is so used in Plowden. When placed within single quotation marks it is used in that sense here.

[102]H. 14 H. 7, 17, pl. 7, Kingsmill; similarly: M. 18 E. 4, 16, pl. 18: *infra*, p. 160, nn. 175 and 176; Thorne, in *Ill. Law Rev.*, XXXI, 211-13.

inence,[103] for the decisions in fact turned only on the answers to these questions: Is the case in the same mischief as that for which the statute provided? Is the result a legally reasonable and beneficial one?[104] An accurate formulation of the principle that during the Year Book period lies back of extensions by 'lequity de lestatut' is that given by Paston in the early fifteenth century: 'lex beneficialis rei consimili remedium praestat, odiosa autem casu quo efficitur vlterius non extendit.'[105] That a statute was penal or abridged the common law did not mean that it must necessarily be denied extension: these categories supplied a useful rule of thumb, and the cases in which extension was denied undoubtedly fell within them, but an act must be taken strictly only when a liberal application led to an undesirable result.[106] This absence of

[103]No more than is given the assertions of counsel in many cases that the situation before the court did not fall within the express provisions of the statute: see Pole's contention in the Derby eyre: R. V. Rogers, 'Intervention at Common Law,' *Law Quart. Rev.*, LVII, 403-4, n. 19, which is typical. Dr. Chrimes (*op. cit.*, pp. 256-58) emphasizes a distinction between acts declaratory of the old law, which were to be equitably interpreted, and those introductory of new law, which were not to be so taken. But that played at most a minor role in the Year Books; indeed, it was very often held that acts which remedied a mischief and thus enlarged the common law were to be taken liberally: *infra*, pp. 143, 146, 155, nn. 120, 129, 152. Moreover, in Everard Digby's case, in which Dr. Chrimes understands (p. 258) that Kingsmill won 'acceptance for his view that a statute which abridged common law (therefore introductory of new law) was not to be interpreted equitably,' the decision in fact went against him and the act though in abridgment of common law was extended: Plowd. 59ᵛ, 178; Chrimes, *op. cit.*, p. 298. During the Year Book period the question whether statutes in derogation of the common law were to be strictly construed is illusory: cf. Allen, *Law in the Making*, pp. 378-79, n. 5, and the literature there noted.

[104]Cf. *infra*, p. 51, nn. 106 in fine, 107.

[105]M. 7 H. 6, 11, pl. 16: *infra*, p. 143, n. 120, §4.

[106]Similarly in the medieval Roman law: Engelmann, in *Festschrift für Karl Binding*, II, 541: 'Auch der anerkannte Grundsatz, dass "odiose" Gesetze nicht analog anzuwenden sind, schliesst nach der Meinung der italienischen Rechtslehrer die analoge Anwendung von Strafgesetzen nicht aus. Denn sie urteilten hier nicht vom einseitigen Standpunkt des Delin-

INTRODUCTION 51

rules, which has been noticed above in connection with ancient demesne, is characteristic of the judicial approach to legislation in a private-law scheme.

That acts of Parliament had achieved a new status by the middle sixteenth century, however, is reflected in the fact that the distinction between 'penal' and beneficial statutes then took its place as an objective rule of primary importance.[107] As parliamentary enactments were removed from

quenten, sondern vom Standpunkt der Rechtsordnung, von dem aus die Anwendung einer Strafbestimmung auf einer gleichstrafwürdigen Delinquenten nicht als "odium," sondern als im öffentlichen Interesse erwünscht, als "favor publicus" erscheint.'; *idem, Die Wiedergeburt der Rechtskultur,* p. 159. The same is true of statutes *contra jus commune:* Engelmann, *op. cit.,* p. 167: 'Im gegensatze zu dieser zunächst verherrschenden und von den Kanonisten allgemein befolgten Lehre haben viele Rechtslehrer, um billigen Bestimmungen des Statuten—und Gewohnheitsrechts gegenüber dem gemeinen Recht geltung zu verschaffen, die Meinung vertreten, dass auch Statuten wie Ortsgewohnheitsrecht *"contra jus commune"* nach allgemeinen Grundsätzen analog anzuwenden seien . . .' In sixteenth-century England when the distinction between 'penal' and beneficial statutes crystallized into definite form it then became difficult to account for the cases in the Year Books that had extended both penal acts and those in derogation of the common law: the cases then appear as exceptions to the rule that such statutes must be taken *stricti juris: infra,* pp. 51-53, nn. 107, 109.

[107]Crompton, *L'Avthoritie . . . des Covrts,* fols. 17, 20ᵛ; Jenk. 185, 221: 'Quae derogant communi legi, stricti interpretantur.' Its strength is revealed by the number of times it is read back into the early cases, so that those in which the 'penal' character of an act had been neither mentioned nor discussed now were taken to have been decided wholly on that ground. This had been true to a limited extent in the late fifteenth century (as the hypothetical cases put in H. 14 H. 7, 17-19, pl. 7, indicate), but it first becomes general in the sixteenth: cf. H. 11 H. 4, 50, pl. 28 with Plowd. 205; M. 27 H. 6, 1, pl. 3 with 6 Rep. 4ᵛ; M. 27 H. 6, 8, pl. 7 with Plowd. 17ᵛ and 8 Rep. 119ᵛ; H. 10 H. 6, 8, pl. 29 with Plowd. 10; M. 7 H. 6, 5, pl. 9 (*Select Cases in the Exchequer Chamber,* p. 38) with Plowd. 36ᵛ and Hatton, *Treatise concerning Statutes,* pp. 35-36; M. 5 H. 7, 7, pl. 16 with Plowd. 109ᵛ, 205; the Year Book cases cited *infra,* p. 156, n. 159 with the *Discourse's* explanation of them; the interpretation of Westminster 2, ca. 11 in the cases cited *infra,* n. 69, and p. 158, n. 168, and the analyses in the text of the *Discourse.* Cases in which 'penal' statutes had been extended during the Year Book period are vouched in support

the ambit of private law and were no longer to be handled
in essentially the same manner as common-law rules, the
formulation of regulations governing their application naturally became necessary. Attention has already been called
to the appearance, in the sixteenth century, of a distinction
between general and express statutes, which was substituted
for the simple private-law approach found earlier in the cases
of ancient demesne and Ireland, and also of a distinction
between affirmative and negative acts that was useful in other
ways. With respect to the extension of statutes beyond their
words, the distinction between 'penal' and beneficial acts
served a comparable purpose. But this rule, like its companion
attempts to deal with statutes on a new basis, was often
unsatisfactory and, in addition, had not always been observed
in the past.[108] The eighth chapter of the *Discourse* notes the

---

of the statement that such statutes may be taken by equity (see the cases
cited in the margin of Plowden's *Commentaries* at the pages noted *infra*,
pp. 52-53, n. 108), and form the explanation for the anomalous group of
decisions that permits some 'penal' statutes to be taken by equity since
'they have been so put in ure': *infra*, p. 157. Similarly, though the statutes
1 R. 2, ca. 12, and 9 E. 3, st. 1, ca. 3, were 'penal,' that had not been an
obstacle to their extension in the Year Books (*infra*, p. 149, n. 140), but
they offered difficulties in the sixteenth century: Brooke, *Escape*, 9:
'. . . ou gardeine de Fleete ad home en prison en execucion et luy per-
mytte descape, action de Dett gyst vers le gardeine per lestatute de Anno
1 R. 2, capitulo 12 . . . et nota que lestatute ne parle mes tantum del
gardein de Fleete, ideo quere si viscount en countie, ou auter gaoler suffre
tiel escape, videtur que action sur l'case gist la, car ceo fuit al comen
ley en tiel case . . . tamen mittitur in vsu vers vicount & huiusmodi.';
Parlement & Statutes, 24: 'Dett lestatute de 9 E. 3, [st. 1], ca. 5 [3] est que
cesty executor que primes venit per distres respondra, vncore ponitur in
vsu que cesty que venit per Capias respondra, quod nota, et hoc
videtur per vn equitye.'; similarly, *infra*, n. 57; 10 Rep. 83: 'Et sicome ceux
statutes auoient este mise in vre solonque lexpresse puruieu coment que
damage ad accrue al subiect . . .' The evolution is similar to that described
in the discussion of affirmative and negative statutes, *supra*.

[108]Plowd. 46: 'ne fuit sure ground que penall statute ne sera prise per
equity car en plusors cases nous veyeromus le contrarie.'; similarly, Plowd.
10, 17, 36, 47, 53, 59-59ᵛ, 82, 124, 178; Hatton, *op. cit.*, p. 66: 'I suppose most

exceptions, amply supported by precedent, that were quickly
made to the rule that 'penal' statutes must not be extended
beyond their words,[109] and similarly in Plowden many cases
were brought forward to show that a 'penal' statute may be
extended, for though it is 'penal against one, yet it is beneficial to all others,'[110] or, in the words of Chief Justice Montague, 'although it restrains the liberty of the tenant in tail,
Sir, every statute which shall be extended by equity restrains
someone, and is penal to someone, but yet inasmuch as it is
beneficial to the greater number, it shall be taken by equity,

---

of those Statutes Penal which are devised to supply a defect in the Common
Law, or to remedy a great mischief in the Commonweal, are extended by
Equity unto cases under Majority or parity of Reason with the Statute
established . . .'; p. 68: 'I suppose that those Statutes Penal, or Restrictive
of the Liberty that the Law otherwise giveth to man, as are in the most
wise mens judgments either equally, or more beneficial than they are penal,
may be extended by Equities, as the Statute of Westminster 2, ca. 1 . . .';
Crompton, *L'Avthoritie . . . des Covrts*, fol. 15: 'Quant estatut est fait
de redresser couin ou vn inconuenience que fuit al common ley, coment
que est penal, vncore auter cases in mesme le mischiefe serront pris per
equitie de dit estatute . . .'

[109]A statute, though 'penal,' may be taken by equity when: (1) it
declares the common law, but not fully; (2) it is the express meaning of
the statute makers (Plowd. 82v: 'Et issint le efficacy del estatutes nest
solement en les parols del estatutes, mes en lentent del estatutes, le quel
entent touts foits doyt este graundment pense, & les parols doient este encline
a ceo, & sur semble reason penall estatute serra extende per equitie, si
lentent del feasors de ceo poit este issint perceiue.'); (3) it has so been put
in ure (*supra*, n. 107); (4) the penalty is just and not *in terrorem* (Hatton,
op. cit., pp. 65-66: *infra*, p. 157, n. 163); (5) when greater reason demands
it (Hatton, *op. cit.*, p. 66: *supra*, n. 108); and (6) the statute takes away
a common law that was 'penal' or 'slavish' (Plowd. 53v: 'Car coment que le
statute icy restraine vn principle del ley . . . vncore serra extend per
equity, entant que fuit fait pur restraint del liberty que le commen ley
done en preiudice de auters.'; Hatton, *op. cit.*, p. 64: 'In the restraint of
rigour, there is greater favour than in some Statutes favourable, or giving
men priviledg or preheminence; for these do but increase a man's good
Estate, those other save the Head, preserve Liberty, deliver from Pains
Corporal and Pecuniary, and sometimes also from the not of Ignominy
. . .').

[110]Plowd. 36v, 54: *infra*, n. 100; 82.

and so is this statute, for it tends to the suppression of deceit and to the advancement of truth.'[111] The need for these arguments indicates the strength the distinction had acquired but also that it was, like the others that emerged contemporaneously, inadequate. One must not conclude, however, that it represents the fruit of three centuries of effort toward the formulation of a satisfactory rule: on the contrary, it was a pioneer attempt to treat statutes on a public- rather than a private-law level and as such an understandably imperfect and stumbling first step toward meeting a problem that had not pressed for solution earlier.

As the sanction behind statutes rather than their content is stressed, they lose their separateness and form a cognate group that must be dealt with as a whole. In response to this need the distinctions mentioned above became prominent and took their places as authentic rules of statutory interpretation. The change is no less apparent, however, in the transformation of 'lequity de lestatut' to 'equity.' In the Year Books, each statute had been considered individually and

[111]Plowd. 59ᵛ, 82ᵛ: *supra*, n. 109 (2); 468: '. . . & a dire que le ley est penal en ceo case, sir, Issint il est en lauter case, mes Equitie ne sache ascun diuersitie enter penal leyes & auters, car lentent . . . doit este ensue, & prise pur ley, cybien en les parolles del penal leys come auters.'; 2 And. 26 (?P. 37 Eliz.): '& quant les fesors de le dit estatute expresse plainment lour intent come ils font ycy nest reson de extende les parols de lestatute pluis ouster que ils purporte &c. Et fuit dit ouster que ceo estatute est penall ley & pur ceo ne doit estre extende pluis ouster que le letter cary mes doit estre prise stricte, & sur ceo (come grownd) mults des cases fuerunt myses d'ont graunde store sont en liuerrs & pur ceo nest necessary de remember ycy ascun de eux: car le grownd nest que fallacy &c.'; Hatton, *op. cit.*, pp. 23-24: '. . . all Statutes, in a manner, are Penall to some; but if they be beneficial to very many, and punish a few, they are to be counted gracious, taking that denomination of the prevalent quality.'; pp. 66, 68: *supra*, n. 108; p. 72: 'And to be short, there are few Statutes Penal, which may not be expounded by Equities, that are beneficial to the Commonwealth, or more part of good men, and Penal but to a few, not worthy to be favoured in such cases, if it so please the Judges of the land to agree.'; 2 Brownl. 108.

cases that were in the same mischief as that for which an act had provided, though they were not expressly included within it, were considered to be within the equity of that statute.[112] But in the sixteenth-century reports 'equity' appears unconnected with particular enactments, and clearly it is not accidental that Aristotle's general principle of ʼεπιείχεια was then for the first time taken to form its foundation.[113] Extensions of acts to analogous cases were now made by judges in the light of a controlling *Equitas:*[114] 'the wise judges of our law deserve great commendation for having made use of it to enlarge the letter according to its discretion.'[115] Plowden's pages are filled with illustrations of this judicial power, which had not been so described in the Year Books, but his interest must be attributed to the increased rigidity that attached to the words of acts of Parliament and the corresponding need

---

[112]For example, H. 14 H. 7, 13, pl. 2: 'Tremaile: . . . car issint est in plusieurs cases quand vn chose ad este purueue per *Statut*, chose in mesme le mischief ad este remedy per l'equite de cel *Statut*. Come per *Statut de Glocester cap.* 7. est ordone que *lou tenant in dower alien, cesty in le reuersion aura brief de casu prouiso:* & per cel *Statut* est solement parle de tenant in dower; vncore per l'equite de cel est pris que de alienation fait per le tenant per le curtesie, ou a terme de vie, il en le reuersion aura brief *d'Entre in consimili casu,* pur ceo que est in ouel mischief. Mesme la *Ley* est, ou executor per le *Statut de Anno 4 E. 3. cap.* 7. auoit brief de *trespas de bonis asportatis in vita testatoris,* administrators sont pris per l'equite de cel; vncore le *Statut* ne parle de administrators: mes pur ceo que est in ouell mischief, est reason que il sera prise per l'equite de cel: issint in plusieurs cases'; *infra,* p. 145, n. 128; p. 146, n. 129.

[113]Loyd, in *Univ. of Penn. Law Rev.,* LVIII, 77; Allen, *op. cit.,* p. 373; Plucknett, *Concise History,* p. 298. For the application of this new principle to circumstances requiring the restriction of statutory words see *infra,* pp. 77-80.

[114]Plowd. 467: 'Equitas est verborum legis directio efficacius, cum vna res solummodo legis cauetur verbis, vt omnia alia in aequali genere eisdem caueatur verbis.'; the matter may be viewed as well from the other side: 'Et issint quaunt les parols enact vn chose, ils enact touts auters choses que sont en semblables degrees.'

[115]*Ibid.* See also Coke's definition: *infra,* p. 64, n. 136.

for some method of escape from their binding force—not to
the fact that the subject had 'a peculiar fascination for him'
or because 'he was a specialist in these matters.' On the other
hand, however, statutes were not yet thought to be exact
formulas emanating from supreme parliamentary authority
nor were they (though the attitude adopted toward them was
quite different from that current in the fourteenth century
and they themselves were more carefully phrased and replete
with enumerations, exceptions, provisos, and saving clauses)[116]
yet conceived in the same spirit as modern legislation. The
inclusion of analogous cases within an act was, to be sure,
no longer wholly incidental to the simple administration of
law or justice between party and party, but results similar
to those that had been reached earlier were still obtainable,
though now by means of a wide power that courts possessed
to extend statutes in the interests of substantial justice.[117]
Here was a new departure, but the judges of the sixteenth
century, reading the old cases in the light of contemporary
ideas of parliamentary authority, were immediately aware
that their predecessors had enjoyed similar powers to exactly
the same degree.[118]

In the sixteenth century, then, the extension of an enactment to a situation not within its precise words could be
justified by means of the doctrine of a controlling 'equity'
which was 'no part of the law, but a moral virtue which cor-
rects the law.'[119] This was a more generalized form of the
Year Book concept of 'lequity de lestatut,' which in turn
reflects the new attitude toward statutes which were now
being recognized as a body of material to be treated as a

[116]Plucknett, *Concise History*, p. 288.

[117]*Supra*, n. 60.

[118]Plowd. 467.

[119]*Infra*, p. 79, n. 165.

whole; but other explanations were also offered. The *Discourse* met the difficulties by a theory grounded upon 'reason & the commen lawe.' Statutes that confirm the common law may be taken by equity to include similar cases, just as the common law itself advances *ad similia*;[120] and so, too, may statutes that resolve a difficulty at common law by choosing between conflicting rules, for when 'doutes are determyned by parlyament, it shalbe said that that was the commen lawe, for so muche as it is presumed that which they doe to be upon beste reason.' Statutes which 'come in encrese of the commen lawe,' by broadening a particular remedy beyond its recognized common-law area, may be taken to indicate that the remedy may be further extended to others in like mischief, 'for synce the commen lawe is grounded upon commen reason yt is good that that which augmenteth commen reason shulde be augmented.'[121] These cases were perhaps sufficiently clear, though it must be noted that no similar systematization had taken place in the Year Books; but where the common law had not dealt with a situation at all (which was most often true) there the reason of the statute may unaided serve to extend it to similar but unmentioned cases, 'for the reason of the lawe is the soule & pythe of the lawe, yea, the verie lawe itselfe.'[122] Thus the *ratio* of the statute is its important part, and the extension of an act was explained as an application of its 'sence' or 'reason' (*quia ratio legis est*

[120]M. 13 H. 7, 5, pl. 3, Mordant; similarly in medieval Roman law: Thorne, in *Speculum*, XI, 456; Engelmann, *op. cit.*, p. 140: 'Rechtssätze der Statuten und des Gewohnheitsrechts, welche mit dem gemeinen Recht übereinstimmen oder welche gemeinrechtliche Begriffe oder Grundsätze voraussetzen, sind im Sinne der gemeinen Rechts auszulegen oder zu ergänzen.'

[121]Landis, in *Harvard Legal Essays*, p. 216.

[122]*Infra*, p. 147.

anima legis),[123] rather than as a simple equalization of similar situations made without theoretical justification in the course of the administration of justice.[124] The *Discourse* clearly does

[123]Plowd. 465. The *ratio legis* is not merely the particular reason that led to the adoption of the specific statute, though it may on occasion be that: *infra*, p. 148, 'when the mischiefe & cause why an estatut was made doeth faile, there doeth the lawe ytselfe faile.'; Cases sur lestatute de 13 E. 1, 7 Rep. 7; 2 Inst. 11; Van Hove, *op. cit.*, pp. 296-97; Lefebvre, *op. cit.*, p. 57. It is often identical with the 'reason' that extends a common-law rule to a novel case or itself forms the basis for decision when a new situation emerges for decision: [Egerton], *Speech . . . touching the Post-nati*, pp. 42-58, 84-85, esp. 53: 'No lawe euer was, or euer can be made that can prouide remedie for all future cases; or comprehend all circumstances of humane actions which Iudges are to determine: Therefore, when such happen, and complaint is made; what shall Iudges doe? Shall they stay for a Parliament? *Interim patitur iustus.* they must therefore follow *Dictamen rationis;* and so giue speedie iustice.' This 'reason' may be regarded as inherent in acts of Parliament themselves (*infra*, p. 147: 'the reasonableness that is in them,' and similarly Plowden and West: *infra*, p. 77, n. 162) or as the broad reason ('le *voier* reason del remedie: *infra*, p. 59, n. 124) or purpose that lies behind the act: Plowd. 59ᵛ: 'en oppression de fauxitie & en auauncement del veritie'; 82: 'pur le conseruation de tranquility, peace, & concorde'; *ibid.:* 'en repressing del vice & graund inconueniences'; 1 And. 350: 'pur le aduantage & benefit de les subjects.' These are but two ways of saying that the statute can be applied to all cases that may reasonably and usefully be included within it, and thus the 'reason' of a statute and 'lequity de lestatut' reach identical results. With the growth of emphasis upon the intention of the legislator the *ratio legis* becomes simply the *ratio legislatoris*—the reason for the enactment of the particular act. For a similar change (from *mens legis* to *mens legislatoris*) in the canon law of the sixteenth century see Lefebvre, *op. cit.*, pp. 61-66, 194, n. 1; also *infra*, p. 60, n. 127; p. 78, n. 163 in fine.

[124]Lefebvre, *op. cit.*, p. 42: '. . . un double principe était affirmé, l'un traditionnel, reconnaissant la possibilité d'étendre la loi audelà des termes mêmes de cette loi en vertu d'un principe qui lui était extérieur: l'équité, et l'autre inclinant vers le possibilité d'étendre la loi en vertu de la loi elle-même, ou de la *mens legis*.' Under this view the distinction between 'penal' statutes, which must be confined to their words, and beneficial acts, which need not be so understood, becomes irrelevant: Lefebvre, *op. cit.*, p. 59: 'la loi, même pénale ou corrective, doit d'étendre aussi loin que porte sa *ratio*.'; Engelmann, *op. cit.*, pp. 169-71. A similar result is reached by emphasizing the broad purpose of the act: Heydon's case, 3 Rep. 7ᵛ (26 Eliz.): 'Et fuit resolue per eux [les barons del Eschequer], que pur le sure & voier interpretacion de touts statutes en generall, (soient ils

not visualize a statute as a rigid pronouncement of law in the Austinian sense, to be applied literally and no further; nevertheless, it is evident that extensions to analogous cases raised more difficulties and thus required a more complex explanation than the lawyers in the Year Books had felt themselves obliged to formulate.

As acts of Parliament take on the attributes of modern legislation, the intention of the legislator must grow in importance and take the place of the equity, conjectured purpose, or reason that had controlled earlier. It is therefore significant that only during the middle years of the sixteenth century did the intention of the makers begin to form the justification for extending a statute beyond its words.[125] The *Discourse* had recognized that statutes must be taken *ex mente legislatorum*, and that the intention of the makers, whether secured directly 'by theire lyvinge voice,' or inferred from the actions of judges who had been 'mooste neerest the statute,' or from the words of the act itself, was important, but such considerations there occupied a position subordinate

---

penal ou beneficiall, restrictiue ou enlarging del common ley) 4 choses sont destre discerne & consider, 1. Que fuit le common ley deuant le fesans del act. 2. Que fuit le mischiefe & defect, pur que le common ley ne prouide. 3. Quel remedie le parliament ad resolue & appoint, pur curer le disease del common weale. Et 4. le voier reason del remedie. Et donques le office de touts Judges est, touts foits a faire tiel construction que represse le mischiefe & aduance le remedie, & a suppresser subtile inuentions & euasions pur continuance del mischiefe, *& pro priuato commodo*, & a adder force & vie al cure & remedie, solonque le voier intencion del fesors del acte *pro bono publico*.'; 4 Rep. 50: *infra*, p. 66, n. 139; 11 Rep. 71ᵛ: '. . . car office des Judges est a faire tiel construction que represse le mischiefe & aduance le remedie, & a suppresser touts euasions pur continuance del mischiefe.'

[125]There had been scattered examples earlier, for an argument based upon conjectured intent is too obvious never to have been invoked: *infra*, pp. 139, 151, nn. 109, 143. But the change from the usual fifteenth-century approach (M. 3 E. 4, 14, pl. 8: 'Jenney: . . . deins le equitie & issint deins l'entent de cel statute, ou autrement serra graund mischiefe . . .') is striking.

to 'reason,' which was itself sufficient warrant for extension. Similarly, 'yf it maie be expresselye gathered to be the meanynge of the statute makers,' a 'penal' statute could be extended, but this was only one of several exceptions to the general rule.[126] In Plowden's *Commentaries*, however, legislative intent was more heavily stressed: statutes were to be read 'according to common reason, and common intendment, and according to the minds of the makers.'[127] The phrase 'the cases which are in the same mischief as those which are remedied by a statute are taken by the equity of that statute,'[128] and other variations of the maxim *ubi eadem est ratio ibi idem ius*, gave way to another: 'for everything that is within the intent of the makers of the act, although it be not within the letter, is as strongly within the act as that which is within the letter and intent also.'[129] The tract attributed

[126]Actual intent may of course be utilized, and is controlling from Hengham's day to that of Lord Nottingham (1678): *infra*, p. 152, n. 145; but that will not often be available. It will be noted that the author of the *Discourse* was quite aware (*infra*, p. 151) that the actual intention of the legislature is undiscoverable in any real sense: 'so manie heades as there were, so many wittes; so manie statute makers, so many myndes.'; see M. Radin, 'Statutory Interpretation,' *Harvard Law Rev.*, XLIII, 870; Landis, 'A Note to Statutory Interpretation,' *ibid.*, p. 888; J. A. Corry, 'Administrative Law and the Interpretation of Statutes,' *University of Toronto Law Jour.*, I, 290; C. B. Nutting, 'The Ambiguity of Unambiguous Statutes,' *Minnesota Law Rev.*, XXIV, 509.

[127]Plowd. 10. As this becomes recognized the preamble is taken to indicate not the mischief existing at the making of the statute, and thus the purpose or 'lentent' of the act, but the *ratio legislatoris: infra*, n. 28; similarly, though the common law before the enactment of the statute is still sought, that throws light upon 'lentent del feasors' rather than 'lentent del statut': *supra*, n. 123 in fine.

[128]*Select Cases in the Exchequer Chamber*, p. 66 (the translator has missed the point of the passage).

[129]Plowd. 366ᵛ; 13ᵛ-14: 'Et issint lestatute [Westminster 2, ca. 1] ne parle des heires les donees en taile, mes des donees mesmez . . . & vncore ad este aiudge que le alienation lissue en taile ne serra pluis preiudicial a son issue que le alienation le primer donee serra a son issue, car les auncient peers del ley veyant que fuit ouel mischiefe, pristeront ceo come ouel ley,

to Hatton is more explicit: 'For when the words express not the intent of the Makers, the Statute must be further extended than the bare words, but ever it must be thought that the meaning of the Makers was such, when there is any proceeding other than the words bear, for it were an absurd thing to make an exposition go further than either the words, or the intention of the Statutaries reached unto.'[130] This new approach was immediately projected backward—a not unusual procedure in the common law—and it was recognized that in the past, when judges had extended the words of

---

& issint intenderont & construeront les ments des feasors del estatute, de mere necessitie, en auoydance del mere mischife.'; 82ᵛ: 'Et vncore lestatute est penal: mes pur ceo que les expositors del estatute pristeront lentent del feasors de ceo destre tiel s. a doner damages en cases semblable, ceo est le cause de ceo. Et issint lentent del feasors del estatutes direct les parols & equitie de eux . . .' The process may be seen to advantage in the reinterpretations of Littleton: cf. Litt. §731 (Co. Litt. 382) with Plowd. 57ᵛ; Litt. §685 (Co. Litt. 359ᵛ-60) with Plowd. 204ᵛ; Litt. §21 with Co. Litt. 24ᵛ.

[130] *Op. cit.*, pp. 28-29; p. 14: *infra*, n. 113; 1 And. 335-36: 'Pur consideration de [cest case] & touts auters Cases del Leys queux sont ambiguous, est necessary de consider ceux parts ensuants come vn erudite en le Ley escry, scil. bona, mala, vtilia, inutilia, conuenientia & inconuenientia. Et si soit bone ou male, profitable ou improfitable, conuenient ou inconuenient, & sur eux de expounder le Statute en cest point, & si il serra prise strict ou pluis largement . . . & primis si due reuerence soit done a le Parliament quel consist (come est conus) sur grand number de learned & discrete persons de Spirituality, Temporality, & Erudites en le Ley de dieu, & les Leys de terre, ne doit estre pense que ils intend de fair vn Ley per quel ils monstre lour intent playnment in parols de statute de toller vn chose, ou prouider counter les mischiefs queux fuerunt vses deuant le Ley fait, & vncore ils intend & mene clerement conter les parols de le Statute, & encounter ceo que est plainment expresse & declare per Record fait de lour agreements . . . si soit bone ou male, conuenient ou inconuenient, ne besoign ascun grand consideration, car certenment a ceo tener pur opinion est absurd; car n'est auter que tener en opinion que les fesors de le Act ceo intend, & que conter lour parols & determination ils auterment intend, le quel est en eux (si fuit voyer) ignorance & folly, ou auterment craft ou disceit, le quel nul reason poit reasonablement prouer . . . car si leys serra issint expound sans auter reason, n'est que male course de inducer ascun chose d'estre deins vn statute que ne vnques fuit intend.'

statutes, 'the reason for their interpretation has always been
founded upon the intention of the makers of the act, which
they have collected sometimes by considering the cause and
necessity of making the act, sometimes by comparing one
part of it with another and sometimes through extraneous
circumstances. So that they have ever been guided by the
intention of the makers, which they have always taken
according to the necessity of the matter and according to
that which is consonant with reason and good discretion.'[131]

Plowden's use of the word 'interpretation' must be re-
marked. The word had been used earlier, though in other
connections, and there is every indication that not until his
period did extensions of the words of statutes become judicial
'interpretations' or 'constructions' of them. The appearance
of the term 'interpretation' provides another indication of
the growing sanction back of acts of Parliament, for as enactments acquire formal rigidity their words must be saved by
regarding departures from them as 'interpretations' made by
judges. These were founded, as has been indicated, upon
reason or equity—words substantially synonymous with
justice—and in the later sixteenth century they were being
made as well in the light of the intention of the legislature.
In Plowden this is taken in its widest sense—as the desire to
reach results 'beneficial a le common weal' or to avoid
'enconuenience & mischiefe'—and under so broad a concept
of legislative intention, similarly equivalent in all respects to
that of justice, acts could be boldly extended, or (as will be
shown later) narrowly restricted, without difficulty. The
words 'lentent del feasors,' therefore, though they reveal a

---

[131]Plowd. 205ᵛ; 57ᵛ: 'Et issint les parols ambiguous ount este expounde
touts foits solonque lentent de feasors . . . ceux parols sont doubtous &
incerteine per le letter, mes le entendement de eux est . . . et tiel ad este
le exposition touts temps puis, per lentent del feasors.'

wholly different approach from that customary in the Year Books, did not immediately lead to results contrary to or more limited than those that had been reached earlier by means of 'lequity de lestatut' or those that were contemporaneously achieved by 'equity'—by reliance upon the general purpose of the act or the *ratio legis*. Indeed, the last quotation shows that they were alternate methods for reaching the same end.[132] An act may still extend to similar cases, though now that is explained as well by the presumption that the legislature could not have intended to permit the continuance of a mischief 'en equall degree.'[133] The legislators alone know what they had intended, and therefore 'the life of the statute rests in their minds,' but 'if they are dispersed, so that their minds cannot be known, then those who may approach nearest to their minds shall construe the words, and these are the sages of the law whose talents are exercised

[132]Cf. it with the formula for finding the 'reason' or 'sence' of the statute: Plowd. 363: 'Et adeprimes ils disoyent que actes de parlyament sount leyes positiue que consyst de deux partes. Le primer est, les parolles del act. Le auter est, le sence, car le letter sans le sence nest le ley. Mes le letter & le sence ensemble sont le ley. Et chescun que voet estre apprise de le ley positiue doit auer intelligence de ambideux. Et le voy de apprender le sence est de consider le commen ley, que est auncyent a tout positiue ley, come *Browne* dit, & ad a faire en lexposition del ley positiue, & per ceo les mischiefes & inconuenyences que sont en le letter sount destre pence: & per reason escheue, & ceo est en le mettre al letter del positiue ley tiel sence que excludera touts rigours & mischiefes, & estoiera oue equitie & bon reason.' Similarly in Heydon's case, *supra*, n. 124: 'le voier reason del remedie' is presumed to be synonymous with 'le voier intencion del feasors.'; see also *infra*, p. 82, n. 171.

[133]Plowd. 82ᵛ: *supra*, n. 129; 178: 'Et pur ceo nest ascun cause ou presumption al contrary mes d'presumer, et prender, que les feasors del act entendount de ayder les patentees . . . & nyent de permitter ceo myschiefe remayne que fuit en equall degree.'; 59ᵛ: '. . . entant que ceo statute fuit fait pur oppression del couyn, il serra extende per equitie, & nosmant, pur ceo que lentent & mentes del feasors del statute doyent este prise destre enclyne . . .'; the legislature is presumed to act 'en oppression de fauxitie & en auauncement del veritie,' or 'pur el conseruation de tranquility, peace, & concorde': *supra*, n. 123; *infra*, pp. 82-83, nn. 171 and 172.

in the study of such matters.'[134] Finally, judges must, since the words of statutes are to be extended in the light of the legislative will, approach that as closely as may be by acting as the lawmaker would have acted had the case presented for decision been brought before him rather than the court.[135] Legislative intent, since it differed only verbally from the other reasons brought forward to explain the extension of statutory words, did not lead to their abandonment. Coke, it is true, used the doctrine of 'equity' sparingly;[136] the explanation most frequently offered by him for the extension of the words of an act (whether it be 'penal' or beneficial)

[134]Plowd. 82. Hatton, *op. cit.*, pp. 29-30: '. . . especially seeing a great part of them [the legislators] are by election, namely all of the Lower House, and then by the law Civil, the Assembly of Parliament being ended, *Functi sunt officio,* and their Authority is returned to the Electors so clearly, that if they were altogether assembled again for interpretation by a voluntary meeting, *Eorum non esset interpretari.* For the Sages of the Law whose wits are exercised in such matters, have the interpretation in their hands, and their Authority no man taketh in hand to control: wherefore their Power is very great, and high, and we seek these Interpretations as Oracles from their mouthes.'

[135]Plowd. 467ᵛ: 'est bone a toy (Lecteur) quecunque soies, que lies le letter del statutes, de imaginer que le Institutor del ley est present, et demaunds de luy le question pur lequite, et quant auois en tien ment demaund ceo, dones toy mesme responz quel vous imagine le Institutor de le ley voet auer done sil suissoit present . . .'; Allen, *op. cit.*, p. 374. In slightly modified form this is modern doctrine: E. Bruncken, 'Interpretation of the Written Law,' *Yale Law Jour.*, XXV, 135; De Sloovère, in *Univ. of Penn. Law Rev.*, LXXXVIII, 531, 539.

[136]4 Rep. 59ᵛ: '. . . de quel Judgement ieo obserue que les Barons adiudge le dit act de *36. E. 3.* destre prise per equitie, car le dit act parle solement de offices retorne en le Chauncerie, et le dit office fuit retorne en le Eschequer, que sans question fuit deins lentention & meaning del Act.' 5 Rep. 14ᵛ; 9 Rep. 12; 10 Rep. 101ᵛ: *infra,* p. 65, n. 137. His definition shows the influence of post-Year Book thought: Co. Litt. 24ᵛ: '*Equitie* is a construction made by the judges, that cases out of the letter of a statute, yet being within the same mischiefe, or cause of the making of the same, shall be within the same remedie that the statute provideth: and the reason hereof is, for that the law-makers could not possibly set downe all cases in expresse terms.'

was the purpose of the statute or the legislative will or intention, sometimes secured from the preamble or title, but often simply drawn from the circumstances Plowden had enumerated.[137] But, in the reports of the seventeenth century, arguments based upon 'equity'—often synonymous with the actual or presumed intention of the makers as revealed by the act, but occasionally used in its older sense—continued

[137]*Supra*, p. 62. 4 Rep. 3: '. . . si le iointure fuit fait deuant mariage que lentent des feasors del act fuit que el ne refusera . . .' (cf. *infra*, n. 96, §4); 59ᵛ: *supra*, n. 136; 6 Rep. 37: 'Car coment que nest ascun expresse clause de restraint de Leases . . . vncore tiel leas est encounter le intention & equitie del dit act . . . come appiert per le preamble, lestatute fuit fait encounter vnreasonable Leases, et est vnreasonable que vn lessee ferra a son pleasure wast & destruction, que est encounter le bien publique.'; 43: 'lentent del statute . . . (come appiert per le preamble) fuit a restorer le auncient common ley & a extirper & extinguisher touts subtill inuentions, imaginations, & practices . . .'; 7 Rep. 19ᵛ: '. . . fuit lentendment del act a gratifier le subiect, que lou nouel prouision fuit fait pur le leuier del debt le Roy in pluys speedy & beneficial manner . . .'; 8 Rep. 72ᵛ: '. . . mes cest statute fuit fait a relieuer cesty que ad droit, & a suppresser tort & daduancer droit . . .'; 137ᵛ: 'deins les parols & entention del act.'; 9 Rep. 25ᵛ: '. . . & que tout le consideration de cest case consist principalment sur le voier construction del dit statute de *32. H. 8.* & pur ceo le final intention del Act, & le puruieu del ceo, sont destre consider . . .'; 10 Rep. 57ᵛ: '. . . car *parliamentum, testamentum, & arbitramentum* sont destre prise solonque les ments & intentions de ceux que sont parties a ceo.'; 60ᵛ: '. . . car les feasors del act entendont non solement aduancement de religion . . . mes auxy encrease de bone hospitalitie & auoiding de dilapidations . . .'; 81: *infra*, n. 109; 101ᵛ: '. . . deins le equitie de ceux parols . . . car . . . *Quando verba statuti sunt specialia, ratio autem generalis, generaliter statutum est intelligendum:* et appiert per le preamble que lestatut fuit fait pur auoiding de periury, extortion, & oppression, trois haut horrible et odious crimes, & pur ceo pur suppressing de eux, et pur aduancement de veritie et Justice, le parols del act aueront benigne & fauorable interpretation; *in hijs enim quae sunt fauorabilia animae, quamuis sunt damnosa rebus, fiat aliquando extentio statuti.'*; 104: '. . . *et hijs non obstantibus,* pur ceo que lestatute fuit fait pur speedy execution de Justice, & serra expound fauourablement de effecter lentencion & purpose des fesors del act.'; 11 Rep. 30ᵛ, 33ᵛ, 34: 'Et est frequent in nostre liures que penall Statutes ount este prise per intendement, au fine que ils ne serront illusorie, mes prendra effect solonque lexpresse intention des feasors del act.'; 34ᵛ; 69: '. . . appiert per les parols del act, que le pleine intent des fesors de ceo fuit . . .'; see *infra*, p. 81, n. 170.

to be found useful.[138] The other explanations are found as
well, and in addition the results to which equity, purpose,
reason, and intention all led could be reached by a 'benigne
& fauourable interpretation.'[139] As legislative intent narrowed
in scope and became less clearly identified with the 'auauncement del veritie' or 'le conseruation de tranquility, peace &
concorde,'[140] and as the purpose or intention of the statute

[138]W. Jones 174 (3 Car.): '. . . & Whitelock dit que pur aduancement
de common justice il fuit bien a extender cest statute per equity a tant,
que poet per reason & bon construction . . .'; 371 (11 Car.): '. . . que
admitt, que les parolls del 31 H. 8 n'extende . . . tamen per equity il
serra, car l'entention del statute de 31 H. 8 fuit . . .'; 435 (15 Car.):
'. . . deins l'entent & equity del statutes.'; 439 (15 Car.): '. . . deins lequity
& compasse de cest statute . . .'; Hardr. 208 (13 Car. II); 2 Keb. 328, 330
(19 & 20 Car. II); 10 Mod. 282 (1 Geo. I); Corry, in *Univ. of Toronto Law
Jour.*, I, 295; Allen, *op. cit.*, pp. 377-78. A careful examination of the late-
seventeenth- and early-eighteenth-century reports with a view toward
tracing the decline of the doctrine would be of great value.

[139]3 Rep. 7ᵛ: *supra*, n. 124; 4 Rep. 50-50ᵛ: 'Et pur ceo fuit dit que le
feoffee del feoffee . . . est hors del dit act; Et fuit dit que issint auoient
semblable statutes estre construe que sont *stricti Iuris* . . . Mes fuit adiudge
. . . acts de Parliaments que done remedie en tiels cases, dieu defend
que ils ne auer benigne & fauourable interpretation, & extend a aduancer
le remedy proportionalment al mischiefe & defect del ley, solonque le
intention & meaning des fesors del acte . . .'; 106ᵛ: '. . . et si tiel construction ne serra fait, le mischiefe intend destre remedie per lact remaynera encounter le intent & meaning del act.'; 5 Rep. 5ᵛ: *infra*, p. 66, n. 140;
14ᵛ: '*Nota* Lecteur, le dit Act . . . ad estre construe beneficialment a
preuenter touts inuentions & euasions encounter le voyer intent des feasors
del act.'; 60: '. . . & acts de parliament faits en preuention ou suppression
de fraud doient auer benigne interpretation . . .'; 6 Rep. 72ᵛ-73: '& ieo
acquaint *Popham* chiefe Justice que cest resolution, & il bien allow de
ceo, & dit que fuit bien fait a construe le dit act in suppression de fraude.';
9 Rep. 25ᵛ: *supra*, n. 137; 10 Rep. 101ᵛ: *supra*, n. 137; 11 Rep. 71ᵛ: *supra*, n.
124; 76: '*Nota* Lecteur, come est obserue en le case . . . le dit act . . .
ad este touts foits construe beneficialment a preuenter touts inuentions &
euasions enconter le voier intention de mesme lact.'; Latch 12; 2 Sid. 28;
2 Sid. 63; March N.R. 36; see *infra*, p. 84, n. 176.

[140]5 Rep. 5-5ᵛ: '. . . . & touts Acts de Parliament, cibien priuate, come
generall, serront prise per reasonable construction, destre collect hors del
parolx del Acts memes, solonque le voyer intention & meaning des feasors
del Act.'; [W. Noy], *A Treatise of the Principall Grounds and Maximes*

came to be more rigidly limited by its words,[141] the last-named grew more frequent, developing naturally into the liberal or equitable construction of beneficial acts characteristic of the early eighteenth century.[142]

Though that century and much of the seventeenth fall outside the scope of the present essay, there was evidently no acceptance, prior to Blackstone's day, of the rule that, Parliament having spoken only of specific things and specific situations, all others were *casus omissi* within the maxim *casus omissus habetur pro omisso*. As Parliament became the sovereign and the duty of the judge was recognized to be merely to determine what Parliament has said and to 'apply' it, omitted particulars could no longer be supplied, since that would amount to a usurpation of or incroachment upon the power of the legislature.[143] This is a view of the judicial

---

of the Lawes of the Kingdome (London, 1642), p. 21: 'All Acts of Parliaments, as well private as generall, shall be taken by reasonable construction [to] be collected out of the words of the Act only, according to the true intention and meaning of the makers.'

[141]W. Jones 422 (14 Car.): 'Il tient que nest deins le equity ou intention del statute, il dit que fuit trope general ground a mitter cases sur statutes, ou choses fueront prise per equity, mes chescun statute estoy sur son particular reason, sur consideration del parts del statute, le mischief deuant, & que choses fueront intende destre remedy per le dit statute; & il prist cest ground, quant commencest oue particular enumeration, la nul auter chose serra prise per equity . . .'; Hardr. 186 (12 & 13 Car. II): 'It is not within the words of the exception, and why should it be said to be within the meaning?'

[142]Corry, in *Univ. of Toronto Law Jour.*, I, 296.

[143]Jones *v.* Smart, (1785) 1 T.R. 52, *per* Buller: 'We are bound to take the act of parliament as they have made it; a *casus omissus* can in no way be supplied by a court of law for that would be to make law.'; Wilson *v.* Knubley, (1806) 7 East 135, *per* Ellenborough: 'To extend it [the act] . . . would be to legislate and not to construe the act of the legislature.'; Fletcher *v.* Lord Sondes, (1826) 3 Bing. 580, *per* Best: '[If a "penal" law is extended by construction] the fate of accused persons is decided by the arbitrary discretion of judges, and not by the express authority of the laws.': see J. Hall, 'Nulla poena sine lege,' *Yale Law Jour.*, XLVII, 168,

function that differed fundamentally from that which had prevailed earlier, and one that in recent years has been the subject of increasingly vigorous attack. Its acceptance marks both the final abandonment of the powers of equitable construction assumed by judges in the sixteenth century (and thus of the older undifferentiated practice best described in terms of 'lequity de lestatut') and the beginning of a long series of apologetic explanations for their past use.[144]

IV

The preceding section has traced in outline the impact of sixteenth-century thought upon the activities of the courts in extending statutes to analogous cases. The converse operation of imposing limitations upon statutes, which was equally transformed after the Reformation Parliament, will now be considered.

---

but note the action was on a special resignation bond. A good many cases are collected in Corry, *op. cit.*, p. 298; Landis, in *Harvard Legal Essays*, p. 217; at this same time the rule appears that denies recourse to *travaux préparatoires*: Plucknett, *Concise History*, p. 299 (cf. p. 294), for it is dangerous to conjecture what a statute was intended to say (as against what it said) from external evidence (G. Bowyer, *Readings Delivered before the Honourable Society of the Middle Temple* [London, 1851], pp. 47, 80; Holdsworth, *Some Makers of English Law* [Cambridge, 1938], pp. 294-97), for that might lead judges to step outside their proper function. The growth of these ideas parallels the development of the new concept of sovereignty which Prof. McIlwain has often contrasted with the old: most recently in *Constitutionalism & the Changing World* (New York, 1939), pp. 26-85, 196 *et seq.; Constitutionalism Ancient and Modern* (Ithaca, 1940).

[144]These appear in most treatises on statutory interpretation (e.g., Maxwell, *op. cit.*, pp. 220-21), and are often repeated: F. J. de Sloovère, 'The Equity and Reason of a Statute,' *Cornell Law Quart.*, XXI, 591-95; Chrimes, *op. cit.*, p. 296. It is sometimes said that Coke had already used these explanations (Maxwell, *op. cit.*, p. 221 n.; Allen, *op. cit.*, p. 376; De Sloovère, *op. cit.*, p. 592) but these references are incorrect (*infra*, p. 152, n. 146) and their appearance must be postponed until the eighteenth century: Landis, *op. cit.*, p. 215.

During the Year Book period no difficulty was experienced in disregarding a parliamentary enactment which, though reasonable and practicable in general, led to injustice or raised technical difficulties in a particular instance. Despite the words of the act, the situation presented for decision was said to be simply 'extra casum statuti' or 'hors de cas de statut,'[145] though this may on occasion be put in other but equivalent phrases—that the facts before the court were not within 'lentent del statut,'[146] or, more rarely, 'lentent del feasors del statut.'[147] These cases have usually been described as 'exceptions out' of statutes, made through an exercise of judicial discretion, but that is to draw a sharper distinction than would have existed in the minds of contemporaries and to blur over the slow development, in the course of the sixteenth century, that is accurately reflected in the changing language of the reports.[148] The attention of Year Book

[145]Plucknett, *Statutes,* pp. 57 *et seq.;* Y.B. 8 Edw. II, 2 (Selden Soc.), p. 88; H. 46 E. 3, 2, pl. 3; H. 11 H. 4, 51, pl. 28; M. 18 E. 4, 16, pl. 18: *infra,* p. 160, n. 176. The same language is used later: 2 Inst. 414 (19).

[146]M. 10 H. 6, 8, pl. 30.

[147]H. 21 H. 7, 17, pl. 28. Dr. Chrimes (*op. cit.,* pp. 293-95) adds P. 4 E. 4, 4, pl. 4, and M. 15 H. 7, 13, pl. 1, but these illustrate not restrictive but extensive interpretation made in the light of the presumed intention of the legislature.

[148]Cf. R. Bellewe, *Les Ans dv Roy Richard le Second* (London, 1585), p. 95, and *Champerty,* 15 with Plowd. 465ᵛ; M. 4 E. 4, 31, pl. 12 with 9 Rep. 26ᵛ and Co. Litt. 381ᵛ: *infra,* p. 163, n. 184; Littleton's simple language with that of Plowden and Coke: *infra,* p. 163, n. 185; Litt. §685 with Plowd. 204ᵛ: '. . . quel exposition del *Littleton* del dit statute (fuit dit) est foundue sur lentent del feasors del act & sur bone reason,' and Co. Litt. 360: 'Here it appeareth, that acts of parliament are to be so construed, as no man that is innocent, or free from injurie or wrong, be by a literall construction punished or endamaged.'; similarly, though in the Year Books it had been sufficient to say that depending upon the penalties contemplated some acts did, though others did not, bind infants and married women (note that the author of the *Discourse* still felt it necessary to state [*infra,* p. 111]: 'an enfant also or feme covert shalbe bounden by an estatute lawe'), in the sixteenth century these classes of persons must be

judges was directed primarily to the attainment of a practical
and legally sound result in the case at hand, and, as they
were engaged in the administration of justice wholly within
the ambit of private law, they were not troubled by the
difficulties that would subsequently be raised. Similarly, in
the absence of the sanction that was later to make every
departure from the precise words of parliamentary acts an
example of judicial will, it was not yet necessary to posit broad
judicial powers in order to bring the express words of the
legislature into harmony with natural justice. Thus, driving a
distress out of one county into another when the land was held
of a manor in the second county was not trespass, 'notwithstanding the statutes of Marlebridge and Westminster the
first';[149] the exaction of a small sum of money as bar fee was
not extortion under the statute of 23 H. 6, ca. 9, for that pay-
ment 'cannot be understood to be within the case of the statute';[150] a chaplain was not bound by the general provisions of
the Statute of Labourers, 'because you cannot compel a chaplain to be in your service by the statute.'[151] There are no
indications that these were recognized as 'constructions' of
the acts in question or as 'exceptions out' of them made by

'excepted out' of statutes: *Doctor and Student*, fol. 29: *infra*, p. 81, n. 170;
Plowd. 205: 'Et issint lestatut de Westminster 2, capitulo 25 enact . . .
Vncore si vn feme couert oue son baron vouch record in assise & faile, el
ne serra attaint disseisoresse . . . Car lentent del feasors del act ne fuit
a conuicter feme couert deste disseisiresse . . . Et issint home veyera aiudge
plusors foits que estatutes ont este fait que ont done peine a chescun que
faira tiel act, ont este expound de extender a nul feme couert, ne enfant.';
1 And. 251: *supra*, n. 52; see also: *infra*, p. 82, n. 171; Thorne, in *Ill. Law
Rev.*, XXXI, 205-7.

[149]M. 1 H. 6, 3, pl. 9 (Y.B. 1 Hen. VI [Selden Soc.], p. 30): *infra*, n. 43.
Sixteenth-century explanations of the cases are there printed.

[150]H. 21 H. 7, 17, pl. 28; Plowden (465ᵛ) regards this as an example of
'Epichaia siue Equitas.'

[151]M. 10 H. 6, 8, pl. 30.

judges. A more striking example is afforded by a group of decisions that permitted acts of Parliament phrased in unambiguous terms to be completely disregarded since they led to results that were considered improper.[152] No principle of jurisprudence or political theory that might serve as an explanation was offered, nor did the reporters note these cases as especially important or distinguish them in any way from the other adjudications of *meum et tuum* they set down in their books.

The administration of justice within the scheme of private law may be further illustrated by a series of cases concerned with royal grants. In Henry VI's reign it was urged that 'King Richard II, after the conquest, by his letters patent which are here before you, granted to one J. S., Chancellor of Oxford, and his successors that they have conusance of all manner of pleas moved in the king's court in which one of the parties was both clerk and resident,' and that therefore, in an action of trespass brought against Thomas Chase, the chancellor, since he was 'a clerk, that is, *Doctor Theologiae*, and resident within the University,' he was entitled to act as judge in his own case.[153] Opinion was divided:[154]

[152]McIlwain, *High Court of Parliament*, pp. 296-97; Plucknett, *Statutes*, pp. 66-71; *idem*, 'Bonham's Case and Judicial Review,' *Harvard Law Rev.*, XL, 35-36; Thorne, 'Dr. Bonham's Case,' *Law Quart. Rev.*, LIV, 550; cf. the sixteenth-century explanation for *Cessauit*, 42: *infra*, p. 75, n. 160.

[153]M. 8 H. 6, 18-21, pl. 6; Brooke, *Patentes*, 15.

[154]'Cottesmore: . . . vncore me semble que le grant est void: car le Roy est lie par son serment a faire ses liges droit: & par son grant il ne peut me forecloser de m'action. Car jeo pose que vn home fuit en debte a moy, & le Roy luy grant que jeo n'aurai jamais accion vers luy: cest grant est void . . . Martin: . . . que le conusance n'est pas grant: car le brief est port vers le Chancelier meme, & il n'y ad clause en le chartre *licet fuerit Pars*, issint que il ne peut auer conusance sinon que il fuit specifie par expresse parols: & s'il fuit expresse, *licet fuerit Pars*, vncore me semble que il n'aura my la conusance sinon que le Roy luy aueroit grante, s'il meme fuit party que il peut faire vn autre Juge: car quand il est party il ne peut

estre Juge indifferent a luy mesme. Rolfe: . . . Et me semble que il n'est impertinent que la conusance soit grant, & que il soit son juge demene: car s'il fait en autre forme que la *Ley* veut la party auera brief d'*Error:* donques n'est nul mischief al party, car autre remedy il n'ad coment que vn estrange soit son juge . . . Babington: . . . il [le grant] sera pris *stricti juris,* ne en nul autre forme que le done est, & nul sera son Juge demene forsque le Roy, & vncore il done son Jugement par mene, come par nous & autres juges . . . Cottesmore: Jeo pose que conusance de touts maners des ples deins la ville de *Saint Albons* soit grante al Baily de meme la ville, & brief fuit porte vers vn de la ville, & le Baily demanda la conusance & soit grante, & puis meme cesty vers que le brief fuit fuit esleu Baily de meme la ville: jeo di que en cest cas le demandant ou le pleintif aura vn *Resommons* pur ceo que le Baily ne peut estre son Juge demene . . . Rolfe: A ceo que *Monmaistre Cottesmore* ad dit . . . jeo di que ils n'auront jamais *Resommons,* ne la ou la *Court* faile de droit, & tiel droit que appert al *Court,* que ils ne poyent faire, come si le tenant vouche vn foreine a garrante, ou plede vn ple qui port date hors del Jurisdiction, icy gist *Resommons* . . . en ceo cas [that put by Cottesmore] gist brief d'*Error* apres Jugement & nemy *Resommons.* Martin: Me semble le contrary de ceo que vous dits . . . car s'ils feront mys a brief d'*Error* grand inconuenience a ensuira; car jeo pose que ils ne veulent recorder vn defaut ou ils doiuent, & ils ne veulent jamais doner Jugement, donques ne peut la party auer brief d'*Error,* & donques sera il sans remedy: *consequens falsum est,* ils auront vn *Resommons* . . . si le Roy voule que il aura conusance quand il meme fuit party, ils le voulent auer expresse en sa chartre . . . Strange: Me semble que estoit oue raison que vn sera son Juge demene, & s'il fait autre que droit, il sera amende en la forme come *Rolfe* ad dit: mes . . . tiel chose ne peut passer del Roy sans special parolls: s'il fuit grante per obscures parolls, & peut estre entende a nous que le Roy ne fuit asserte de ceo quand il le grante, nous ne deuons pas ceo allower . . . Rolfe: . . . n'est pas inconuenient que vn home soit Juge demene . . . Me semble que il gist en grant le Roy a faire home estre son Juge demene, & que nul inconueniencie ensueroit, car s'il me fait autrement que la *Ley* veut, j'aurai brief d'*Error* . . . Babington: Si le Roy grante a vn home conusance de touts maners [de] ples *licet esset fauorabilis* a luy meme: mes s'il grant *licet fuerit Pars,* adonques le ple sera tenu par vn tiel son Seneschal & son depute: donques sera le Seneschal Juge quand son Maistre est party, & ceo veut la chartre le Roy, & ceo est nul inconueniencie, car le *Ley* entendra que il veut estre Juge indifferent auxybien come nous entre le Roy & autres . . . Et auxy inconuenient est a vn home d'estre son Juge demene come ad este adjuge, & ministre d'execute son jugement, & ceo ne peut estre. Car jeo pose que le Roy grante a le Baily d'*Oxenford,* que ils auront conusance dun ple, & ils ont conusance dun ple, & les parties sont a issue deuant eux, & ils agardont vn *Venire facias,* puis ils memes font cel, & returnent deuant eux memes, si ceo appert per le record, il est merement error, & pur ceo que ils ont malement fait, ils seront amercis: & ils memes ne purront amercir eux memes . . . Martin: Me semble a meme l'entent

Rolfe and Strange believed that the writ of error provided a sufficient safeguard, Martin and Babington that it did not, but obviously the discussion turned upon private-law considerations, and those who were inclined to permit a man to be judge in his own case took that position not because so ordered in a royal grant but because to do so was not prejudicial or 'inconuenient.' The letters patent, being general (and thus not conferring an express authority upon the Chancellor to decide cases to which he himself was party), supplied a convenient means, which was seized upon by a number of judges and serjeants, for escaping a direct adjudication of the problem, but if express words had been used there are indications that they would not have been sufficient.[155] A patent containing the phrase *licet fuerit pars*, it is said, would be 'impertinent' and 'void,'[156] and here a parallel may be

---

... que si conusance soit grante a vn home *licet fuerit Pars*, que cel grant est void, sinon que il soit specifie que il peut faire autre Juge, car il ne peut estre son Juge demene: car si Fine soit leue a vn *Justice de cest place*, & il meme prende la conusance, cest fine est void ... Strange: Me semble que vn home per grant le Roy peut estre son juge demene, car vn home represent deux homes *diuersis respectibus*. Car jeo pose que vn *Redisseisin* soit directe al Vicont, la il sera Juge & auxy minister ... & il est Juge & executor a son Jugement demene ... & sera entendu que il fist indifferentment donque il est vn home qui fist l'office de ii, & c'est nul impertinency: car sil fait autrement que la *Ley*, la party s'aydera par vn brief d'*Error* ... [mes] il [le Chancelier] n'aura la conusance par ceux obscure parols, sinon que ils furent expres ...'; similarly: T. 38 E. 3, 15-16, [pl. 20]; H. 40 E. 3, 10, pl. 21; M. 2 H. 4, 4, pl. 14; H. 12 H. 4, 13, pl. 3; T. 9 H. 6, 19, pl. 13, Fulthorpe; T. 11 H. 6, 49, pl. 7; M. 12 H. 6, 2-3, pl. 9; H. 35 H. 6, 54, pl. 18; M. 2 E. 4, 19, pl. 13; M. 9 H. 7, 11, pl. 6; *Abridgement of the booke of Assises*, fol. 58v.

[155]*Supra*, n. 36.

[156]M. 21 E. 4, 47, pl. 6: 'Baker: ... Come si le Roy grant a me *cognitionem omnium placitorum licet fuerim pars* d'estre tenus deuant mon bailif, il est bon, *quod tota curia affirmauit*, mes ilz diont que s'il soit grante a tener deuant luy mesme generalment, ceo est void.' Similarly, H. 39 H. 6, 40, pl. 3: 'Choke: ... car coment que le Roy per son prerogatiue puit prendre vn home en sa protection per vn an, ceo n'appert pas grand

drawn between an impertinent grant and an unreasonable custom.[157] There is but one Year Book case holding a statute 'impertinent' and 'void,'[158] and it must therefore be taken with

---

mischief a le party, ne nul disinheritance, pur ceo que apres l'an nient obstant cest *protection* il puit auer *Resommons*, & proceder en suit, mes ou il est eins per iii ans, il puit este per xx ans C ans ou M ans; issint appert al commencement ouertement disinheritance, & tresgrand mischief & inconuenience, que n'est suffrable per *Ley*. Sicome le Roy puit grante a vn chartre dexemption que il ne sera mis en Enquest, &c. & puis vn auter . . . mes s'il grant per son chartre a touts que demeurent en le County, que ils ne seront mis en l'Enquest, cest grant est void pur l'inconuenience: et issint en cest case.' The report has been summarized in Chrimes, *op. cit.*, pp. 281-82, but as has been pointed out (Plucknett, in *Tudor Studies*, p. 170), it is misleading to regard cases like these as illustrations of the supremacy of statute over royal prerogative, for the only point in issue was whether the words of the charter led to an 'inconueniencie': the abstract problem of public law was not raised. It had not yet become simply a question of superiority in Plowd. 236: 'Et coment que le roy ad moults prerogatiues per le common ley touchant sa person, ses biens, ses dets and duities, & autres choses personal, vncore le common ley ad tielment admesure ses prerogatiues que ils ne tolleront ne prejudiceront l'inheritance de ascun.'

[157] M. 35 H. 6, 25-29, pl. 33 (*Select Cases in the Exchequer Chamber*, pp. 114-29): p. 115: '. . . il est encontra resoun et comen droit et in preiudice dune autre persone et issint ici il est encontre resoun quune auera [omit: quune auera] et droit quilz prescriberount quune auera mez biens in plegge par Estraunge et que le properte serra in moy et chargable par autre person issint le prescripcion est voide. Et sir coment que le prescripcion soyt boun, vncore il est voide vers le Roy quar il est except de chescun custome . . .'; p. 116: 'Fortescue: Arguez et moustrez vne Custome que est encontre resoun quar sont plurieus Customez allegez mez nulle incontre resoun et la ley est fondu sur resoun et resoun est ley quar si terre soit departable intre malez ou que le puisne fitz inheritera cest resoun; mez sir si la Cyte de Loundrez voille prescriber que si ascun Estraunge in la Cite defende [insert: se vers] ascun home quil [read: qui] lirra a lui de lui naufrer cest prescripcion est incontre droit et resoun quia licitum est vim repellere . . .'; p. 118: 'Et auxint si home voille prescriber dauer de chescun que demurre sur soun seignourie dauer [omit] vn fyne quant il marie sa fyl ou fitz cel prescripcion intre frank hommez est voide, quod fuit concessum . . .' There are many cases on unreasonable customs: see Allen, *op. cit.*, pp. 504-23.

[158] P. 27 H. 6: *Annuitie*, 41: *infra*, p. 171, n. 211, §9. Coke (*infra*, p. 87, n. 186, and 2 Inst. 587-88) and Blackstone (*Comm.* I, 91) use 'impossible' as the equivalent of 'impertinent,' but that was not the meaning given

caution,[159] but there is no reason to believe that if the Chancellor's patent had been both express and confirmed by act of Parliament the arguments would have taken another course and a contrary result would have been reached. The growing sanction back of parliamentary enactments that appears in the sixteenth century may be seen both in the more complex explanations used to account for the restriction of statutory words—a development which parallels that noticed above in connection with the extension of an enactment beyond its precise scope—and in the recognition of judicial 'interpretation,' which is understood in a very wide sense as the power to bring acts of the legislature into the fullest possible accord with substantial justice. Thus it may be said straightforwardly that 'those that are out of the myschiefe of an estatut are lykewyse out of the compasse of the statute'; that a statute must be taken 'conter les parollz' or 'enconter le texte' to avoid injustice, since it is a truism that 'statutes come to stablyshe lawes, & yf anie iniquitye shulde be gathered of them they doe not so muche as deserve the name of lawes';[160] and that acts of Parliament

---

the word in the Year Book: McIlwain, *The High Court of Parliament*, pp. 270-76, 308; Plucknett, in *Harvard Law Rev.*,XL, 39-41, 55 (n. 71), 59 (n. 88). There are cases disregarding statutes but there is no other using the terms 'impertinent & void.'

[159]3 Rep. 23: '. . . et *Wray* chiefe Justice, et sir *Tho. Gawdie* disoient, que sicome cestuy que est bastard nee nad ascun cosin, issint chescun case import suspition de son legitimation, sinon que il ad auter case que serra come son cosin german a supporter . . .'

[160]*Infra*, p. 162. Plowd. 109ᵛ-110: 'Et issint lez Judges que fueront nostre predecessors, ascun foits ont expound parolz merement enconter le texte. Et ascun foits ont prise choses per equitie de vn text contrarie al text de faire eux agreer oue reason & equitie. Et pur ceo lestatut de Anno 25 E. 3. est, que per lexception de nontenure de parcel, nul brief abatera . . . [*infra*, p. 170, n. 211, §5] quel exposition est merement encounter le text, car le text est que nul brief abatera, & ils abatera ascun briefe, & issint lour exposition exclude le generaltie, & fait lestatute particuler, et

A DISCOURSE

are to be read in the light of reason and convenience, or, in other words, to be so understood that neither injustice nor absurdity ensues.[161] But more usually a distinction was

---

issint ount ceo expounde enconter le texte de fair ceo agreer oue reason. Et en mesme le maner ils ont expound lestatut de *Praerogatiua Regis* . . . le quel exposition est contrarie al texte pur ceo que le text est contrarie al reason, que pur tiel petit tenure home payeroit cy graund charge, que ilz ne pristerount destre lentent del feasors del estatute. Et lestatute de Westminster 2, de Cessauit est, *Fiant breuia de ingressu haeredi petentis, super haeredem tenentis, & super eos quibus alienata fuerint huiusmodi tenementa.* Vncore si le demaundant en Cessauit morust, le heire nauera Cessauit, pur ceo que il nauera les arrerages, & issint lestatut ad este expounde et prise, quel exposicion est merement contrarie al texte a touts purposes, pur ceo que le texte est contrarie a tout reason, a doner action al heire pur vn chose en consideration de auter chose nient due a luy.' Hatton, *op. cit.,* p. 44: 'Sometimes Statutes are expounded by Equities, because Law and Reason repugn to the open sense of the words, and therefore they are reformed to consonance of Law and Reason. The Statute of 25 *E.* 3. That by exception of *non tenure* of parcel, no Writ shall abate . . . The Statute of *Westmin.* 2. of Cessavit . . .'

[161][St. Germain], *Doctor and Student,* fol. 27-27^v: *infra,* p. 80, n. 169; fol. 29-29^v: *infra,* p. 81, n. 170; Plowd. 9: *infra,* n. 43; 13^v-14: 'Et lestatut de Westminster 2, capitulo 3, que done resceits a feme couert, dit, *si vxor ante iuditium venerit parata respondere, et ius suum defendere, admittatur &c.* Et issint ne done le resceit mez ou la feme est *parata respondere,* et vncore ad este aiudge que el, esteant resceiue, priera en aide ou vouchera, & issint ad este resceiue lou el nad este *parata respondere.* Mes les auncient peeres del ley considerant le dit estatute, ont veye que si lestatute serra prise strict accordant as parols, que donques graund enconuenience ensueroit, s. le perde del recompence per le garranty &c. & pur ceo ils pristeront le dit estatute solonque lequitie entende per reason, coment que les parols ne done ceo, & coment que les parols semblant encounter ceo, issint que en touts estatuts il y sont ascun priuate cases exempt hors del general prouisions per lequitie del reason, pur auoidance de pluis grand mischiefe . . . Pur queux cases auant per moy reherse, il appiert que ascun choses pur mere necessity sont exempts & foreprise (per lequitie del reason) hors del prohibition des parols del estatutes . . .'; 18^v: *infra,* p. 120, n. 43; 109^v-110: *supra,* n. 160; 204-5, 465-67; *infra,* p. 169, and pp. 169-70, nn. 209, 211. In the following century: Hob. 346: 'if you ask me, then, by what rule the judges guided themselves in this diverse exposition of the self same word and sentence, I answer, it was by that liberty and authority that Judges have over Laws, especially over Statute Lawes according to reason and best convenience to mould them to the truest and best use . . .'; see *supra,* n. 123.

drawn between the words of an act and its 'meaning,' 'reason,' or 'sence,'[162] or the results to which all these methods of approach led were reached by means of a doctrine of 'equity.'

In the Year Books, though the extension of a statute to an unprovided case was accomplished through 'lequity de lestatut,' that term was never used in the contrary process by which a situation was held not to fall within an act too generally drawn. The legal vocabulary of the reporters contained no word describing the unconnected instances in which statutes had not been literally applied in particular

[162]*Infra*, p. 140. Plowd. 13ᵛ, 18-18ᵛ: 'en chescun ley ilz y ont ascun choses que quant ils chanceont & happont, home poit infringer les parolx del ley, & vncore ne infringera le ley; & tiels choses sont exempt hors del penalty del ley, & le ley eux priuiledge coment que ils sont faits enconter les parolls, car le infringer del parols del ley nest infringer del ley, si entent del ley nest infringe. Et pur ceo les parols del ley de nature, de ley de cest Realm, & dauters realmes, & le ley de Dieu auxi voile yelder & doner lieu a ascuns acts & choses faits enconter les parols de mesme le leyes, & ceo est lou les parols del ley soient infringe pur auoidre greindre inconueniences, ou pur necessity, ou pur compulsion, ou pur inuoluntary ignorance.'; 82, 109ᵛ: *supra*, n. 160; 205ᵛ, 363: *supra*, n. 132; 465, 466: 'Et issint le vicount que ad alien eux deinz lan, & en ceo ad fait contrarie al parols del ley, nad infreinge le ley, mez ad obserue le ley, entant que il ad obserue lentent del ley, & plest bien les Institutors del ley.'; Hatton, *Treatise concerning Statutes*, p. 14: *infra*, n. 113; William West, *The Second Part of Symboleography*, fol. 176: 'By all which we may gather, that the outward words of the law onely are not the law but the inward sence and meaning thereof: For our Lawes (as all other lawes) haue two parts, that is to say, the flesh & soule, the letter resembleth the flesh, the intent and reason, the soule: *Nam ratio legis est anima legis*. The Law may be compared to a nut, whereof the letter resembleth the shell, the sence the kernell, and as the profit of the nut is not in the shell, but in the kernell, so the fruite of the Law is not in the letter, but in the sence: and as he which resteth vpon the shell looseth the fruit of the nut, so he which staieth vpon the letter wanteth the profit of the Law . . .'; 5 Rep. 2ᵛ: *infra*, n. 113; 10 Rep. 100: '. . . est ascauoire que la sont 2. manners des formes, s. *forma verbalis*, & *forma legalis; forma verbalis* estoit sur les letters & sillables del act, *forma legalis* est *forma essentialis*, & estoit sur le substance del chose deste fait & sur le sence del statute, *quia Notitia ramorum huius statuti non in sermonum foliis, sed in ratione radice posita est.*'; 2 Inst. 107: 'a case out of the mischiefs is out of the meaning of the law, though it be within the letter.'; see *supra*, n. 123; cf. *supra*, p. 70.

cases because of the injustice that would ensue. But in the early sixteenth century St. Germain recognized these as examples of that 'Epicaia, the which is no other thing but an exception of the law of god, or the law of reason, from the general rules of the law of man, when they by reason of their generalty would in any particular case iudge against the law of god, or the law of reason'[163]—though he was careful to point out that 'of this term equitie to the intent that is spoken of here, ther is no mencion made in the lawe of Englande, but of an equity deriued vpon certeine statutes mencion is made many tymes and often in the law of England. But that equity is al of an other effect then this is . . .'[164]

[163]*Doctor and Student*, fol. 27ᵛ. St. Germain, like Bracton, borrowed continental terms and distinctions and adapted them to the problems of English legal practice: P. Vinogradoff, 'Reason and Conscience in Sixteenth Century Jurisprudence,' in *Collected Papers* (Oxford, 1928), II, 191: his concept of Epicaia was drawn from Aristotle by way of St. Thomas Aquinas and Gerson: *ibid.*, pp. 192-96; Van Hove, *op. cit.*, pp. 281-89; Lefebvre, *op. cit.*, pp. 193, 197-202. This 'equity' must be distinguished from that found earlier in England (Pollock and Maitland, *op. cit.*, I, 189; Vinogradoff, *op. cit.*, p. 197; Allen, *op. cit.*, pp. 322-27), which, as Vinogradoff pointed out, 'though specifically recognized and sometimes applied in practice, had been taken in a wider sense, including justice and analogy': *supra*, nn. 93 ff. The development on the Continent parallels this closely: Van Hove, *op. cit.*, p. 281: 'A doctrina aequitatis de qua iuristae agunt, multum discrepat epikeia, prout eam ex Aristotele S. Thomas definit, quam tamen latine vocat aequitatem.'; Lefebvre, *op. cit.*, p. 200: 'Mais les glossateurs et les commentateurs ne semblant pas avoir interprété ces textes dans le sens de l'épikie aristotélicienne.' After its appearance in the *Summa Theologica* the doctrine was not revived on the Continent until the late sixteenth century—in the writings of Suarez—in response to current political theory. This is contemporaneous with its appearance in England.

[164]*Op. cit.*, fol. 30. Loyd (in *Univ. of Penn. Law Rev.*, LVIII, 78-79) sees the contrast between the equity of a statute and the equity enforced by subpoena in chancery, but St. Germain is pointing out that Epicaia—an 'exception secretly vnderstood in euery general rule'—has no place in the law of England: exceptions out of statutes are made '[sometime] by the law of reason and sometime by the intent of the makers of the statute . . .'; exceptions from 'the general customs or maximes of the law' by the writ of *sub poena*. It is of 'lequity de lestatut,' which *extends* acts to unmentioned cases, that 'mencion is made many tymes and often in the law of England.'

Later in the century, as has been indicated, the old 'lequity de lestatut' was transformed into the new 'equity,' and, just as extensions were now to be made in the light of an 'equity which is not part of the law, but a moral virtue which reforms the law,'[165] so restrictions could be accomplished by means of that same principle. Though the *Discourse* still uses the term only in the older sense of extension, and thus is close to the Year Book concept of 'lequity de lestatut,' Plowden refers to an equity that enlarges the letter and to its counterpart that diminishes it,[166] Hatton's discussion of the exposition of statutes 'according to equity' deals with both restrictive and extensive interpretation,[167] and Thomas

---

[165]Plowd. 466ᵛ; Allen, *op. cit.*, p. 373. The distinction between law and morals is striking and cannot easily be duplicated in the Year Books (or in other medieval writings: Gierke, *Johannes Althusius*, pp. 277-79; F. Kern, *Kingship and Law in the Middle Ages* [Oxford, 1939], p. 155: I cannot agree with Dr. Chrimes' warning [*op. cit.*, p. 254, n. 1; Kern, *op. cit.*, p. xxvii] that these conclusions must be confined to the early Middle Ages). Due to the fact that in large measure 'ley est resoun et resoun est ley' it was not necessary to posit natural, fundamental, or 'higher' law in order to disregard the words of a royal charter or an act of Parliament: Pickthorn, *Early Tudor Government: Henry VII*, chap. 5. That the Chancellor's charter could not stand 'oue raison' (*supra*, n. 154) and that another granting a protection for a long period of time would lead to 'disinheritance, & tresgrand mischief & inconuenience, que n'est suffrable per *Ley*' (*supra*, n. 156) was sufficient to hold them ineffective, and similarly, though such acts were infrequent, a statute that led to anomaly might be disregarded (*supra*, nn. 152, 158). The Student was quite correct in placing the law of reason first among the six grounds of the law of England. The beginnings of a new era are visible in Plowden's 'moral vertue que reforme le ley' and in his use of the words 'interpretation et construction'; the phrase 'impertinent & voide,' applied to an act of Parliament, appears for the last time in Dr. Bonham's case (*infra*, p. 85), and it was soon replaced by and misinterpreted as an appeal to natural law rather than to Law (*infra*, p. 91, n. 194).

[166]Plowd. 13ᵛ, 467: 'Et issint il appert diuersitie enter les deux equities, car lun abridge le letter, lauter le enlarge, lun demenist, lauter amplifie, lun toll de le letter, et le auter add a ceo. Et issint home ne poet targer sur le letter solement . . .'

[167]*Op. cit.*, pp. 31-62.

Ashe devotes a long chapter to 'ou, & en queux statutes le generality des parols serra restraine par construction fait per equite, & exposition fait sur iceux encounter la lettre & les paroles mesmes.'[168]

Though they had not been necessary before, the reasons examined above and currently used in the sixteenth century for extending an act, in the interests of justice, beyond its words, were used also to restrict its application in order to achieve that same end. But to do less than a statute provided, and thus in effect to disobey it, was a more obvious infringement of legislative fiat than the converse process of doing what the statute provided, and more, by extending its application to analogous cases. Plowden's doctrine of *Equitas*, as applied to restriction, rapidly declined as 'exceptions out' of harsh common-law rules and statutes alike came to be allocated to the chancery,[169] but it remained possible to justify restrictive

---

[168] 'Ἐπιείκεια: *et table generall a les annales del ley* (London, 1609), pp. 172-209; *idem, Abridgment des tovts les cases reportez alarge per Monsieur Plowden* (London, [? 1600]), fols. 6, 23, 74ᵛ, etc. W. Jones 49 (M. 22 Jac.): 'Per ceux cases il appiert que cest statute ad estre prise per equity plus quam parolls en ascun case & en ascun case pluis strict quam parolls . . .'

[169] In St. Germain's book the technical jurisdiction of the chancery was not yet known by the general term 'equity': Pollock, 'The Transformation of Equity,' in *Essays in Legal History* (Oxford, 1913), p. 293; but that identification had been made by the early seventeenth century—cf. *Doctor and Student*, fol. 27-27ᵛ ('. . . sith the deedes & acts of men, for which lawes bee ordeined, happen in diuers maners infinitely, it is not possible to make any general rule of the law, but that it shal faile in some case, & therefore makers of lawes take heede to such thinges as may often come & not to euery perticuler case, for they coulde not though they would. And therefore to follow the words of the law were in some case both against iustice & the common wealthe: wherefore in some cases it is necessary to leaue the woords of the law, and to follow that reason & Justice requireth, and to that intent equitie is ordeined: that is to say, to temper & mitigate the rigour of the law.') with Lord Ellesmere's remarks in 1 Ch. Rep. 6 (13 Jac.): 'The Cause why there is a *Chancery* is, for Mens Actions are so divers and infinite, That it is impossible to make any general Law which will aptly meet with every particular Act, and not fail in some Circumstances.' Early in the sixteenth century St. Germain had

construction by reference to the intention of the makers,[170] behind which lie the presumptions—often unexpressed—that

---

pointed out (*supra*, n. 164) that 'most commonly where any thing is accepted [excepted] from the general customes or maximes of the laws of the realme by the law of reason the party must haue his remedy by a writ that is called Sub pena,' and it was natural, therefore, that Ellesmere (*op. cit.*, p. 12), writing almost a century later, should see the equitable statutory interpretation of the judges as an equal encroachment upon the chancellor's prerogative: 'And the Judges themselves do play the Chancellors Parts upon Statutes, making Construction of them according to Equity, varying from the Rules and Grounds of Law, and enlarging them *pro bono publico*, against the Letter and Intent of the Makers, whereof our Books have many Hundreds of Cases.'; West, *Second Part of Symboleography*: *supra*, n. 162 (and note that this is part of a chapter entitled 'Of the Chancerie'). For Ellesmere the common-law judges were to decide strictly according to the words of the act (1 Ch. Rep. 15) and if an unreasonable result was reached relief was to be had in chancery (*op cit.*, p. 11): '. . . and if this Cause were exhibited to the Parliament it would soon be ordered and determined by Equity; and the Lord Chancellor is, by his Place under his Majesty, to supply that Power until it may be had, in all Matters of *Meum* and *Tuum*, between Party and Party; and the Lord Chancellor doth not except to the Statute or the Law upon the Statute, but taketh himself bound to obey that Statute . . .'; cf. Holdsworth, *A History of English Law*, V (1927), 337; McIlwain, *High Court of Parliament*, pp. 293-95. See also: W. G. Hammond's notes to F. Lieber, *Legal and Political Hermeneutics* (3d ed.; 1880), pp. 286-88; Llewellyn Davies, in *Columbia Law Rev.*, XXXV, 521; Allen, *op. cit.*, pp. 334 (n. 1), 432-33.

[170]St. Germain (*Doctor and Student*, fols. 28ᵛ, 29-29ᵛ), after noting cases in which infants and married women were 'excepted & excused by the law of reason' from the operation of some statutes, adds, 'the cause there as I suppose is for that the minde of the makers of the said estatut shalbe taken to be that that case should be excepted. And in al these cases the parties shalbee holpen in the same court & by the common law, & thus it appeareth that somewhat [sometime] a man may be excepted from the rigor of a statute by the law of reason, and sometime by the intent of the makers of the statute . . .'; fol. 147ᵛ: *infra*, n. 24; Plowd. 10ᵛ: '. . . quel proue que ou les parols del estatute sont generall, come sont en nostre case icy, que touts choses que sont deyns les general parols ne sont prise come le puruiew de le statut, mes tiels choses que les feasors meanont, & issint lentent des feasors est iudge des parols & abbridgera le generaltie de eux.'; 204-5ᵛ (*supra*, n. 148; *infra*, n. 43): 'Issint per ceux cases appiert que les sages del ley cy auant ont construe statutes enconter le letter en ascun apparance, mes en fait ceux que comprehendont en parols touts choses, ilz ont expound de extender forsque a ascuns choses. Et ceux que prohibite

the legislature acts according to reason,[171] and does not intend harsh or harmful results.[172] The concept permitted a good deal

---

que nul facera ils ont enterpretate de permitter ascun a faire. Et ceux que en parols conteigne chescun person, ils ont aiudge de extender forsques a ascun person, & le cause de tiel lour enterpretation ad este touts foits lentent del feasors del act . . .'; 369: *infra*, n. 28; 1 Rep. 15: *infra*, p. 160, n. 176; 3 Rep. 60, 62: '. . . & si les feasors del dit act de *11. H. 7.* vssont estre demaund . . . ils voilent auer responde . . .'; 77ᵛ: 'Ne fuit vnques lentent del feasors del act . . .'; 79, 79ᵛ; 4 Rep. 111: '. . . que ne vnques fuit lentention del acte, car lentention des feasors fuit come appiert per le Preamble . . .'; 7 Rep. 45ᵛ: '. . . que nest pas tolle per general parolx del act, car donques touts interpleaders serront per ceo tolle auxi, que ne vnques fuit lentention del act, mes lentention des feasors del act fuit . . .'; 8 Rep. 119: '. . . & la feme seruiue & enter en le dit manor per force des ditz general parolx; mes fuit adiudge que eux ne extendont al dit manor que fuit specialment nosme: & si issint soit en vn fait, *a fortiori* issint serra en vn act de parliament, que (come vn testament) est destre expound solonque lentention des feasors.'; 130; 9 Rep. 105: '. . . tiels customarie estates ne sont deins le dit Act, pur diuers causes, *1*. In respect del basenes del estate, car in le iudgement del ley ils nont forsque tenancie a volunt, que est cy feble que les fesors del Act de *4. H. 7.* ne vnques entendont a includer ceo deins les generals parols del Act . . .'; 10 Rep. 45ᵛ: '. . . les parols del preamble sont . . . issint que lentent des feasors del act fuit dauoyder recoueries vers tenant pur vie solement . . .'; 81: *infra*, p. 139, n. 109; 81ᵛ-82, 82ᵛ: '. . . lentencion des feasors del act ne vnques fuit a presumer . . .'; 100ᵛ; 11 Rep. 60ᵛ: '. . . le title [del act] est . . . issint que les fesors del act ne intend my ascun abrogation . . .'; 73ᵛ. This is comparable to the extracts collected *supra*, n. 137. See also: *supra*, nn. 127, 129; *infra*, nn. 24, 43, 109, p. 163, n. 185.

[171]Plowd. 205ᵛ: 'Et issint ont qualifie le rigor del parol solonque reason: solonque que lentent del feasors del act serra presume.'; 363ᵛ: '. . . son heire que est soubs le age de 6 ans, il ne fuit entende per les fesors del act que tiel heire serra chase de faire son claime per action ou entre, car il de tiel age nad intelligence a sacher sa droit, ne discretion a faire entre . . . & tiels ne fueront vnques entende per les feasors del acte . . .'; 364ᵛ: 'Et pur ceo laches ne serra impute al enfant, ne ils preiudice per ceo per lentent del feasors que ils collyont sur reasonable entent.'; 465-68; see *supra*, n. 133.

[172]9 Rep. 73: *infra*, p. 164, n. 188; 106ᵛ: 'Act de Parliament ne vnques fait tort . . .'; 107: '. . . & vn Act de Parliament, a que le Roigne & touts ses subiects sont parties & done consent, ne poet faire tort, a cest cause la Dame de Gresham fuit discharge . . .'; 11 Rep. 14: '. . . le Parliament est Court de tresgrand honor & Justice de que nul doit imaginer dishonorable chose, & le *Doctor & Student* fol. *164. ca. 55.* ne poet este

of freedom, but it too was narrowed in scope, for the broad
form of it used in Plowden's *Commentaries*—where it had
been substantially equivalent to justice—was soon restricted:[173]
the intention of the makers must be drawn from the act
itself,[174] and the words of a statute must ordinarily be followed (since they were the best indication of the legislative
will) when no contrary intent appeared and if no unreasonable result would ensue.[175] These rules, like St. Germain's,
should not be understood as invariably observed in practice,
but by the opening of the seventeenth century it could no
longer be easily said that a case presented for decision did

entend que vn statute que est fait per Authoritie de tout le Realme, cibien
del Roy & des Seigniors spirituel & temporall, come de touts les commons,
ferront ascun chose enconter veritie &c.'; 12 Mod. 687 (1701): '. . . and
an act of parliament can do no wrong.' (this last has been given a different
interpretation: Plucknett, in *Harvard Law Rev.*, XL, 55). Similarly, the
king can do no wrong: Plowd. 264ᵛ; 1 Rep. 44ᵛ: '. . . & si le graunt le
roy ferra discontinuance, ceo ferra tort, quel Roy per son graunt ne
poet faire . . .'; 5 Rep. 15ᵛ: '. . . le Roy esteant le test del bien publique
ne poit estre instrument a defeater le puruiew dun act de Parliament fait
pro bono publico.'; 11 Rep. 72: '. . . le Roy ne serra exempt per construction del ley hors del generall paroles des acts faits a suppresser tort, pur
ceo que il est le fountaine de Justice & common droit, & le Roy esteant
le Lieutenant de Dieu ne poet faire tort *Solum Rex hoc non potest facere,
quod non potest iniustè agere*.'; Jenk. 307-8; cf. *supra*, nn. 154, 156.

[173]St. Germain had already noted (Chrimes, *op. cit.*, p. 213, n. 6):
'Truth it is, that sometime the intent of a statute shall be taken farther
than the express letter stretcheth; but yet there may no intent be taken
against the express words of the statute, for that should be rather an interpretation of the statute than an exposition.' Similarly, H. Kantorowicz,
Studies in the Glossators of the Roman Law (Cambridge, 1938), p. 140.

[174]*Supra*, n. 140.

[175]Plowd. 369: *infra*, n. 28; 5 Rep. 118ᵛ: 'Et les Judges disoyent que ils
ne doyent faire ascun interpretation encounter lexpresse letter del statute:
car riens poyt issint expresser le intent dez fesors del act come lour direct
parolx demesne, car *Index animi sermo*, & serra perillous a doner scope a
faire construction in ascun case encounter les expresse parolx, quant lintent
des fesors nappiert al contrary & quant nul inconuenience sur ceo ensueroit.'; Co. Litt. 147: '*Quoties in verbis nulla est ambiguitas ibi nulla
expositio contra verba fienda est*.'

not fall within the intent of the makers of the act, for by that time the facile and frequently drawn distinctions between words and meaning, and words and intention, had become less common. Judges construed general acts so as to avoid anomalous results,[176] but that it was becoming more and more necessary as the century advanced to adhere to the plain language of an enactment may be inferred from the appearance of the statement that exceptions may be made out of affirmative (but not negative) statutes and from the use in this connection of the old rules that certain types of acts—in particular, those that abridged the common law, interfered with the liberty of the subject, or were penal—must be taken *stricti juris*. This had meant that such statutes could not be extended by equity, though it was now understood to permit judges to restrain, by exposition, acts that fell within these categories.[177] They could thus be narrowly construed in a

[176]9 Rep. 26ᵛ: *infra*, p. 163, n. 185; Co. Litt. 11ᵛ: '. . . such interpretation must ever be made of all statutes, that the innocent or he in whom there is no default may not be damnified.'; 360: *supra*, n. 148; 381ᵛ: *infra*, p. 163, n. 184; 2 Inst. 25: '. . . he should have right and no remedy . . . which the law will not suffer, and therefore this case of necessity is by construction excepted out of the statute.'; 110 (1): *infra*, n. 107; 112: *supra*, n. 51. Such constructions may be denied: 9 Rep. 72: '. . . et ilz disoient que feme couert fuit deins les parols del act; et serra grand mischiefe si ascun construction exemptera luy hors del penalty de cest statut . . .'; 11 Rep. 72: *supra*, n. 172; 72ᵛ: '. . . la ley est reason et equitie a faire droit a touts, et a sauer homes de tort & mischiefe, & pur ceo le ley ne vnques ferra construction enconter ley, equitie, & droit.'; 73ᵛ: 'Et fuit resolue, que le ley ne vnques voet a faire interpretation de aduancer vn priuate, et a destroyer le publique, mes touts foits daduancer le publique, et a preuenter chescun priuate, que est odious in tiels cases: et pur ceo est bien dit in *Heydons case* . . .'; for constructions extending the words of statutes: *supra*, n. 137.

[177]*Infra*, p. 86, n. 182. Prof. Corry (in *Univ. of Toronto Law Jour.*, I, 297) notes that the authorities cited by Dwarris for the strict construction of various types of statutes all date after 1700, but there were earlier examples: 8 Rep. 119ᵛ: *infra*, n. 168; 120; Ash v. Abdy, (1678) 3 Swanst. 664; Pound, in *Harvard Law Rev.*, XXI, 398 (note the words of the act, 22 Car. II, cap. 1, §3), 400-401. The *Discourse* had already noted (*infra*, p.

manner that parallels the liberal construction of remedial acts and those of public benefit and utility, to which reference has been made earlier.[178]

The problem that would have been raised if the Chancellor of Oxford's grant had been express and, in addition, confirmed by Parliament, was directly faced, early in the seventeenth century, in Dr. Bonham's case.[179] A clause in a patent confirmed by statute had conferred upon the Royal College of Physicians power to fine (and, consequently, to imprison) unlicensed physicians practicing in London—half the fine to go to the College, half to the king. Acting under this authority the Censors of the College had fined and imprisoned Dr. Bonham, who retaliated by bringing an action of false imprisonment against them.[180] The words of the first clause of the act were straightforward: they could not be evaded by appealing to legislative intent,[181] or, since the

---

156): '. . . penall statutes . . . sommetymes they are taken more straightelie then the wordes are.'; this grows more frequent as the seventeenth century draws toward its close.

[178]Corry, op. cit., p. 296. For the strict interpretation of penal acts in the early eighteenth century see J. Hall, Theft, Law and Society (Boston, 1935), chap. 3; idem, in Yale Law Jour., XLVII, 177.

[179]8 Rep. 114; 2 Brownl. 255. The important words occur at 8 Rep. 118: 'Les censors ne poent este iudgez, ministerz, & parties, iudges a doner sentence ou iudgement, ministers a faire sommons, & parties dauer le moitie del forfeiture, quia aliquis non debet esse iudex in propria causa; imo iniquum est aliquem sui rei esse iudicem: & vn ne poet este iudge & attorney pur ascun des parties . . . Et appiert en nostre liures, que en plusors cases le common ley controllera acts de parliament, & ascun foits adiudgera eux deste ousterment voide, car quant act de parliament est encounter common droit & reason, ou repugnant ou impossible deste performe, le common ley ceo controllera & adiudgera tiel act deste void . . .'

[180]I have set out the facts of the case and analyzed Coke's arguments, in Law Quart. Rev., LIV, 543, and in The Constitution Reconsidered (New York, 1938), p. 15.

[181]Cf. supra, n. 160. It can only be said that if the legislature had foreseen the result to which it led they would not have intended it. This is the

statute was in the negative, by excepting Bonham out of the act.[182] They led, however, to what Coke and his companions considered injustice, since the Censors were at the same time 'iudgez, ministerz, & parties,' and it was therefore held, in language reminiscent of the Year Books, that the first clause of the act was 'void.'[183] Coke seems to be asserting that there were acts of Parliament void *ab initio* since they conflicted with common right and reason, but if this interpretation of his words is adopted one has difficulty in explaining both the absence of the familiar passages in the *Doctor and Student*, and elsewhere, that might have been usefully cited,[184] and his references in the same sentence to repugnant statutes and acts impossible to be performed. Such acts he likewise considered 'void,' but clearly that section of an act which is inconsistent with another portion of it need only be considered ineffective,[185] nor need the authority and validity of a statute that

---

point of Coke's quotation of Herle's remark in Tregor's case (P. 8 E. 3, 30, pl. 26): '. . . ascuns statutes sont faits *encounter ley & droit*, que ceux que eux fesoient *perceiuant* ne voilent eux mitter en execution,' which is parallel to 3 Rep. 79ᵛ: 'Et si les fesors del act vssent este demaunds, si lour entent fuit que tiel fine issint leuie per tiel practise et couin liera les lessors, ils voilent auer responde dieu defend que ils intenderont a patronizer ascun tiel iniquitie . . .' Coke interpolated the italicized words in reporting Tregor's case, and there has been considerable but essentially irrelevant discussion both of Herle's dictum and the meaning of Coke's alterations: McIlwain, *High Court of Parliament*, pp. 286-91; Plucknett, *Statutes*, pp. 68-70; *idem*, in *Harvard Law Rev.*, XL, 35; Allen, *op. cit.*, p. 369.

[182]Thorne, in *Law Quart. Rev.*, LIV, 545.

[183]Similarly, 4 Rep. 13: 'Auxy fuit resolue que si lacte fuit priuate, & que le court doyt accept ceo destre tiel come est alleadge, donques le dit act fuit encounter ley & reason, & pur ceo void: Car come ceo est alleadge ceux que ne offend serront puny, et ceo fuit *condemnare insontem & dimittere reum* . . .'

[184]Holdsworth, *op. cit.*, IV, 280; Pickthorn, *op. cit.*, p. 134; Chrimes, *op. cit.*, pp. 290-91. Coke had used them in Calvin's case: 7 Rep. 12-12ᵛ, 14.

[185]1 Rep. 47: '. . . et appiert en nostre liuers que vn sauant en vn Act de Parliament, que est repugnant al corps del Acte est voide, come en

it is impossible to apply be impugned. Furthermore, the precedents cited in support of his statement are all instances in
which the plain words of parliamentary enactments had
been rejected.[186] Unless the assumption be that the cases fall
far short of the mark, and afford no support for the assertion

---

Plowdens Commentaries fol. 563.b. ou le supposed attainder del Duke de
Norffolke, fuit per Act de Parliament en *primo Mariae* declare destre voide
et nul *ab initio,* sauant les estates et leases faits per le Roy Edw. 6. &c. cest
sauant fuit voide, car quant lattainder fuit declare destre voide, le dit sauant
fuit encontre le corps del Act & pur ceo void, issint en le case *Michaelmas*
6. & 7. Eliz. Dyer 231. est enact per Lestatut de *31. H. 8. cap. 13.* que touts
mesons de religion & lour possessions adonques, ou apres destre dissolue,
serra al Roy en mesme lestate et condicion sicome ils fueront al temps
del fesance del dit Act, sauant a touts estraungers lour interests &c. puis
le dit Act, Labbot de Ramsey graunt vn procheine auoidance dun Esglise
de son patronage & puis Labbey fuit disolue & fuit adiudge que le graunt
fuit voide, & le sauant repugnant al corps de lacte . . .' Coke is making the
point that if the exception to a proposition is coextensive with the proposition itself one or the other must fall, and he assumes (as does the author
of the *Discourse:* p. 133) that the exception or saving clause, being a
modification of the first proposition, is ineffective. The contrary position
has been taken: *infra,* n. 91.

[186] Rep. 118: 'Lestatute de *Westminster 2, ca. 21,* done brief de *Cessauit*
heredi petenti super heredem tenentis, & super eos quibus alienatum fuerit
huiusmodi tenementum, & vncore est adiudge en *33 Ed. 3, tit. Cessauit 42,*
ou le case fuit, deux coparceners seigniors & tenant per fealtie & certein
rent, lun coparcener ad' issue & morust, launt & le neece ne ioindra en
Cessauit, pur ceo que le heire nauera *Cessauit* pur le cesser en temps son ancestor. *Fitz. N. B. 209F,* & oue ceo accord *Plowd. Com. 110* [*supra,* n. 160],
& le reason est pur ceo que en *Cessauit* le tenant deuant iudgement poet
render les arrerages & dammages &c. & reteigne son terre, & ceo ne poet il
faire quant le heire port *Cessauit* pur le cesser en le temps son auncester,
car les arrerages incurre en le vie del ancester ne appent al heire, & pur
ceo que ceo serra encounter common droit & reason, le common ley adiudge
le dit act de Parliament quant a cest point voide.'; see *infra,* p. 170, n. 211,
§3. Prof. Plucknett (*Harvard Law Rev.,* XL, 35-36) remarks that 'in Coke's
telling the story gains an aunt and a niece as well as considerable clarity—
all derived from an unspecified and unidentified source,' but the source is
clearly Fitzherbert's *Natura Breuium* at the page cited. Coke considered
Annuitie, 41 'impossible deste performe,' and therefore ineffective rather
than void *ab initio,* and in Dyer 313 and in Strowd's case the express words
of 1 E. 6, ca. 14, were similarly held ineffective: W. Jones 234; Plucknett,
in *Harvard Law Rev.,* XL, 41-44.

they are intended to sustain, Coke must be understood to say that 'in many cases the common law will control acts of parliament'—that is, will restrict their words in order to reach sound results; and 'sometimes it will adjudge them to be completely void'—that is, will reject them completely if modification cannot serve.[187]

The precedents adduced by Coke showed that courts in the past had disregarded the express words of statutes in certain instances, holding them ineffective in whole or part, and his statement that this had been done when the acts were 'contrary to common right and reason, or repugnant, or impossible to be performed,' was a reasonably accurate synthesis of the cases.[188] Such action was clearly something more than the usual interpretation or construction in the light of 'lentent del feasors,' but nevertheless Coke was able to prove to the satisfaction of his fellow judges that the cases were 'truly vouched' and provided adequate authority. They therefore held the act in Dr. Bonham's case ineffective in so far as it purported to give the Censors power to act as 'judges

[187]Thus the fourth argument is not a dictum, but takes its proper place as one of the five arguments directed toward the interpretation of the act. Coke's use of the word 'void' in the sense of 'ineffective' is frequent: 10 Rep. 27-27v: 'Pur ceo que ils fuerunt *cuidam Capellano*, & nosme nul incertaine; & quant le grant le Roy est noncertain ceo est void, come si le roy license vn a doner xx. markes de rent *cuidam Abbati* le grant est void, intant que nest certaine.'; 10 Rep. 43, 55v, 61v, 67v: '. . . pur le honor del roy et le benefit del subiect tiel construction serra fait que le chartre le roy prendroit effect, car ne fuit intent le Roy a faire voide graunt.'; 110v; 11 Rep. 11; Ellesmere uses the word in the same sense: *infra*, p. 88, n. 188. For the prerogative 'controlled' by common law see Plowd. 236: *supra*, n. 156.

[188]That acts 'repugnant ou impossible deste performe' were void was admitted, for Lord Ellesmere (Moore 828), in his address to Chief Justice Montague, commending those judges who did not declare statutes void for being contrary to common right and reason, made the significant exception, 'I speak not of impossibilities or direct repugnances.' For the statement that Westminster 2, ca. 21, had been disregarded because it was 'contrarie a tout reason' see Plowd. 109v-110: *supra*, n. 160.

to give sentence or judgment, ministers to make summons, and parties to have half the forfeiture,' just as in the Year Books an express grant to decide all cases *licet fuerit pars* might not permit the grantee to be judge in a case in which he himself was party. In that situation there was evidence that the plea must be held by his seneschal,[189] and, similarly, Coke's opinion required that the fine for practicing medicine in London without the certificate of the Royal College of Physicians be recovered through the courts and go wholly to the king.[190] Both his thought and the language in which it was phrased are close to the Year Books, and, like his predecessors on the bench, Coke was concerned only with the application of a statute that led to results 'encounter common droit & reason,' not with the theory that 'an Act of Parliament may be void from its first Creation' because of a conflict between its provisions and fundamental, natural, or 'higher' law. Dr. Bonham's case was the last appearance of the doctrine in its medieval form—one that had been literally going out of court for a century—for to hold an act to be without effect no longer involved merely private-law considerations, as had earlier been true, and Coke's argument was not met, as those of the Year Book judges had been, on that ground.[191]

[189]*Supra*, n. 154.

[190]8 Rep. 120ᵛ-21.

[191]1 Ch. Rep. 11, *per* Ellesmere: 'It seemeth by the Lord Coke's Report, fol. 118, in Dr. Bonham's Case, That Statutes are not so sacred as that the Equity of them may not be examined. For he saith, That in many Cases the Common Law hath such a Prerogative, as that it can controul Acts of Parliament, and adjudge them void; as if they are against Common Right, or Reason, or Repugnant, or impossible to be performed, and for that he vouches . . . And yet our Books are, That the Acts and Statutes of Parliament ought to be reversed by Parliament (only) and not otherwise, Bro. Tit. Error, 65, &c., and 7 H. 6, 28; 21 E. 4, 46; 29 E. 3, 24 . . .' It is notable that Ellesmere was able to produce only instances in which judgments in Parliament had been held not reversible elsewhere:

But, as has recently been observed, the belief would be erroneous that law had already abandoned its claim to being any sort of reflection of factual truth, or an expression of intelligence and moral worth, and reconciled itself to being merely the articulation of the will of a legal sovereign.[192] Coke's authorities were becoming valueless in the face of new habits of thought, and, though the words of his report did not in fact 'import any new opinion' and were, as he said, 'only a relation of such authorities of law as have been adjudged and resolved in former times,' they contemplated, nonetheless, what was in many respects the revival of an obsolescent view.[193] A similar result could be reached by

---

in Brooke's words: '. . . et videtur per lerrour en parlement . . . que ceo serra reuerse per auter parlement, si soit errour, et ne poet estre auterment reuerse.' He was on safer ground (Moore 827-28) in commending Sir Edward Montague and others who had not claimed 'to have power to judge Statutes and Acts of Parliament to be void, if they conceived them to be against common right and reason; but left the King and the Parliament to judge what was common right and reason . . .'; judges were to adhere to the statute, though relief in a difficult case might be had in chancery (*supra*, n. 169), the chancellor acting temporarily for the king or Parliament: [Egerton], *Priviledges and Prerogatives of the High Court of Chancery*, sig. B2v: 'And if any ambiguity, or doubt should bee conceived upon the words and intent of this statute, sith it concernes the jurisdiction of the Kings Courts, which have no power nor authority but from the King whom they serve, one Court ought not to take upon them to Iudge and deside their owne Jurisdiction, and then Bracton's [fol. 34] rule is to be holden: (that is) that the King's interpretation is to be expected, Who is to declare and expound all doubtfull or obscure words in *Chartis Regiis & factis regum*: For all Statutes are *facta regis*, made at the request and by the consent of the Lords Spirituall and Temporall, and the Commons.'; [Egerton], *Observations on the Lord Coke's Reports*, p. 11: 'It is *magis congruum* that Acts of Parliament should be corrected by the same Pen that drew them, than to be dashed to pieces by the Opinion of a few Judges.'

[192]Wormuth, *op. cit.*, p. 62; Ellesmere, *supra*, n. 169.

[193]Coke later regarded *Cessauit*, 42 as 'contrary to itself' (2 Inst. 402), and his decision in Bonham's case as rejecting a statute because of repugnancy: 2 Brownl. 198.

means of the theory that any act of the sovereign that broke
the bounds of natural law was formally null and void,
though, since such a theory had not been needed earlier,
there was a corresponding absence of strictly legal precedent
in the Year Books and later reports that could be urged in
its support. It was, however, soon advanced,[194] though it was
to be a doctrine of diminishing importance in the English
courts.[195] The inroads that parliamentary sovereignty had
made by the eighteenth century are clearly visible in Blackstone: general words in an act may be disregarded if they
lead to collaterally absurd results,[196] but 'if the parliament

[194]Hob. 87 (12 Jac.): '. . . even an Act of Parliament, made against
naturall equitie, as to make a man Judge in his owne case, is void in it
selfe, for *Iura naturae sunt immutabilia,* and they are *leges legum.*' No
authority was cited, and though it was already possible to refer to Coke's
report of Bonham's case, it was not mentioned; H. Finch, *Nomotexnia,
cestascauoir, vn description del common leys dangleterre* (London, 1613),
fol. 19: 'Leyes Positif que sont directment contrarie a les Leys Natif, pard
lour force, & ne sont destre repute ascun leys omnino come ceux que sont
contrarie al Ley de Nature.' The general observations in the older books
(*supra,* n. 184) came into new importance.

[195]Many of the cases are considered by Prof. Plucknett in *Harvard Law
Rev.,* XL, 54-59; see also: E. S. Corwin, 'The Higher Law Background of
American Constitutional Law,' *ibid.,* XLIII, 375 ff. Note the quotation from
Fabian Philipps in McIlwain, *Constitutionalism Ancient and Modern,* p. 154.

[196]*Comm.,* I, 91: '. . . if there arise out of them [acts of Parliament]
collaterally any absurd consequences, manifestly contradictory to common
reason, they are, with regard to those collateral consequences void . . .
where some collateral matter arises out of the general words, and happens
to be unreasonable, there the judges are in decency to conclude that this
consequence was not foreseen by the parliament, and therefore they are
at liberty to expound the statute by equity, and only *quoad hoc* disregard
it. Thus if an act of parliament gives a man power to try all causes that
arise within his manor of Dale, yet, if a cause should arise in which he
himself is party, the act is construed not to extend to that, because it is
unreasonable that any man should determine his own quarrel. But if we
should conceive it possible for the parliament to enact, that he should try
as well his own causes as those of other persons, there is no court that
has power to defeat the legislature, when couched in such evident and
express words as leave no doubt whether it was the intent of the legislature or no.' This is Coke's rule (2 Inst. 112: *supra,* nn. 51, 176) that

will positively enact a thing to be done that is unreasonable,
I know of no power that can control it . . . [the judges are
not at liberty to reject it] for that were to set the judicial
power above that of the legislature, which would be sub-
versive to all government.'[197] This is contemporary with the
abandonment of the doctrine of equitable interpretation
noticed earlier,[198] and with the appearance of the complete
theory of parliamentary sovereignty.[199]

V

There are two copies of the *Discourse* in the Huntington
Library. EL. 2565 is a quarto paper volume which contains
the two parts of William Staunforde's *Exposicion of the
Kings Prerogatiue*, folios 1-83[v] and 87-139,[200] in an unidentified hand, followed after some blank folios by the *Discourse*
(hereinafter referred to as *E*), separately paged 1-18, written
in English, in Thomas Egerton's early hand. It is this text
that is reproduced below. EL. 496 is a smaller paper volume,

'statutes must be so construed, as no collaterall prejudice grow thereby.'
It will be noted that the word 'void' is used in Coke's sense of 'ineffective'—
a fact which has misled Allen (*op. cit.*, p. 372 n.) and Corry (*op. cit.*, p. 298).

[197]*Comm.*, I, 91. Other means were adopted for avoiding the application
of a statute considered undesirable: Plucknett, *Concise History*, p. 303. Note
that the doctrine there noticed becomes important, despite precedent to the
contrary, only in the late eighteenth century.

[198]*Supra*, n. 143.

[199]McIlwain, *Constitutionalism & the Changing World*, pp. 61-85.

[200]The division is discernible in the first printed edition (1567), where
the sixteenth chapter, which ends the first part, is headed 'the laste chapiter,'
and the chapters of the second part are unnumbered. Similarly, the second,
third, and fourth editions (1568, 1573, and 1577), though their chapters are
numbered consecutively throughout, make the original division into
separate parts apparent by preserving unchanged the position of the note
that originally concluded the first part. Staunforde's prefatory letter to
Nicholas Bacon is dated Nov. 6, 1548, and the first part of the *Exposicion*
probably represents his 1546 Lent reading at Gray's Inn.

of 396 folios—Thomas Egerton's commonplace book in his own hand—in law French, written in large part before 1572 but containing many later notes, case extracts, and quotations. The *Discourse* (hereinafter designated *F*) appears in the same ink and hand as the body of the commonplace book, in law French, at folios 368-78, though to it, as well, later additions have been made.

The two manuscripts of the *Discourse* bear a relationship to each other very similar to that borne by two manuscripts of Thomas Marowe's *De Pace*.[201] *F* is a translation and condensation of *E*, omitting its connecting passages and redundant phraseology, and abridging its carefully complete explanations. *F* is never unintelligible or obscure, but it quite evidently is a severely practical though accurate summary, devoid of all grace, from which everything but unadorned substance has been eliminated.

E utilizes Staunforde's *Plees del Coron*, supplying four page references to that text as printed, and therefore 1557 must represent the earliest date at which *E* could have been written. No mention is made of the first part of Plowden's *Commentaries*, though a treatise on statutory interpretation written after 1571 would be unlikely to overlook it. Accordingly, I date *E* between 1557 and 1571, though, as will be indicated below, the earlier decade of that period can be fixed upon with some certainty.

E possesses but two passages written subsequent to the text proper.[202] *F*, on the other hand, falls into two distinct divisions: the *F* text proper, quite evidently written at one date, and subsequent additions to that text, inserted at a somewhat later time. The additions will be dealt with at

---

[201]B. H. Putnam, *Early Treatises on the Practice of the Justices of the Peace in the Fifteenth and Sixteenth Centuries* (Oxford, 1924), pp. 160-62.

[202]*Infra,* nn. 2, 183.

greater length below. The *F* text proper contains not only all the material of *E*, including its two additions, but also some further matter not present in *E*. I incline to the hypothesis that the *F* text proper was summarized from *E* and copied by Egerton into his commonplace book some time after the insertion of *E*'s two supplementary notes, and that, in an effort to have conveniently available all his material on statutes, he incorporated at that same time the additional matter in question. Since this material includes a reference to the eighth year of Elizabeth,[203] and another to Christopher Wray's second reading at Lincoln's Inn in 1567,[204] the construction of the *F* text proper clearly took place after that date. Moreover, 1567 is the year Staunforde's *Exposicion* first appeared in print, and Egerton might then profitably have proceeded to copy *E* into his commonplace book in order to dispense completely with a manuscript volume now superseded in part. I place the *terminus a quo* of the *F* text proper, therefore, shortly after 1567, and thus *E*, its ancestor, may roughly be dated 1557-67. The particular *E* manuscript now in the Huntington Library (which is at least once removed from its original) may be dated a little more closely in the light of Egerton's admission to Lincoln's Inn after 1559.

To establish a *terminus ad quem* for the *F* text proper is somewhat less easy, but I am inclined to believe that it was written before 1572, certainly, and probably several years earlier. As was pointed out above, *F* contains later additions to the text proper—additions which may easily be distinguished both by the ink in which they are written and by the positions they occupy. In every case they have been added in blanks at the ends of chapters or inserted, when space permitted, between paragraphs of the text. Since these

[203]*Infra*, n. 140, §10.

[204]*Infra*, n. 179.

additions consist largely of extracts from cases reported in the first part of Plowden's *Commentaries*, and supply page references to the printed edition, they could not have been inserted before 1571. How soon after 1571 is a question that cannot be answered from the manuscripts of the *Discourse*, but aid is available in the commonplace book, for in it, as well, the Plowden citations are additions, in a later ink, inserted in a manner similar to that described for the *Discourse*. In 1571 Egerton had been at Lincoln's Inn almost a dozen years and was very soon to be called to the bar. Thus the main body of his commonplace book had taken definitive form, and, though he long continued to add to it, the body of material collected during his student period formed a distinct and substantial unit under each head. Evidently he worked carefully through Plowden's volume of reports, after its appearance, copying appropriate passages into their proper places under the heads into which his book was divided, and adding to the *Discourse* extracts concerning statutory interpretation. Very little subsequent to Plowden was added to the *Discourse*, but in the commonplace book the Plowden citations often are followed, but never preceded, by extracts from Brooke's *Abridgement* of 1573-4. I suggest, then, that the Plowden citations were added to *F* shortly after the appearance of the *Commentaries*—perhaps in 1572, but not after the appearance of Brooke. If that is true, the *F* text proper, since it must antedate its additions, may be assigned to 1567-72, though in my opinion the earlier half of that period is probable.

The additional matter that Egerton incorporated into his summary of *E* to form the *F* text proper may now be further considered. I suggested above that the *F* text proper was constructed to abbreviate the unnecessary length of *E* and to make conveniently available in one place all Egerton's notes on questions of statutory interpretation. Fortunately, several pages of memoranda upon the flyleaves of two of his printed books, now preserved in the Huntington Library, permit a portion of this new matter to be seen in its original form.

Doubtless one of the first books that Egerton acquired after his admission to Lincoln's Inn was the essential *Nouuelle Natura Breuium* 'du Iuge tresreuerend Monsieur Anthoine Fitzherbert,' in Tottel's edition of 1560.[205] He covered its flyleaves at both front and back with notes and tags of general reading, the more lengthy from Lambert Daneau's *Ethices Christianae*, St. Augustine's *De Civitate Dei*, and Giacomo Concio's (or Aconcio's) *Stratagemata Satanae;* but he used them also for legal notes, and particular attention may be called to two leaves devoted to notes on the interpretation of statutes. At the beginning of the volume a flyleaf, unfortunately badly damaged by dampness, is headed 'Nota ou statute sera construe enconte<r les parollz>.'[206] It contains cases placed there by Egerton from time to time—perhaps several at once—obviously after 1560 but prior to the appearance of the first part of Plowden's *Commentaries*, for, as in both the *Discourse* and the commonplace book, references to Plowden's printed volume are added in a later ink and inserted between paragraphs. Of the eleven separate notes on the page, four appear as part of the new matter added to the summarized *E* text to form the *F* text proper.[207] As will be noted, they were incorporated in the order they appear, and are in almost identical words. The omitted cases, though collected by Egerton, apparently did not qualify later for inclusion in the *Discourse*. Those interpreting Prerogativa Regis had been

[205]The title-page is dated 1553: *S.T.C.* 10960; J. H. Beale, *A Bibliography of Early English Law Books* (Cambridge, Mass., 1926), p. 153 (T 345).

[206]*Infra*, Appendix I.

[207]*Infra*, n. 211.

discussed by Staunforde, 'the best expositor of a statute that
hath been in our law,'[208] in his *Exposicion*, and thus were available in print after 1567. I suggest that the others, illustrating
as they do more obvious matters, did not merit transfer to *F*.
The verso of the flyleaf is headed 'Quant roy sera lye per
statute' and contains eight cases.[209] It evidently was written
after Sir John Ratclyffe's case (1564-5), which it mentions.
None of its cases appears in the *F* text proper, and I am inclined to date the page after 1567, though even this makes
Egerton's failure to incorporate the notes into the *Discourse*
hard to understand. The absence of a corresponding chapter
may have made their inclusion troublesome, or perhaps the
availability of Staunforde's *Exposicion* may again supply a
sufficient explanation.

Egerton's copy of Littleton's *Tenures*, in Tottel's edition
of 1557, preserves several other extracts that were afterward
incorporated into the *F* text proper.[210] On the leaf following
the colophon, Egerton noted cases concerned with the sub-
sumption of later situations under prior statutes, and these
appear as a group in the *F* text proper. Examination reveals
that the same language is used, the same blanks for the later
insertion of chapter numbers are left, and the identical cases
are cited.[211]

The foregoing conclusions may now be summarized.
Shortly after his admission to Lincoln's Inn—perhaps as early
as 1560—Egerton copied the *E* text of the *Discourse* into the
last blank pages of a volume which already contained a copy
of Staunforde's *Exposicion*. During his apprenticeship he

[208]Francis Bacon's speech as counsel for Calvin in the case of the Post-
Nati: *Works*, ed. Spedding (London), VII (1859), 676.

[209]*Infra*, Appendix II.

[210]*Infra*, Appendix III.

[211]*Infra*, n. 140.

compiled, in the customary manner, a commonplace book in which he placed under appropriate heads summaries of the cases he read or heard. Since his book contained no division for cases involving statutes, these as has been indicated were collected elsewhere, though two notes were added to *E*. When in 1567 the printed edition of the *Exposicion* superseded Egerton's manuscript copy, he thereupon proceeded to dispense completely with the volume by copying the *E* text of the *Discourse* into his commonplace book. In the process he reduced its unnecessary length, partly by putting it into law French, partly by omitting merely rhetorical portions, and at the same time incorporated his accumulation of pertinent material, none of which is of a date later than 1567. To this—the *F* text proper—he added after 1571 a good many excerpts from Plowden's volume of reports, easily distinguishable by the positions they occupy and the ink in which they are written, though doubtless some few additions had been made from other sources in the interim—for example, a sentence from Thomas Marowe's reading on Westminster I, ca. I. By 1572 the *F* text of the *Discourse*, as we have it, was complete, for very little was added subsequent to the Plowden extracts. Brooke's *Abridgement*, for example, was not utilized. Mention may be made, however, of two later tags: one from Lambert Daneau's *Ethices Christianae* (1577), the other from Adam Blackwood's *De Iure Regni apud Scotos*—the second of which could not have been entered before 1581.[212] Both were placed in the inner margins

[212]His commonplace book was by his side again in the next century, as the close correspondence between the first chapter of the *Discourse* and some pages of his only unquestioned printed work, the celebrated Exchequer Chamber opinion in Calvin's case, indicates: *infra*, n. 9. For the authorship of *Certaine Observations concerning the Office of the Lord Chancellor* (London, 1651), 'composed by the Right Honorable, the most learned, Thomas Lord Ellesmere, late Lord Chancellor of England,' and for that of *The Lord Chancellor Egerton's Observations on the Lord*

of otherwise completely filled leaves, and illustrate Egerton's characteristic fondness for concise expression rather than any methodical attempt to supplement the *Discourse*.

The text of the *Discourse* here printed is that of *E*, which has been reproduced as it stands, except that abbreviations have been expanded, capitalization and punctuation have, in general, been modernized, and marginal comments and citations have been so labeled and placed in the notes.[213] The portions of *E* omitted in *F*, since they are formal rather than substantial, have not been indicated. The additional matter found in the *F* text proper has been edited as above, placed in the notes, and so identified; the two subsequent additions to *E*, and those to the *F* text proper, have likewise been placed there, but distinguished by insertion within slanting dashes: /. . . . ./. Reconstructions of the missing portions of the notes printed in the Appendixes appear within pointed brackets. Additions to these notes—made after 1571—I have distinguished, as above, by slanting dashes. Here, as throughout, the material within square brackets has been supplied by the editor.

Year Book references are to the 1679, or vulgate, edition, long associated with the name of Serjeant Maynard, but,

---

Coke's Reports (London, n.d. [1710?]), see Holdsworth, *op. cit.*, V, 272-73, 478, n. 1. *The Priviledges and Prerogatives of the High Court of Chancery* (London, 1641), 'written by the Right Honourable Thomas Lord Ellesmere, late Lord Chancellour of England,' apparently is a memorandum to which an extravagant title has been attached: *Catalogue of Hargrave Manuscripts in the British Museum* (London, 1818), No. 240 (9), No. 269 (1); Holdsworth, *op. cit.*, V, 271.

[213]In the particular *E* manuscript in the Huntington Library the marginal notes of its ancestor proved too bulky to be accommodated there, and were placed in the body of the page, marked by indentation, a line or bracket in the margin, and generally by the word *Nota*. These are clearly notes to the text and have been so treated.

where the books of particular years have been re-edited, references have been supplied. References to Magna Carta are to the third reissue, 1225; statute references, to the Record Commission's *Statutes of the Realm*.

A Discourse

A Discourse upon the Exposicion & Understandinge of Statutes &c.

Proclamacions. Ca. 1

All that lawe which ys posytyve consisteth either in proclamacions or in actes of Parlyament.[1] In proclamacions as yf

[1][This identification of positive law and legislation, also apparent in Plowden (363: quoted *supra*, n. 132; 365: '. . . il est bone pur expositors de ceo acte ore, de approcher cy pres al reason del common ley, quel est le chiefe master en exposicion del parols del leyes positiue, come poyent'), represents a complete departure from the long medieval tradition (O. Lottin, *Le droit naturel chez Saint Thomas d'Aquin et ses prédécesseurs* [Bruges, 1931], p. 28; S. Kuttner, 'Sur les origines du terme *droit positif*,' *Revue historique de droit français et étranger*, 4th Ser., XV, 728-40) which identified positive law with human law generally: H. 33 H. 6, 9, pl. 23: 'Prisot: . . . car ne puit este vn positiue [ley] mes tiels que fuit ajuge ou fait per *Statut*.'; M. 8 E. 4, 12, pl. 9, Yelverton: *supra*, n. 9; J. Hawarde, *Les Reportes del cases in Camera Stellata*, ed. W. P. Baildon (1894), pp. 78-79; S. B. Chrimes, *English Constitutional Ideas in the Fifteenth Century* (Cambridge, 1936), pp. 197 (n. 3), 198, 207. Behind this change may be glimpsed the final separation, accomplished in the sixteenth century, of the court of Parliament, 'le quel est le pluiz haut & digne court que le Roy ad,' from the other courts of the realm (*supra*, n. 16), and of the product of legislation from that of adjudication, which made Prisot's easy conjoining of judgment and statute (not infrequent during the fifteenth century: T. 7 H. 7, 16, pl. 1: 'Fineux: . . . car vn Act de Parlement n'est forsque *Judicium*, & vn Act come vn Jugement . . .') unusual enough to merit remark early in the seventeenth: [Thomas Egerton], *The Speech of the Lord Chancellor . . . touching the Post-nati* (London, 1609), p. 37: 'And *Prysot* saieth, *fol. 9: There cannot be a positiue Lawe but such as was iudged or made by Statute*. Wherein I note also that hee equalleth a Iudgement with a Statute.'; 55: 'And in their Iudgements they [the civilians] are guided by Arrests and former Iudgements, as may appeare in the books of many that haue collected such Arrests. And they attribute so much to such former Iudgements, That as *Prysot* equalleth them to a Positiue Lawe, so they hould, That *Sententia facit Ius, & res iudicata pro veritate accipitur, & legis interpretatio legis vim obtinet*.'
The division of legislation into parliamentary, which required the 'threefold consent,' and nonparliamentary is usual in the sixteenth century (*infra*, n. 5), and is repeated by Egerton: *infra*, n. 9.]

the prynce by his counsell have thought good & expedient to publyshe anie thinge as a lawe.[2] But therin hathe bene doubted of what effecte such proclamacions have bene, and what payne he that breaketh them shulde have. And some saie that the payne ys the losse of his alledgyance.[3] As for thaucthoritie of them an acte of Parlyamente was made in 31 H. 8,

[2]*E* (fol. 1): /*Nota.* M. 4 H. 3, *Dower*, 179: En briefe de dower le tenaunt plede quod le demaundant est sub potestate regis Francie & residens in Francia et prouisum est a consilio regis quod nullus de potestate regis Francie respondeatur in Anglia antequam Anglici respondeantur de iure suo in Francia, & le attorney le demaundant ceo ne potuit dedicere, ideo sine die./
F: M. 4 H. 3, *Dower*, 179: Proclamacion plede en dishablement del person le demaundant.
[F. W. Maitland, *Bracton's Note Book* (London, 1887), II, pl. 110; W. Staunforde, *Exposicion of the Kinges Prerogatiue* (London, 1567), fol. 39-39ᵛ; Jenk. 3.]

[3][Fitzherbert, *Nouvelle Natura Breuium*, 85*C*: 'Et si subiect fait enconter cell [proclamation] ceo est vn contempt, & il ferra fyne pur cell al roy.'; Dyer 296, pl. 19 (M. 12/13 Eliz.); R. Crompton, *L'Avthoritie et Ivrisdiction des Covrts* (London, 1594), fol. 14: 'Nota que le Roy ne poit per son proclamacion alter le ley, mes poit faire proclamacion que si ascun fait conter le content de proclamacion, que incurgera le indignacion de sa Maiestie, mes sur pain de forfeture de son terre, ou perder de son vie, sans parliament ne poit.'; but see fol. 16ᵛ: 'Nota per mesme le reason que le roigne per son absolute authoritie poit committer home al prison durant son pleasure a demurre la, come patet, *Stamf[orde, Plees del Coron]*, 72. Issue & per sa proclamacion el poit ordeine, que si ascun fait conter le content de cel proclamacion que serra imprison, & vncore *vide 42 Li. ass. 5*, que commission issist hors de Chauncery a seiser les biens dun A. & son corps sans auter proces de le suit agarde void.'; 12 Rep. 75; H. Finch, *Nomotexnia, cestascauoir, vn description del common leys dangleterre* (London, 1613), fols. 27ᵛ, 28ᵛ: 'Offences al Roy ouster Treason . . . sont . . . (3) A disobeyer le commaundement del Roy per son Proclamation en *Anglois*. (4) A disobeyer ascun chose prohibit per ascun Estatute.' With regard to this last, see: M. 35 H. 6, 6, pl. 9: 'Ashton: Et issint touts cases on vn *statut* defend vn chose, si ascun home ferra le contrary de ceo il ferra fine, car il est vn contempt.'; Chrimes, *op. cit.*, pp. 195 (n. 1), 201 (n. 3); G. Barraclough, 'Law and Legislation in Medieval England,' *Law Quart. Rev.*, LVI, 87-88; 9 Rep. 39ᵛ: 'Car les parols del Act sont, les Ordinaries facent deputer, &c., & le refusel a faire ceo est contempt al Roy . . .']

[ca. 8], which ys now repealled.[4] Howbeit yt ys certen that the readers affirme that by the commen lawe yf the ordynaunce that was made had bene in supplement or declaracion of a lawe, that that had bene good, beinge ordeyned by the Lordes & never consented to by the Commons. As the statute of Merton, the Lordes were assembled about the maryage of Elyanor & not sommoned to a Parlement & yet hathe that the face of an estatute, & yet ys not called a statute but Prouisiones Merton. So lykewyse de Bigamis where yt saieth *omnes de consilio concordauerunt,* yt provethe that at the begynnynge it was no statute.[5] And so ys thexposicion of

---

[4][1 E. 6, ca. 12, §4. Though the Statute of Proclamations conferred on the crown powers it already possessed, the *Discourse* regards the statute as having supplied the sole authority for proclamations. So Crompton, *op. cit.,* fol. 14: '*Vide 31. H. 8. ca. 8.* que fuit ordeine per parliament, que proclamacion fait per Roy per aduise de certain de son counsell nosmes in mesme le acte, duist este obey & obserue come vst este done per acte de parliament, & puis *34. H. 8. ca. 23.* vn auter estatut fuit fait, consernant loffendors de primer act, mes per *1. E. 6. ca. 12.* sont repeals, per que estatuts appiert, que proclamacion ne lye, come act de parliament sans este issint ordein per parliament, car si sic, les dits estatutes de roy H. 8. fuerunt faits in vaine.'; and Coke, 11 Rep. 87ᵛ: 'Et ou le Roy E. 3. in le *39.* an de son raigne per son proclamation command le exercise de Archerie & Artillery, & prohibite le exercise de casting de stones & barres & le hand & foot balles, cockfighting, *& alios ludos vanos* . . . vncore nul effect de ceo ensuist, tanque diuers acts de Parliaments . . .' Similarly, as the *Discourse* and Crompton (*supra,* p. 104, n. 3) indicate, the provision of the statute that proclamations should not infringe 'any actes, comen lawes, standinge at this present tyme in strength and force, nor yet any laufull or lawdable Customes of this Realm,' is taken to mark the bounds of nonparliamentary legislation under all circumstances: 12 Rep. 75; E. R. Adair, 'The Statute of Proclamations,' *English Hist. Rev.,* XXXII, 34-36; K. Pickthorn, *Early Tudor Government: Henry VIII* (Cambridge, 1934), pp. 414-18; T. F. T. Plucknett, *A Concise History of the Common Law* (3d ed.; London, 1940), pp. 45-46.]

[5][See 30 Liber Assisarum, pl. 5: 'Shardelowe: Et ceo que vous parles del statut *de Bigamis,* ceo ne fuit vnques ascun statut.'; *Abridgement of the booke of Assises* (London, 1555), fol. 6; cf. 5 Rep. (Preface), p. 13: 'The Statute of Bigamis, in anno 4 E. 1. Obserue how the king by advise of his Councell (*that is by authoritie of Parliament*) expounded how the said councell should be vnderstood . . .'; Coke similarly interpreted a

Gloucester.[6] And in H. 19 H. 3, Fitzh[erbert, *Natura Bre-uium*], 32D yt is said, *Et prouisum fuit coram domino rege, archiepiscopis, episcopis, comitibus, & baronibus quod nulla assisa vltime presentationis de cetero capiatur de ecclesiis prebendatis ne de prebendis.*[7] And in [P.] 39 E. 3, fo. 9 [7, pl. 3], thoughe the statute[8] which saieth that the defendant in a *premunire* shulde answerre in propre parson were never proclaymed in the countreye nor the Commons never agreed unto it, yet saiethe Thorpe, *que quant toutes les seigniours sont assembles ils poient faire vn ordynaunce et cel serra*

---

reference to the council in a Year Book of Edward III: *infra*, n. 145; for further discussion of de Bigamis see 9 Rep. 16-17.]

F (margin): /Vide Acton Burnel, anno 11 E. 1, *le roy per luy & toute son counselle ad ordeyne &c.*/

[For the contemporary requirement that a statute have the 'threefold consent' see: M. 4 H. 7, 18, pl. 11; T. 7 H. 7, 14-16, pl. 1; [St. Germain], *Doctor and Student*, fol. 146: 'there is no statut made in this realme but by the assent of the lords spiritual and temporal & of al the commons . . .'; Plowd. 79: '. . . car 3 choses fount ceo vn act. s. lassent de les seigniors, de les commons & de Roy, & lun ou deux sans le tierce ne fait ceo vn act.'; C. Hatton, *A Treatise concerning Statutes, or Acts of Parliament, and the Exposition thereof* (London, 1677), pp. 7-8: his reference is to Plowd. 209, on which see 4 Inst. 113; Prynne, *Brief Animadversions on . . . the Fourth Part of [Coke's] Institutes* (London, 1669), pp. 55-57 (cf. 2 Inst. 551); Crompton, *op. cit.*, fol. 12ᵛ (misnumbered 13): 'Les auncient estatutes come *Magna charta*, & auters estatutes sont, quod Rex statuit, & bon, car est implie, que les Seigniors & Commons assentent. *Parliament Brooke. 76.* & lestatute de finibus 27. E. 1. est statuimus & ordinauerimus.'; Co. Litt. 159ᵛ; 8 Rep. 20ᵛ; Jenk. 177: 'Act de Parliament mentioned destre per Roy & Seigniors est nul et void. 21 E. 4, 46, 49.'; H. G. Richardson and G. O. Sayles, 'The Early Statutes,' *Law Quart. Rev.*, L, 557 ff.; Chrimes, *op. cit.*, pp. 234-35; F. L. Baumer, *The Early Tudor Theory of Kingship* (New Haven, 1940), pp. 147-52.]

[6] [Richardson and Sayles, in *Law Quart. Rev.*, L, 568; Sayles, 'The Sources of Two Revisions of the Statute of Gloucester, 1278,' *Eng. Hist. Rev.*, LII, 467.]

[7] [Maitland, *op. cit.*, III, pl. 1117; Bracton, *De Legibus*, fol. 241ᵛ; Fitzherbert, *Graunde Abridgement* (London, 1565), *Darrain Presentment*, 23.]

[8] [38 E. 3, st. 2; see: Richardson and Sayles, in *Law Quart. Rev.*, L, 559; Plucknett, *Concise History*, p. 292; *idem, Statutes*, p. 34.]

tenus come estatute. But for anie thinge that is in alteracion or abrydgement they have no power, and therfore a readinge that I have seene reherceth apon the statute de Bigamis, yt was agreed by the Counsell in 16 E. 4 that a protteccion shulde lye for them that were in a vyage royall, in an assyse or wrytte of entre, and that houlden of no force.[9] [Fol. 1ᵛ]

[9][4 Rep. 35ᵛ: 'Et pur ceo si le Roy graunt Protection en *Quare impedit,* ou *Assise,* oue *non obstante* de ascun ley al contrarie, cest graunt est voide; car per le common ley Protection ne gist en nul de ceux cases pur le perde que poit eschier al plaintife per tiel graund delay, et pur ceo le *non obstante* ne poit auayler . . . come est rule en [H.] 39 H. 6, 39, [pl. 3].'; *supra,* n. 156; Co. Litt. 130ᵛ-131.]
  F (along inner margin): /Legis interpretatio, legis vim obtinet. Ad. Blacuod[ae]us, [. . . *pro Regibus Apologia* (1581)], pa. 119./[Quoted: [Egerton], *Speech . . . touching the Post-nati,* p. 55: *supra,* p. 103, n. 1.]
  [At pp. 13-15 of this *Speech,* Lord Ellesmere's reliance upon the first chapter of the *Discourse* is evident, though it will be noted that, in the interests of prerogative, the distinction between declaratory or supplementary provisions and those that abridge existing law is not reproduced.
  'Of the strength of Proclamations, being made by the King, by the aduise of his Counsell and Iudges, I will not discourse, yet I will admonish those that bee learned and studious in the Lawes, and by their profession are to giue counsell, and to direct themselues, and others, to take heede that they doe not contemne or lightly regard such Proclamations.
  'And to induce them thereunto, I desire them to looke vpon, and consider aduisedly these few Proclamations, Prouisions, or Ordinances, which I will point out vnto them; and of what validitie and force they haue beene houlden to bee in construction of Lawe, albeit they be neither Statutes, nor Acts of Parliament.
  '*M. 4. H. 3.* in *Dower,* the Defendant pleaded, *Quod petens est de potestate Regis Franciae, & residens in Francia: Et prouisum est à Consilio Regis, quod nullus de potestate Regis Franciae respondeatur in Anglia antequam Angli respondeantur de iure suo in Francia.* This the Plaintifes Atturney could not denie; and thereupon the Iudgement was, *Ideo sine die.*
  '*Anno 20. H. 3.* certaine Prouisions and Ordinances were made which were called *Prouisiones Merton,* where the King assembled his Archbishops, Bishops, Earles, and Barons for the Coronation of the King, and his wife Queene *Elenor;* and the words be, *Prouisum est in Curia Domini Regis apud Merton coram Wilihelmo Cantuariensi Archiepiscopo, & Coepiscopis, Suffraganeis suis; Et coram maiori parte Comitum & Baronum Angliae ibidem existentium pro Coronatione ipsius Domini Regis & Helionorae Reginae, pro qua omnes vocati fuerunt: Cum tractatum esset de Communi vtilitate Regni super articulis subscriptis. Ita prouisum fuit*

Ca. 2. Parlyament & Acte de Parlyament &c.

The moost auncient court & of greatest authoritye ys the kynges hyghe court of Parlyament, the authorytie of which ys absolute & byndethe all maner of persons bycause that all men are pryvie & parties therunto.[10] Unto thys courte some come by reason of theire tenure, some by vertue of wrytte, & some bycause of theire offyce.[11] By reason of tenure all

---

& concessum, tam à praedictis Archiepiscopis, Episcopis, Comitibus, & Baronibus, & alijs. De viduis primò &c.

'*Fitzherbert* citeth a Prouision made *Anno* 19. *H*. 3. in these words, *Et prouisum fuit coram Domino Rege, Archiepiscopis, Episcopis, Comitibus, & Baronibus, Quod nulla Assisa vltimae praesentationis de caetero capiatur de Ecclesijs, Praebendatis nec de Praebendis.* This Prouision was allowed and continued for Lawe, vntill *W*. 2. *Anno* 13. *Edw*. 1. *ca.* 5. which prouides the contrary by expresse words.

'*Anno* 6. *Ed*. 1. the King and his Iudges made certaine Explanations of the Statute of *Gloucester,* which are called, *Explanationes statuti Gloucestriae:* And these be the wordes, *Postmodum per Dominum Regem & Iusticiarios suos factae sunt quaedam Explanationes quorundam articulorum superius positorum.* Which Explanations haue euer since been receiued as a Law.

'There is a Proclamation by King *Ed*. 3. bearing *Teste* at *Westminster Anno* 15. *Ed*. 3. And Iudge *Thorpes* opinion *Pa*. 39. *E*. 3. 7. both of which I will now forbeare to report, and wish the Students to reade the same in the printed Bookes, where they shall see both the effect and the reason and the cause thereof; They are worth their reading, and may informe and direct them what iudgement to make of Proclamations.']

[10][*Doctor and Student*, fol. 146v: 'And euery statut there made is of as strong effect in the lawe as if al the commons were there present personally at the making thereof . . .'; Sir Thomas Smith, *De Republica Anglorum*, ed. L. Alston (Cambridge, 1906), p. 49; R. Hooker, *Of the Laws of Ecclesiastical Polity*, in *Works* (Oxford, 1888), VIII, vi, 11; Crompton, *op. cit.*, fol. 17: 'Chescun sera lye per act de Parliament, si son droit nest saue, car chescun est priuie al act de parliament. 21 H. 7. 4. per Vauisor.' As Crompton's citation indicates, there had been anticipations of this position in the Year Books (the important words are printed *supra*, n. 17, but cf. Brooke, *Extinguishment & Suspension*, 22), but the statement has a varying content: *supra*, pp. 13 *et seq*.]

[11][The relationship between this chapter of the *Discourse* and the *Modus tenendi parliamentum* will be noticed: it may thus be included among the

archebisshoppis, bysshoppis, abbottes, pryors, earles, & barons appere yf that they be sommoned by the space of 40 daies before the Parliament. By writte knightes of the shyres & burgesses of Parlyament doe come; by wrytte also citizens of cyties & barons of the Cynque Portes doe appere, and so is yt of those that are of the kynges Counsell, whose charges the kynge shall beare, by which it maie appere the sayenge of those to be false which saie that none of the Counsell oughte to be in the Parliament Howse. There commethe also by writte directed to deanes & archedeacons of every dean-erie and archedeaconrie twoo proctors of the clergie, and eiche of those that doe so come by eleccyon doe bringe twoo warrantes with them, whereof the one remeynethe with themselves, the other is inrolled by the clerke of the Parlya-mente. By thys yt maie be gathered the convocacion howse hathe bene somme tyme parcell of the Parliament, but now it ys not so, for Phyllpotte[12] that was burned for herysie, when that he was called to his answerre, shewed that his wordes which he had spoken were said in the convocacion howse, and forsomuche as by a lawdable custome of the reallme the Parlement was a place of free speache & that also was a member of the Parlyament, he therfore desired the freedome & libertye of the howse. Howbeit yt was to hym by the Lorde Ryche & Lorde Wynsore then saide that thoughe they came by a writte of sommons of the Parlya-ment, that yet notwithstandinge they were no parcell nor member of the Parlyamente, for they, as Newton saieth,[13]

---

works that drew upon the *Modus* during the revival of historical and legal studies in the Elizabethan age: M. V. Clarke, *Medieval Representation and Consent* (London, 1936), pp. 365-67, 374-92.]

[12]*F:* Phylpottz case en temps Mary.

[13][M. 20 H. 6, 12, pl. 25 (*Select Cases in the Exchequer Chamber* [Selden Soc.], p. 86).]

have no power over the layetie but onlie to charge the spirit-
ualltie by dysme, or to make institucions provinciall, as
holidaies, fastinge daies, & suche lyke, and therfore thoughe
an acte of Parlement passe without theire consente yet it ys
fyrme & good. By this it is easye to be knowne who shalbe
bounden by an acte of Parlement & whoe not, for those
whose presence is there requysyte are [fol. 2] bounden,[14]
exceptinge alwaies our soveraigne lorde the kynge, for he
shall not be bounden onlesse he be named, but he shall take
advantage of an estatut thoughe he be not named.[15] An alyene
ys not bounde by our estatutes,[16] & so I saie of those of
Irelande or those of ancient demesne, for they come not to
the Parlyament.[17] But thoughe those of Irelande be not
bounden by our Parliament because they have a Parliament

[14][Presumably areas summoned but not actually represented. In this way
the purely legal theory of 'plena potestas' is supplemented: see Chrimes,
op. cit., p. 80, n. 2; Miss Wood-Legh's note to L. Riess, *The History of the
English Electoral Law in the Middle Ages* (Cambridge, 1940), p. 21, n. 4;
infra, n. 27: 'dumtamen summoniti sunt.']

[15][T. 35 H. 6, 62, pl. 1, Ashton; T. 12 H. 7, 20, pl. 1, Mordaunt; Keilw.
35, pl. 3; Plowd. 239v, 240-41; 11 Rep. 68-68v. But, in the sixteenth century,
this formula was being transformed: *infra*, Appendix II; Plowd. 235-237v, 251v-
252v; 5 Rep. 14v, 15v; 7 Rep. 21, 32, 32v; 11 Rep. 70v, 72, 72v, 75, 75v; Jenk.
307-08; P. Birdsall, 'Non Obstante,' in *Essays in History and Political Theory
in Honor of Charles Howard McIlwain* (Cambridge, Mass., 1936), pp.
57-59.]

[16]*E* (fol. 2): Vide per lalyene [P.] 13 E. 4, [9, pl. 5].
[Chrimes, *op. cit.*, pp. 256, 269.]

[17]*E* (fol. 2): Et per ceux de Irelande vide [M.] 1 H. 7, fo. 2, [pl. 2] &
[M.] 2 R. 3, fo. 1 [12, pl. 26] & T. 1 [3] H. 7, p. 10, [pl. 3].
F (margin): [P.] 7 H. 6, 35, [pl. 39]: Martin [Newton]: [Hommes en
Ancien demene] ne serrount [en]pledes per accions dones per statute.
E (fol. 2): Et per ceux en auncien demesne vide 22 E. 3; vide Gloucester,
ca. 13.
[22 E. 3 may refer to 22 E. 3, *Corone*, 276—a precedent commonly cited
in discussions of the effect of statutes upon married women (9 Rep. 73;
Hob. 98). If so *E*'s copyist has mistaken it, perhaps because of the position
it occupied in the margin, for a case upon ancient demesne; it may however
be an erroneous reference to the case in 21 E. 3 noted *infra*, n. 19.]

of theire owne, yet notwithstandinge when they are in Englande, as they are subiecte to the kynge, so are they subiecte unto his lawes. And further yf yt be suche an estatut as makethe a lawe, as that statute that gyvethe the expenses of Parlyament & defaultes,[18] and infantes accions of accompte againste the garde[i]n,[19] byndethe them of auncient demesne.[20] So ys it yf theye be expresselie named in an estatut, as maie appere by the statute de [blank] and the statute de Yorke,[21] but as for taxes, fyftenes, aides, relieffes, or suche lyke, they are not bounden, for the kinge maie charge his demesne tenauntes without anie Parlyament. An enfant also or feme covert shalbe bounden by an estatute

[18] [12 R. 2, ca. 12; 23 H. 6, ca. 10. But see P. 7 H. 6, 35, pl. 39: 'Newton: Hommes en *Ancien demene* ne poient estre enpledes per actions dones per le *statut*, car ils ne sont parties al fesance del *statut*, ne al election des Cheualiers, des Burgeses, ne ils ne seront contributories a lour expences.'; Dyer, 373[v] (M. 22/23 Eliz.); Hob. 47-8 (10 Jac.); *Registrum Breuium Originalium*, fol. 261; Fitzherbert, *Natura Breuium*, 14E, 228C; Crompton, *op. cit.*, fol. 5[v]; Coke, *Complete Copyholder* (London, 1764), p. 226; W. Lambard, *Archeion* (London, 1635), p. 258; W. Blackstone, *Tracts* (3d ed.; Oxford, 1771), pp. 233-36; L. C. Latham, 'Collection of the Wages of the Knights of the Shire in the Fourteenth and Fifteenth Centuries,' *Eng. Hist. Rev.*, XLVIII, 457-59.]

[19] [Marlebridge, ca. 17. See: H. 21 E. 3, 10, pl. 30: 'Et dit fuit per Willoughby que l'heir aura son recouery [against a guardian in socage] per pleint de accompt en le court *d'Ancien demesne*. Et cum hoc concordat tota Curia.'; 1 And. 74: *supra*, p. 25, n. 44.]

[20] *F* (margin): [P.] 27 H. 8, 12, [pl. 33]: le counterplee de voucher done per Westminster 1, ca. 39 [40] gist la.
[H. 14 H. 7, 18, pl. 7: 'Keble: . . . jeo pose que en *Ancien demesne* in brief de *Droit clos*, il fait sa protestacion in nature d'vn *Formedon*, [&] il aura l'auerment que est done per cest *Statut* [1 H. 7, ca. 1].'; Keilw. 101[v].]

[21] [The Statute of York expressly provided that its provisions override all charters and franchises: Plucknett, 'Parliament,' in *The English Government at Work, 1327-1336* (Cambridge, Mass., 1940), I, 122, n. 1. The blank in the text may be filled by Gloucester, ca. 13 (*supra*, p. 110, n. 17, §3), expressly naming London, which, though it was not ancient demesne (P. 7 H. 6, 31-33, pl. 27; M. 8 H. 6, 3-4, pl. 9; T. 37 H. 6, 27, pl. 3; Plowd. 124), enjoyed similar special customs: 1 And. 71.]

lawe, as maye appere by the statute of Cessers[22] & by the statute of Merton.[23] Howbeit some have said that upon the statute of Westminster 1, [ca. 4], of wreckes, he shall not be concluded thoughe the yeare & the daie passe before he put in hys proofe.[24] And here also it is to be noted that yf anie of those that be choosen burgesses be a man atteynted, that duringe the whoalle tyme of hys attaynder he can not be burgesse of the Parlyamente.[25] Those that come to the Parliament by reason of theire office are the twoo clerkes of the Parlyament, the chiefe cryar of Englande, the chiefe usher, the chauncellor, the treasourer, the chamberlayns & barons of the Exchequer, the justices of the kynge, the stewarde

[22][Gloucester, ca. 4. See: P. 20 H. 6, 28, pl. 22: 'Newton: Femme couert que tient de moy cesse per deux ans, durant le couerture vre, j'aurai *cessauit* vers luy. Ad quod concessit Paston.'; *Doctor and Student*, fol. 147ᵛ; Dyer, 104ᵛ, pl. 13; Plowd. 364ᵛ; 6 Rep. 4ᵛ; 8 Rep. 44ᵛ; 9 Rep. 85-85ᵛ.]

[23][Merton, ca. 3: M. 9 H. 4, 5, pl. 19; Hob. 96; but more probably ca. 6: the precedents are examined in Doctor Hussey's case (Moore *v.* Hussey), 9 Rep. 71ᵛ, Hob. 93, 1 Rol. 445, 2 Brownl. 59, 91.]

[24][Plowd. 360, Saunders; 365; *contra*: Plowd. 364ᵛ, 372; Sir Henry Constable's case, 5 Rep. 108ᵛ; M. Dalton, *Officium Vicecomitum: The Office and Authority of Sheriffs* (London, 1682), pp. 79, 91-92; cf. *Doctor and Student*, fols. 155ᵛ-157ᵛ. But neither an infant nor a married woman is within Westminster 2, ca. 25: T. 4 H. 7, 11, pl. 6: 'Haws: Et le *statut* couient auer construction reasonablement. Et est vn *statut de Westminster second ca. 25*, que done, *Si vn plede record en Assise & est certifie, Nul tiel record, per ceo il sera atteint disseisor &c.*, vncore enfant n'est pris deins cest *statut* & vncore le *statut* general.'; *Abridgement of the booke of Assises*, fol. 146; S. E. Thorne, 'The Equity of a Statute and Heydon's Case,' *Ill. Law Rev.*, XXXI, 206, n. 9. In the sixteenth century this becomes an exception out of the statute made in the light of 'reason' or the intention of the legislature: *Doctor and Student*, fol. 29-29ᵛ: *supra*, p. 81, n. 170; fol. 147ᵛ: 'the law presumeth that it was not thintent of the makers of the statute that he should haue that punishment.'; Plowd. 10ᵛ: *supra*, p. 81, n. 170; 205: *supra*, p. 70, n. 148; 205ᵛ, 363ᵛ, 364ᵛ: *supra*, p. 82, n. 171; 2 Inst. 414 (19); Hob. 95-96. Similarly an infant is not within Westminster 2, ca. 11: Plowd. 364.]

[25][M. 1 H. 7, 4, pl. 5.]

of Englande also, who by reason of his office oughte to place the Lordes; the porter also ought to see there be but one doore at which they goe in or out. As for the expences of those that shalbe knightes of shyres or burgesses of townes, or barons of the Cynque Portes represent in Parliament, that is, for a knight of the shyre a marke by the daie to be levied of the shyre by distress. Cytizens also were accompted peeres with the knightes of the shyre. Burgesses & barons of the Portes had never above x s. apiece and for the[26] [fol. 2ᵛ] levienge of that they were wont to have a writte under the great seale directed unto the warden. And as they doe beare theire charges, in lyke maner also doe they paie the fyne that is for their defaulte. For the firste daie the burgesses shalbe called & yf they appere not then the boroughe shall paye C s., yf at the second daie the knightes of the shyres make defaulte, the shyre shall paie C li., yf the thirde daie baron of the Cynque Portes make defaulte, those of the Cynque Portes shall paie C markes. At the fourthe daie yf the proctors of the clergie make defaulte, the bysshoppe shall paie C li., and so shall abbottes & bysshoppis yf they at the fyfthe daie make defaulte. But what yf all the bysshoppis make defaut, or what yf all the lordes spirituell & temporell be absente, yet it ys saide that the kynge with his commonaltie maie kepe the Parlyamente alone, for the Commons have everie of them a greater voice in Parlyament then hathe a lorde or bysshoppe.[27] [Fol. 3]

26[The words 'and for the' are repeated, forming the first three words of fol. 2ᵛ.]

27[*Modus tenendi parliamentum* (Clarke, *op. cit.*, p. 382): 'et hoc patet quia rex potest tenere Parliamentum cum communitate regni sui, absque episcopis, comitibus et baronibus, dumtamen summoniti sunt ad Parliamentum, licet nullus episcopus, comes vel baro ad summonitiones suas veniant.'; cf. Chrimes, *op. cit.*, pp. 145-59.]

F (margin and at foot): /T. 7 H. 8 en Doctor Standysh case que [le] clergye est subiecte al temporall jurisdiccion &c. Les justices disoient que

Ca. 3. De Queux Partibus Estatute Consyste & de Preamble Destatute

As every thinge in tyme hathe founde his perfeccion so
have our estatutes also, for at the begynnynge the maner of
theire statutes was no more but to put in writinge the pur-
vyewe or bodye of the statute, but synce it is growen to
greater perfectenes. And the statutes for the moost parte
consyste of three partes: that ys, the preamble, the bodye,
& the provisoes of the statute. As for the duetye of the preamble, that is no more but to shewe the cause whye the
statute was made & what was the myschief at the commen
lawe. Wherein althoughe the common lawe be mysrecyted
yet is not that to purpose, for it is not the wordes of the
preamble that have the effecte of an acte of Parliament, but
it is the bodye of the statute that hathe that force.²⁸ And

---

le roy poit assets bien tenir son parlement per luy & ses temporall seigniours
& per ses commens tout sans son spirituall seigniours, car les spirituell
seigniours nont ascun place en le parlement chamber per reason de lour
spiritualtye, mes solement per reason de lour temporall possessions &c./
[Keilw. 184ᵛ.]

²⁸[Francis Bacon's argument in Chudleigh's case (II. 31 Eliz.), in *Works*,
ed. Spedding (London), VII (1859), 625: 'And whereas a wise man has
said, *nil ineptius lege cum prologo, jubeat non disputet:* this had been true
if preambles were annexed as pleading for the provisions of laws; for the
law carries authority in itself: but our preambles are annexed for exposition;
and this gives aim to the body of the statute; for the preamble sets up the
mark, and the body of the law levels at it.' The preamble throws light
upon the common law prior to the statute (Bacon, *The Learned Reading . . . upon the Statute of Uses* [London, 1642], p. 27: 'The Preamble
of the Law was justly commended by *Popham* chiefe Justice in 36 *Reginae*,
where hee saith, that there is little need to search and collect out of
Cases before the statute, what the mischiefe was, which the scope of the
Statute was to redresse, because there is a shorter way offered us, by the
sufficiency and fulnesse of the Preamble . . .'), and thus upon the intention
of the framers: Plowd. 10ᵛ, 369: 'Et pur apprendre le puruiew le melious,
le preamble del act est deste consider, le quel *Dyer* terme deste vn cliff
de ouerer les ments del feasors del act, & les mischiefs que ilz entend de

therfore the statute of Westminster 2, ca. 4, that begynneth, *In casu quando vir implacitatus &c.*, doeth indede mysrecyte the commen lawe, for the mischiefe was not when he alone loste by defaulte, for then she might have had an assyse, but the mischiefe was when he & she togeather loste by defaulte, for then was she without remedye.[29] Notwythstandinge whiche recytell yet ys the purviewe of the statute taken as the mischief was indede. So upon the statute of Merton, ca. 4, the wordes are *feoffauerunt libere tenentes suos de paruis tenementis in magnis maneriis*, and yet yf the feffement were of grette tenementes & smalle maners the remedie ys all one, for the statute therein did but recyte the specialltie of the case, as peradventure the bylle where upon the statute was made; yet did not exclude the generaltie of the purviewe.[30]

remedier . . . Et tiel est le office del expositors de insuer lentent del feasors, expresse a eux per plain termes.'; there had been anticipations of this in the Year Books: P. 4 E. 4, 4, pl. 4: 'Et lopinion de Choke, Illing-worth, & Yelverton fuit . . . chescun statute fait, couient estre prise solonque l'entent de ceux que ceo feceront, la ou les parollx de ceo sont doutes & nemy en certein, & solonque le rehercel de le statute.', but references to the preamble, and to its value in ascertaining not 'what was the myschief at the commen lawe' but the legislative intent, do not appear regularly until the sixteenth century: 3 Rep. 77ᵛ; 4 Rep. 111; 10 Rep. 45ᵛ; *supra*, n. 127. At the same time, as the *Discourse* indicates, the preamble itself becomes common and more elaborate; see also: Plucknett, *Concise History*, p. 288.]

[29]E (margin): H. 10 H. 4, *Disseisin*, 7; M. 40 E. 3, [46, pl. 31], per Thorpe; M. 48 E. 3, [31], pl. 20, per Belknap in *dum fuit infra etatem*.
[The reference is to Westminster 2, ca. 3: *In casu quando vir amisit &c.* See: *Abridgement of the booke of Assises*, fol. 16ᵛ; *Vieux Natura Breuium* (London, 1580), fol. 132: 'Mes en cas que si home recouera deuers le baron sole terre que est de droit la feme par defaut, ou par accion trie, & le baron deuie, la feme auera vn assise & nient *cui in vita*, pur ceo que el ne fuit my party al iudgement, & fuit ouste per le recouerie de son franktenement.'; Plowd. 43ᵛ, 57ᵛ; 6 Rep. 8ᵛ; 2 Inst. 342; T. F. T. Plucknett, *Statutes and Their Interpretation in the First Half of the Fourteenth Cen-tury* (Cambridge, 1922), p. 49, n. 2.]

[30][11 Rep. 33ᵛ: 'Et ou lestatut de *21. H. 8. cap. 15.* parle in le preamble de leases faits pur graund fines *for the incomes &c.*, & le puruieu est, *That*

So upon Westminster 2 [1], ca. 2, it ys saide, *quant clerke est pris &c.*, by which it maie be gathered that the auncient lawe was that immediatelie as sone as he had bene taken he shulde be delivered to the ordinarye, howbeyt that ys not lawe, for at this daie he shalbe arraigned firste.[31] In lyke maner the statute of Gloucester, ca. 2, recytethe that in an assyse of mordancester *sil alledge feffement &c.*, yt is not true, for the feffemente of the auncester with warrantie was never anie plee in an assise of mordancestor, because it doeth goe in traversinge the poynte of the wrytte.[32] Infynite other examples maie be put, but these shall suffice to prove that the preamble of an estatute hathe not the force of an estatute as to make that lawe which yt recytethe, but that indede the lawe shalbe taken as yt was.[33] And unto this purpose it apperteignethe also that ys saide that althoughe the preamble

---

all such Termors shall or may falsifie, ad estre touts foits prise que lestatute extend a leases faits ou pur petit fine, ou pur nul fine.']

[31]*E* (margin): Staunf[orde, *Plees del Coron*], 131.

[32]*E* (margin): H. 20 H. 6, 21 [19, pl. 14], Yelverton; H. 13 H. 4, *Ayde* [*Aiel*], 9; M. 27 E. 3, [8, pl. 14], *Mordancestor*, 11; P. 14 E. 3, [Y.B. 14 Edw. III (Rolls Ser.), p. 135], *Cosinage*, 5 [6]; H. 14 E. 2, *Cosinage*, 12.
[2 Inst. 291 (2).]

[33]*E* (fol. 3): Vide que per le preamble destatute 2 & 3 E. 6, ca. 24, il appiert que le receuer des felons biens serra felonie & vncor est certen que le ley ne fuit issint, vide *Corone*, 126 & 208.
[Similarly, Staunforde, *Plees del Coron*, fol. 43ᵛ; Jenk. 28, but see R. Crompton, *L'office & aucthoritie de Iustices de Peace* (London, 1587), fol. 37ᵛ: 'Resceit de biens imblées conusant que sont inblées fait le resceiuer accessorie al felony come *Windham* justice dassise dit in son charge al assise al *Stafford*, 27 Eliz. *Vide* [M.] 9 H. 4, fol. 41 [1, pl. 3], et 25 E. 3, 39, & *vide* 2 & 3 E. 6, ca. 24'; W. Fulbecke, *A Parallele or Conference of the Civill Law, the Canon Law, and the Common Law* (London, 1601), p. 103: '. . . and if goods be stolne and I.S. knowing they be stolne receiueth them, in this case, though he receiue the goods onely, and not the felon himselfe, yet he is accessarie to the felonie.'; cf. B. H. Putnam, *Proceedings before the Justices of the Peace, Edward III to Richard III* (Ames Foundation), pp. cxli-cxlii.]

recyted be more speciall or more generall then the statute recitethe, that [fol. 3ᵛ] yet it shalbe taken accordinge to the purviewe & not the preamble. As Westminster 1, ca. 5, was made onlie for the free eleccion by Kynge John disturbed, but yet it is generallie taken for all other eleccions so that they shalbe free. So upon the statute of Gloucester, ca. 7, althoughe the mischiefe were onlie for feffementes with warrantie, yet because the wordes are generall, *si feme done ou vende &c.*, they are generallie taken for all feffementes aswell without warrantie as with it.³⁴ Contrarywyse, upon the statute of Wynchester, ca. 1, althoughe the preamble recyte, *pur ceo que de iour en iour robberies, homycydes, arsons, &c.*, yet for homycide concealed there was no remedie because that the remedie gyven by the purviewe is by restitucion which can not be in homycydes. So that theffecte of the estatute lyethe in the bodye & bowells of the statute, & therfore we will speake of that. [Fol. 4]

Ca. 4. Quant les Parollz Sont en Laffirmatyue & Quant en le Negatyue

The force & effecte, as I have saide, beinge to be considered upon the bodie of the statute, you muste therin consider whether it be in the affirmative or in the negative, for that makethe a difference to divers purposes. One ys that an estatute in the affirmative doeth not take awaie neither the commen lawe nor other statutes that were made before.³⁵

³⁴[11 Rep. 33ᵛ; 2 Inst. 309.]

³⁵*E* (margin): P. 10 E. 4, 7, [pl. 18; Y.B. 10 Edw. IV (Selden Soc.), pp. 63, 64], Chocke; [H.] 3 H. 7, 2 [1, pl. 1]; [P.] 46 E. 3, 12, pl. 12; M. 50 E. 3, 24, pl. 4 [5], Han[imer].

F: /T. 4 H. 7, 11, [pl. 6], Vavasor: [Et Sir, vn *Statut* en le affirmatiue ne defetera ascun chose:] issint lestatute [1 E. 3, st. 2, ca. 17] que voit que vicomtes del counties deliueront enditements a les justices de peace per indenture, vncore sils ne sount issint, il nest voide./

And therfore notwithstandinge that processe of foriudger be geven in a wrytte of mesne,[36] yet is not the processe that was at the commen lawe taken awaie.[37] And in lyke maner was the case adiudged in the Archesse, that notwithstandinge the statute 21 H. 8, ca. 5, commanded the ordinary to commytte the admynistracion to the nexte of kynne, upon payne of x li., yet yf he woulde forfaicte that x li. he mighte commytte the admynistracion to whome he woulde, for that the statute in the affirmative tooke not awaie the power that he had by the commen lawe.[38] But this grounde faylethe there where possiblie the statute in the affirmative & the commen lawe can not stande togeather, & then the statute takethe awaie the commen lawe. As the statute of Magna Charta, ca. 19, willethe that the constables that take for castell garde shall have 40 daies respite, & the statute of Westminster 1, ca. 31 [32],

F (along inner margin): /Precepta affirmatiua non obligant ad semper, sed pro loco & tempore, varias interpretationes variaque temperamenta et limitationes accipiunt, ex circunstantiarum varia ratione. Negatiua vero semper, & omni loco & tempore, nulla circunstantiarum habita ratione, obligant. Quia in affirmatiuis actus virtutum explicantur. In negatiuis actus peccatorum & vitiorum, qui semper sunt en malo coniuncti [vt libro 2 Ethicon docet Aristoteles] & ideo fugiendi. Danaeus, *Ethices Christ[ianae]*, lib. 2, pa. 132./

[36]*F:* Westminster 2, ca. 9.

[37]*E* (margin): [M.] 13 E. 2, *Mesne*, 68.
E (fol. 3ᵛ): Vide Hankford, [P.] 7 H. 4, 13 [12], pl. 8. Lestatute que done le *elegit* [Westminster 2, ca. 18] ne tolle le *capias* que fuit al commen ley: [T.] 15 [17] E. 4, [4], p. 3.
[11 Rep. 64: *supra*, p. 40, n. 73.]

[38]*E* (margin): 43 [Liber] As[sisarum], pl. 22; H. 8 H. 4, 20, pl. 7, in fine; 44 E. 3, 3, [M. 24 E. 3, 37, pl. 55], *Assise*, 131; vide seme matter sur lestatut de York: 30 Lib. Assisarum, pl. 5; 15 E. 3, *Assise*, 132[?].
[Crompton, *L'Avthoritie . . . des Covrts*, fols. 16, 21: 'Lestatute *21 H. 8, ca. 13,* parle que nul person desglise, ou tiel home espiritual prendra lesse pur ans pur vie, ou a volunt &c. sur paine de forfait pur chescun mois, que il occupie ceo x. l. al Roy, & informer, mes nota, que le lesse nest fait voide per dit estatut, come ad este ruled *Dier 358.*']

willethe that yf he be paide in thexchequer, then he shall
paie it out of hande. Here the statute in the affirmative
takethe awaie the lawe before, for it can not stande togeather
that he that shulde paie mentenaunt shulde have also 40 daies
respyte.[39] But, contrarywyse, the statute in the negative:
that deniethe & takethe awaie also the commen lawe. Another
difference betwene these ys that upon a statute in the affirmative there is no accion grounded, for it ys commonlye receyved for a grounde amonge the readers that *ex nuda pro-
hibitione non oritur actio.*[40] And therefore upon Magna
Charta, ca. 6, *haeredes maritentur absque disparagatione,*
althoughe the heire had bene disparaged yet was there no
accion gyven tyll afterwarde, upon the statute of Merton,
[ca. 6].[41] And so the same statute of Magna Charta, ca. 7,
willethe that the wyfe, after the deathe of her husbande, shall
have *maritagium suum et dotem suam & hereditatem suam,*
yet hathe she no more remedie by the statute then she had
at the commen lawe. But where such an estatute is in the
negatyve, there the partie shall not onlie frame an accyon
upon the statute,[42] but he that transgressethe the wordes of

[39][11 Rep. 59, 62ᵛ-63; Jenk. 2.]

[40][Hervey's Inner Temple reading on Magna Carta (Harvard Law
School Library MS), fol. 8: '. . . est vn common dit que null accion est
foundue sur vn estatut quest en laffirmatyue &c. et vncore cest estatute
(Magna Carta, ca. 7) est en laffirmatyue . . .'; illustrations of this statement
are difficult to find: the rule seems never to have been widely accepted.]

[41][An action was supplied but as was pointed out (Litt. §108; Co. Litt.
81-81ᵛ; 1 Rep. 87ᵛ-88; *infra,* n. 146; cf. *infra,* n. 198) 'ne fuit vnques view ne
oye que ascun action fuit port sur cel statute de Merton pur cel disparagement enuers le gardeine . . .']

[42]*E* (margin): [M.] 35 H. 6, 8 [6, pl. 9], Ashton.
[10 Rep. 75ᵛ: 'Et auxy deste obserue, que quant ascun statute prohibite
ascun chose &c. si ascun implead auter, coment que soit in course dun
legal proceeding, vncore le partie grieue auera action sur lestatute vers le
partie que sua enconter lestatute, coment que les parols de lestatute ne

the statute shalbe amercyed. As the statute of Marlebridge, ca. 4, saiethe *nullus de* [fol. 4^v] *caetero ducere faciat distric-* *tiones &c.*, yf anie man offende the wordes of the statute, you maie have your accion & he shall be amercyed.[43] There is

done ascun action al partie, mes ceo est vn consequent et chose imply in chescun chose prohibite per ascun statute . . .']

F:/Marow sur Westminster 1, lectura 2 [B. H. Putnam, *Early Treatises on the Practice of the Justices of the Peace in the Fifteenth and Sixteenth Centuries* [Oxford, 1924], p. 295] que accion ne gist sur statute en le negatyue sil ne soit per expresse parollz destatute./

[43] [The statute of Marlebridge, ca. 4, made it a trespass to drive beasts distrained in one county to another county, but when the land upon which the distress was taken was held of a manor in the second county, the defendant was permitted to justify: Plucknett, *Statutes*, pp. 61-62; M. 1 H. 6, 3, pl. 9 (Y.B. 1 Hen. VI [Selden Soc.], p. 30; Thorne, in *Ill. Law Rev.*, XXXI, 206, n. 11). However, a contrary view had been taken in H. 30 E. 3, 5, and in P. 22 E. 4, 11, pl. 30: 'Pigot: Moy semble que il ne poit justifier en tiel maner, car il est restreint per lestatut que est en le negatif, que voit que *nullus de caetero*, issint le statute ne poit estre construe sinon *stricti juris* . . . & auxi le statut est en le negatiue, pur ceo il ne poit justifier, pur ceo auise a vous, car il est peremptory per vous [the judges]. Genny: Moy semble que il bien poit justifier, car coment que le statut soit en le negatif, l'entent de le statut fuit pur cel cause, car deuant cel statut a chescun temps que home voilloit auer distres ou pur rent seruice, coment que le manor fuit en mesme le county . . . il voile a tout temps auer chase le distres en auter county . . . & pur cel mischief fuit le statut fait . . . Et a ceo que vous dits que le statut est en le negatif, issint est le statut de maintenance, que nul doit maintener, & vncore nient obstant, son prochein amy maintenera, & auxy home de le ley, & issint auters statutes. Hussey: Moy semble que il ne poit justifier, pur ceo que le statute est en le negatif nient obstant est dit en vn roll *Anno 1 H. 6.* que le Seignior bien poit chaser le distres hors del county, lou il fuit prise en auter county lou le manor est, & pur ceo nous voillomus voier notre presidents . . . Pigot: S'il poit justifier il est graund mischief, car il n'ad ascun replegiari . . . car nul poit faire replegiari forsque le Vicont de le county . . .' No judgment is noted, but the position urged by Pigot was not adopted in Keilw. 50, pl. 3 (P. 18 H. 7), and it was not adopted later: Plowd. 9^v: '. . . le statut de Marlebridge prohibite que nul ducera distresse d'un countie en auter countie, vncore il est tenus en 30 E. 3. que lou le Abbesse de Wylton auoit vn manour en vn countie, que el puissoit amesner distresse prise en auter countie, en terre tenus del dit manour, en mesme le countie ou le manor fuit, nient obstant que lestatute est en le negatyue, et ceo pur le enconuenyence et absurditie que auterment ensuera.'; 18^v:

yet another difference to be marked where the statute is in
the affirmatyve & where not. And that is yf the thinge pro-
hibited by the statute doe concerne iurisdiccion or suche
other lyke and yt be done contrarie, then is the thynge so
done voide & *coram non judice.* As the statute of Magna
Charta, ca. 12, saiethe, *assisae non capiantur nisi in comitatibus
suis,* yf they be contrarie to that prohibicion houlden elsewhere, then is the houldinge voide & *coram non judice.*[44] So
the statute of Articuli super Chartas, [ca. 3], willethe that
the stewarde of the kinges howse shall not houlde plee of
trespasse done without the verge; yf he doe contrarye to
that statute he is then punyshable & the plee voide.[45] Neither
is this onlie true in iurisdiccions, but also in other thinges
forbydden by statutes in the negative. But this grounnde

similarly 'en auoidance del mischiefe & inconuenience.'; 204^v: similarly 'mes
les Juges ont prise lentent del feasors del act nient de extender a celuy
seignior, mes ou le seigniorie & tenancy auxi sont en vn mesme countie.';
2 Brownl. 260; 2 Inst. 106: '. . . note hereby a case out of the mischiefs is
out of the meaning of the law, though it be within the letter.']

[44][M. 38 H. 6, 18, pl. 36: '*Assise de Mordancestor* fuit porte en le *Comon
Place.* Laicon demanda jugement [si] le court voile conustre car il dit
le *Statutum de Magna charta* est *Assisae non capiantur nisi in propriis
comitatibus suis.* [It was urged that] le *Statut* n'est my issint, mes le *Statut*
est, *Capiantur,* & nemy en le negatiue . . . Et puis le court dit, que si le
Statut soit, *non capiantur,* cest court n'aura conisance, &c.'; M. 39 H. 6, 19,
pl. 28: '*Assise de Mordancestor* en le *Comon Bank* de terres en Bucks.
Laicon reherce le *statut de Magna carta, ca. 12.* que veut que *Recognitiones
Assisae capiantur in comitatibus suis,* & il proue per son brief que le terre
est en le County de B. . . . Billing: A le *Comon ley l'Assise* puit auer este pris
en auter County, & le *Statut* n'est en le negatif . . . Et puis *agarde fuit per
Prisot* que le defendant [? demandant] ira a Dieu.'; Brooke, *Mordauncester,*
12; 2 And. 181.
    Magna Carta, ca. 12, is quoted in affirmative form by Littleton (M. 8 E.
4, 16, pl. 21), indicating a continuance of the lack of knowledge on the
part of judges and lawyers of the wording of statutes: Plucknett, *Statutes,*
pp. 105-12; Sayles, *Select Cases in the Court of King's Bench under Edward
I* (Selden Soc.), III, xvi.]

[45][Plowd. 37^v; Le case del Marshalsea, 10 Rep. 77.]

failethe even in iurisdiccions, for the statute of Magna Charta, ca. 12 [11], saiethe, *communia placita non sequantur curiam nostram*, yet yf at this daie they houlde plee of formedon in the kinges benche it is not voide.[46] So upon the statute of Gloucester, ca. 8, yf they of the commen place doe houlde plee of dette under 40 s. yt is not voide, yet ys the statute in the negative, *null &c.*, but the cause ys, these by a meáne maie houlde iurisdiccion.[47] Nowe, contrarywyse, an estatute in the affirmatyve is of no suche force. As Westminster 1, ca. 5, that willeth al eleccions to be free, yet yf they be by compulsion they are not voide. There are divers cases wherein this grounde ys broken, but those maie be marked by readinge.[48] [Fol. 5]

[46][Plucknett, *Statutes*, p. 62; M. 10 H. 6, 13, pl. 43, Chantrelle; 36 H. 6, 34, pl. 34; M. 22 E. 4, 33, pl. 11: 'Brigges: Coment que les justices de Bank le Roy tient plee d'vn formedon, & iudgment soit done en meme le court, il est forsque error, coment que le statute est *quod communia placita non sequantur &c. curiam nostram*, & nemy *coram non judice.*'; H. 1 H. 7, 12, pl. 18; H. 14 H. 7, 14, pl. 3: 'Nota que Fineux Chief Justice disoit . . . come ou *Statut de Magna carta c. 11. est, Communia Placita* [&c.], vncore si *Formedon* soit porte in le *Comon Banc*, & per certain cause remue icy, nous aurons la determination de cel . . . Issint de choses destre determinez deuant Justices de paix, si cel case soit remue in *Banc le Roy* . . .'; Keilw. 106: '*Praecipe quod reddat* en banke le Roy, et iudgement est done la sur cest briefe cest est error, et nemy void iudgement, pur ceo que les Judges de banke le Roy per vn forme poient tener plee de terre.'; Crompton, *L'Avthoritie . . . des Covrts*, fols. 67ᵛ, 68; 2 Inst. 23 (5); cf. M. 1 R. 3, 4, pl. 9.]

[47][M. 19 H. 6, 8, pl. 19 (18); H. 14 H. 8, 15, pl. 2 & 17, pl. 5, Brooke, *Iurisdiction*, 45; Crompton, *op. cit.*, fol. 101; Thorne, 'Notes on Courts of Record in England,' *West Virginia Law Quarterly*, XL, 359, n. 35.]

[48]*F* (at foot): /P. 2 Eliz., Plowd. 206: Lestatute anno 34 & 35 H. 8, ca. [26], voit que *touts accions sur ascuns statutes serrount sue per originall briefe deuaunt les justices de Wales a lour sessions deins lour lymittes &c.* Et sur ceo fuit argue que tiels accions ne poient este sue en le courtes le roy al Westminster. Quar coment que les parollz sont en laffirmatiue, *que serrount sue &c.*, vncore en eux vn negatyue est implye, *viz.*, et nemy allyors &c. Come Westminster 2, ca. 4, voit que demaundant en *quod ei deforciat* vouchera *acsi esset tenens in priori breue*, & en ceo negatiue est include, *viz.*, et non aliter, & pur ceo si primer breue fuit *scire facias*, il

Ca. 5. Come Parollz Sera Expounde en vn Statute &c.

For the further exposicion of an estatute there is well to be considered the wordes, the sentence, & the meanynge thereof, for sommetymes it shalbe construed straictelie—that is, accordinge to the wordes & no further. Sometymes the wordes by equytye are stretched to lyke cases. Sommetymes they are exponded againste the wordes. And sommetymes there happen cases upon statutes for which there is no wordes in the statute, and then is the exposicion made at the commen

---

ne vouchera. Sic lestatute 27 H. 8, ca. [10], que home auera le possession en mesme maner come il auoit luse, implye & non auterment. Sic lestatute anno 31 H. 8, ca. [13], que monasteryes viendront al roy en mesme le state que donques ils fueront, implye & nemy en auter estate. Mes per Sanders & le melleur opinion, le ley est contrary, vncore les cases suisetes ils agree quar le dit statutes create choses que ne fueront a le commen leye, et pur ceo ils serront fait & pris en lorder lymitte per lestatute, & nemy auterment. Mes en ceo case per statute anno 27 H. 8, [ca. 26], Gales fuit unite a Angleterre & pur ceo accions foundue sur statutes per choses surdantes la fueront suable al Westminster deuaunt lestatute 34 & 35 H. 8, et pur ceo le dit statutes veignount apres ne tolleront le iurisdiccion de les courtes sinon per expresse parolls restreignaunt ceo. Nota cest diuersitye./
[Plowd. 113; Hatton, *Treatise concerning Statutes*, pp. 83-84: 'For Statutes in the affirmative, imply a negative, when they be constitutive of new Law, and there is no Law nor Statute beforehand to the contrary thereof: but where there is a former Statute or Law contrariant, it is not taken away by implying a negative in an affirmative, as 27 H. 8. *Wales* was united to *England*, and 34 & 35 H. 8. Authority was given to the Justices in *Wales* affirmatively, giving them Jurisdiction to try all Penal Statutes. This taketh not away the Authority that Judges had before in other of her Majesties Courts: And though some say, that a Statute in the affirmative defeateth nothing, yet am I not of their mind, for the cause and reason aforesaid. And further, because I know the Statute of 31 H. 8. gave the King the possessions of divers Colledges in such state as they then were; and though the possessions of some of them came not to the Kings hands three or four years after, nevertheless all the Leases granted between the time of the Statute and the Kings entry, are void by this Statute. So that this affirmative defeateth with great reason.'; Crompton, *op. cit.*, fol. 15; 11 Rep. 59ᵛ; 2 Inst. 200 (4).]

lawe. Of all these yt shalbe speciallie spoken hereafter. But firste for the bare wordes of an estatute, yt is plaine that so muche as the worde by his propre signyficacion doethe sygnyfye, unto so muche the statute doethe extende. As *dysparagement* is a worde properlie conteyninge under it all the species of disparagement & therfor all disparagementes are conteigned under the same: Magna Charta, ca. 6.[49] So by proper significacion under *ecclesia* all the members of the churche are conteigned: Magna Charta, ca. 1. So commen is this and everie chapiter shewethe an example, & reason sheweth that that which by propertie of grammer speache maie be taken, ought to be taken, onlesse the meanynge of the statute or somme grette reason doe importe otherwyse.[50] As upon Merton, ca. 1, the worde *dos,* althoughe it doe compryse all dower, yet is it not taken but for dower *ad hostium ecclesie,* the reason is shewed for that she may enter into that.[51] And so upon the statute of Marlebridge, ca. 13, which saiethe *allocetur ei essonium vnicum,* yet it is taken but for the commen essoine, for, althoughe it doe signifye properlie all kynde of essoines, yet notwithstandinge yt is mooste commenlie by use of speache taken for the commen essoyne.[52] As *fee* is alone taken for fee simple,[53] or a lease for lyfe without more by commen use of speache is taken for your owne lyfe.[54] For use, as it is *optimus magister* & *omnium doctorum praecepta superat,* so is it diligentlie

---

[49][Litt. §109; Co. Litt. 80-80ᵛ.]

[50][Plowd. 122, 125, 127ᵛ; cf. *infra,* n. 66.]

[51][Litt. §§39, 43; Co. Litt. 34ᵛ-37ᵛ; 4 Rep. 1ᵛ.]

[52]*E* (margin): [H.] 19 H. 6, 51, [pl. 11].
[Brooke, *Parlement & Statutes,* 48; similarly, Marlebridge, ca. 19: M. 2 E. 4, 17, pl. 9; 5 E. 4, Long Quinto, 70; 2 Inst. 126, 137.]

[53][Litt. §293; Plowd. 11; 11 Rep. 39.]

[54][Litt. §56.]

to be observed of the statute makers.[55] As this worde *terra* in statutes is not onlie taken for landes, but for all kynde of tenementes, and that by a contynuall use of the statute makers: Westminster 2, ca. 4; statute de Religiosis;[56] Magna Charta, ca. 36.[57] So is *feoffare* commenlie taken not onlie for a feffement, but for a graunte, lease, release, fyne, or other maner of covenauntes, & signyfyethe as muche as this worde *alienare:* Marlebridge, ca. 6;[58] Gloucester, ca. 7; Westminster 2, ca. 4. And so thoughe *rapina,* of his propre significacion, ys robrye,[59] yet by use we see the statute makers have taken [fol. 5ᵛ] yt for hym that takethe awaie goodes by trespasse: Marlebridge, ca. ultimo [ca. 28]; Westminster 1, ca. 36 [37].[60] So by verie use & custome you shall see these wordes

[55] [1 And. 77 (T. 19 Eliz.): 'Les parols de le statute sont d'estre intend accordant a le commen *understanding and speech* que passe enter person & person, & nemy en le darke sense accordant al operation del ley.'; [Egerton], *Speech . . . touching the Post-nati,* p. 62: 'And wordes should bee taken *sensu currenti:* for vse and custome is the best expositor both of lawes and wordes; *Quam penes arbitrium & ius & norma loquendi.'* In the construction of deeds, the rule is very common: 4 Rep. 35; for the medieval Roman law: W. Engelmann, *Die Wiedergeburt der Rechtskultur in Italien* (Leipzig, 1938), pp. 152-53.]

[56] [M. 3 E. 4, 12-15, pl. 8; Brooke, *Parlement & Statutes,* 50.]

[57] [Brooke, *Exposition de certen parolx,* 16: Nota in veteri libro intrationum que le briefe de elegit est *quod liberet medietatem terre et tenementorum in balliua sua,* et vncore lestatut de Westminster 2, ca. 18. ne parle nisi de medietate terre sue, et ne parle de hoc verbo *tenementum,* et ideo, vt videtur, statutum illud intelligitur de terris & tenementis per hoc verbum *terra* tantum, et vide antiquo libro Intrationum, et nouo libro intrationum, que le quarte parte dun mese fuit extende per vn elegit, et vncore mese nest terre, et sic vide lentent del paroles del statute, et sic habetur in vsu, de faire extent de moitye de rent & huiusmodi.'; Brooke, *Elegit,* 13. A similar result might be reached through 'lequity de lestatut': Plowd. 178ᵛ: *'Elegit medietatem terrae suae* est done per lestatute de Westminster 2, ca. 18, vncore per lequity de ceo per *Elegit* il auera le moity del rent.']

[58] [2 Inst. 110 (4).]

[59] [Bracton, *De Legibus,* fol. 150ᵛ; Staunforde, *Plees del Coron,* fol. 27ᵛ.]

[60] [The French version of Westminster 1, ca. 37, uses the word 'roberie,' but as the equivalent of trespass: 2 Inst. 236.]

in feodo & hereditate put in statutes where indede it was but for lyfe: Gloucester, ca. 4; Westminster 2, ca. 5, ca. 15 [25], & ca. 41 [42]. So thoughe *boscus* doethe properlie signyfye nothinge but woodde (naye, not woodde neither properlie, for it is but a worde knowen onlie to our lawyers), yet in Charta de Foresta, ca. 4, it is not onlie taken for the libertie which he hathe in trees, but also for the libertie which he hathe in the place where the woodde growethe. Somme worde there is also unproperlie taken for that that the statute makers woulde have it, so *facere* hathe bene put for *reficere:* Magna Charta, ca. 15. So *conuictus* hathe bene put for *attinctus:* Magna Charta, ca. 22.[61] So *locus certus* hathe bene put for *species loci certi:* Magna Charta, ca. 11. So *defunctus* hathe bene put for *executor defuncti:* Magna Charta, ca. 18. So *resommoniatur* hathe bene used for *reattachiatur:* Westminster 2, ca. 35.[62] Sommetymes also wordes are improper, but then it is by somme figure of speache, as by metonomya *ecclesia* was put pro *hominibus ecclesiasticis:* Magna Charta, ca. 1; and sommetyme *ecclesia* hathe bene put pro *ordinario ecclesie,* as in Magna Charta, ca. 18.[63] So upon Merton, ca. 5, *vsura* is taken for a penaltie.[64] And unto this grounde it apperteinethe when one tence is taken for an other, one number for an other, one gender for an other, or such lyke. As upon Charta de Foresta, ca. 4, these wordes *qui habent* in

[61][2 Inst. 37; 4 Rep. 46-46v.]

[62][2 Inst. 441 (11). See also Dyer 125v: 'Et en nostre ley [in construing deeds] vn parol serra construe diuers temps en le sence dun auter, sicome reuertera serra pris pur remaynera, *& encontra.* Item discendra serra pris pur reuertera per [M.] 6 E. 2, [Y.B. 6 Edw. II (Selden Soc., 1921), pp. 32-39, *Entré congeable,* 55], in casu de receite. *Et hoc verbum recipere terram* serra pris *pro reintrare, in eodem libro, & in 8 libro Assisarum,* [pl. 34], returnera serra pris pro *reintrare* vel *habere terram* pur le condicion enfreint . . . [many examples cited].'; Plowd. 140v, 171 (deeds).]

[63][The citation is incorrect.]

[64][T. 35 H. 6, 61, pl. 1; Plowd. 236v; 2 Inst. 89.]

the present tense are taken also for the wordes [*qui*] *habue-runt*. And so upon the statute of 32 H. 8, [ca. 16], those that have anie letters patentes of our soveraigne lorde the kinge were taken also for those that shall have anie graunt. So upon the statute De frangentibus prisonam,[65] *iudicium requirit* was taken for *iudicium requirebat* in the preter tence.[66] And so upon Westminster 2, ca. 5, *que fuit de aduocatione* is taken for the future tence *que fuerint de aduocatione*.[67] In lyke maner sommetyme the singuler number is put for the plurall, as upon Merton, ca. 3, *eundem conquerentem* is put for *eosdem conquerentes*.[68] So upon Magna Charta, ca. 3 [2], *et releuium nobis debeat* & yet *si releuia debeant* it is so taken also. So contrarywyse the plurall is taken for the synguler, as Merton, ca. 3, saieth *assumptis secum custodibus*, and yet

---

[65][23 E. 1.]

[66]*E* (margin): Staunf[orde, *Plees del Coron*], 32; [T.] 40 E. 3, 20 [30, pl. 7].
[M. 35 H. 6, 11, pl. 17: 'Littleton: A ma entent ceux parolls *si qui fuerint* serront pris come ils poient, solonque l'entendment del condition, & nemy per order del Gramar: car en diuers cases le *praeterit tempus* seruira per le *praesens tempus*. Come en cas si vn voile faire vn fait del feffement, le comen fesance de charters est, *Dedi, concessi*, or si cest serra pris solonque le vray rule de Gramar, il donera deuant le fesance del fait, le quel ne serra issint pris; mes il sera pris come il puit estre en Ley, & come il puit estre entende, & ceo est per le *praesens tempus* . . .' (for the words 'dedi, concessi, et hac presenti carta confirmavi,' see Thorne, 'Livery of Seisin,' *Law Quart. Rev.*, LII, 345-47); M. 35 H. 6, 16, pl. 25: 'Moile: . . . car en plusors cases en les ancien *Statutz* nous prismus le statut tout auter que le lettre est: car nous deuons prendre accord au comen entendement, & accord al entent que il fuit fait, & nemy solonque les parols. Et auxi jeo ay commonier oue vn Maistre de Gramar, & il dit moy que souent fois le *praeterit* temps sera pris pur le present temps, & vn parol pur auter, & toutes sera saues & excusez per figures & rules en Gramar.']

[67][T. 27 H. 8, 19, pl. 6; Brooke, *Exposition de certen parolx*, 5: 'Nota per *Audeley* chaunceller que ascun foitz ceo parol *esteant* serra pris pur le future temps, sibien come pur le present temps . . .']

[68][Co. Litt. 154ᵛ.]

yf there be but one coroner, it is good ynoughe.[69] So upon Westminster 2, [fol. 6] ca. 6, *implacitatus* ys taken also yf divers be impleaded. And as for the masculyne gender to be conteyned under the femynyne there are [those] that mayntayne it by propertie of speache, in so muche that it is a rule amonge the cyvilians, *masculinum sub se continere foemininum*.[70] As upon Merton, ca. 7, *quis* conteynethe *quam*,[71] and upon Marlebridge, ca. 6,[72] & Westminster 2, ca. 35, *puer* is construed pro *femella* & *primogenitus* pro *primogenita*.[73] So upon Westminster 2, ca. 6, which I have cyted, *implacitatus*

[69]*E* (margin): 23 Lib. Assisarum, pl. 7.

[H. 14 H. 4, 34, pl. 52; H. 39 H. 6, 40-42, pl. 4; Plowd. 86ᵛ, 393; 2 Inst. 84; Jenk. 288. Similarly under 1 H. 5, ca. 3: M. 9 E. 4, 37, pl. 15: 'Moile: S'il forge vn fait il est en case de statute de forger de faux faits, &c.' But under Westminster 2, ca. 11, the plural is not taken for the singular: H. 20 H. 6, 17, pl. 4: 'Paston: Le *statut* purque les auditors ont lour pouuoir veut, *auditors*: & jeo ne veya onques ascun jugement fait per vn commissioner seul sans compagnon. Purque &c. Yelverton: Sir, en *Redisseisin* le *statut* veut, per le *vicecomes, assumptis secum coronatoribus*, &c. & vncore suffit si vn coroner soit la: issint icy. Purque &c. Fortescue: Vraiement jeo croy que non, si non que ne sont plusieurs coroners en la county.'; T. 20 H. 6, 41, pl. 17: '*Newton per auis de touts ses compagnons dit*: . . . issint vn auditor aperluy n'est pas juge de record . . . Et auxi le *statut* parle d'accompt deuant auditors.'; T. 4 H. 6, 25, pl. 3; T. 7 H. 7, 15, pl. 1: 'Fineux: . . . come ii arbitrators, & vn d'eux oue l'assent de l'autre fait agard, donq ceo n'est nul arbiterment, pur ceo que ambideux ne donont arbitrement . . .'; Thorne, 'Courts of Record and Sir Edward Coke,' *Univ. of Toronto Law Jour.*, II, 43-46; see also Plowd. 69; 10 Rep. 100ᵛ-101; Cro. Eliz. 672 (41 Eliz.); *infra*, n. 168; 2 Inst. 380 (5).]

[70][For the conflicting medieval Roman-law rules see: *Tractatus Vniversi Juris* . . . (Venice, 1586), index, *s.v. Masculinum an & quando concipiat femininum;* also the collection *Tractatus vtilissimi de Statutis* (Lyons, 1552); S. Schard, *Lexicon Iuridicum* (Cologne, 1593), p. 594: 'Masculinum compraehendere foemininum, non est perpetuum, praesertim in poenalibus & odiosis.']

[71][Both *E* and *F* read *quam;* cf. 2 Inst. 93.]

[72][Plowd. 82: 'Marlebridge est, si home enfeffe son fits, per collusion que &c., vncore sil enfeffe son frere ou soer esteant son heire apparant, il serra deyns le equitie del estatute.']

[73][Westminster 2, ca. 35, includes both expressly: 9 Rep. 72ᵛ; 2 Inst. 437.]

is taken for *implacitata* also. And so of others in lyke maner.[74] [Fol. 6ᵛ]

Ca. 6.   Come vn Sentence Sera Expounde en Estatute &c.

But those construccions that are to be considered of the sentence are somwhat more to be regarded then that which is of the bare wordes. And here I call the sentence that which ryseth of the wordes beinge waighed togeather. Wherein is to be sene the relacion of wordes, the couplinge of the same, what maie be gathered of them by implicacion, & divers suche other thynges. But nowe first here is a rule to be remembered, and that is, where there is that fourme of speache which the logycians call *indefinitum*, that then yt is as thoughe it were universall, for the rule is that *indefinitum aequiparatur vniuersali*.[75] So upon the statute of Marlebridge, ca. 28, where yt is said *habeat easdem acciones*, yt is thus construed, *vt habeat omnes easdem acciones* which his predecessor mighte have. So upon Westminster 2, ca. 2, where

[74][Brooke, *Exposition de certen parolx*, 16: '. . . et lestatute de Merton [Mortmain: De Viris Religiosis] que done entry *proximo domino*, vncore si feme soit seigniores, el poet enter pur mortmain.' Similarly, *capitali domino* in Westminster 2, ca. 9: Brooke, *Parlement & Statutes*, 102; 1 And. 13: '. . . car *homines* est parol que contene suis luy cybien le female come le male.'; Plowd. 86ᵛ: *infra*, n. 160. But 'by propertie of speache' the feminine does not include the masculine, though it may be taken so by equity: M. 7 H. 6, 10, pl. 16: 'Cheine: . . . car le *statut de Praerogatiua Regis*, [ca. 6], . . . est beneficial, & chose semble serra pris [per] l'equity, & autre est de statut penal, que sera pris *stricti juris*, ergo cel *statut* serra auxybien entende des males come des females . . .'; Jenk. 95.]

[75]*E* (margin): 40 Lib. Assisarum, pl. 23, Candish; 3 Lib. Assisarum, pl. 20[?].
[The phrase 'Indefinita locutio aequipollet vniuersali' appears in the *glossa ordinaria* to the decretal Rex Pacificus, Sept. 5, 1234, of Gregory IX, which forms the prooemium to the *Decretales Gregorii IX, s.v. in iudiciis*; c. 22 X, de privilegiis, v, 33 (Innocent III, 1215): 'Verba generalia generaliter sunt intelligenda.' This is, of course, another form of the general principle 'Vbi lex non distinguit neque nos distinguere debemus.']

it saiethe *coram justiciariis*, it ys taken *coram omnibus justi-ciariis*.[76] And this rule procedeth generallye to be true, onlesse the matter of it selfe do perswade us to contrarie sence. Then muste be considered for the relacyon of the wordes in a sentence, and therin ys the grounde approved true, that *relatiuum semper reflectitur ad proximum antecedens, nisi contrarium ex subiecta materia colligi possit*.[77] As upon the statute of Magna Charta, ca. 3, the wordes *antequam homa-gium eius acceperit* are not there referred unto the lande, & yet was that the nexte antecedente, but that it shulde not be so construed maie elsewhere be evidentlie proved.[78] And this grounde is not onlie true in statutes, but also in wryttes, deedes, pleadinges, & suche lyke. As yf a writte be *ad respon-dendum A, B, & C apprenticio suo, suo* shall here be referred to B as unto the nexte antecedente.[79] So yf it be anye adiec-tyve or addicion, the relacion is to the nexte, as yf it be *prece Alicie nuper vxori Johannis de Norton Dauye*, this worde *Norton Dauye* hathe relacion to the husbande John & not to Alyce the wydowe of the same John.[80] So yf a writte be

[76]F: /[H.] 6 H. 7, 14, [pl. 6]: iour done *partibus predictis*, et pris *omni-bus partibus predictis.*/
[Cf. M. 12 H. 4, 9, pl. 18, Skrene; T. 11 H. 6, 54, pl. 23.]

[77][T. 9 H. 6, 28, pl. 30 (*Select Cases in the Exchequer Chamber*, p. 61): 'Martyn: . . . quia ad proximum antecedens fiet relacio nisi impediatur sentencia.' Dyer, 14v, 15v, 46v; Plowd. 127v; 2 Rep. 71; Finch, *Nomotexnia*, fol. 3v; [W. Noy], *A Treatise of the Principall Grounds and Maximes of the Lawes of the Kingdome* (London, 1642), p. 2.]

[78][2 Inst. 10-11.]

[79]E (margin): M. 4 H. 6, 1, [pl. 3].

[80]E (margin): M. 4 H. 6, 4, [pl. 9]. Le liuer est contra per Babington.
F: Le liuer est contra per Babbington, s. que serra referre al person nosme en le breue & a nul auter.
[The words 'Norton Dauy' were held to refer to Alice rather than John, though this departure from the general rule 'ne puist estre auterment entendue, mes que le baron est mort, & en les auters cases le maister et pere serront entendues destre en vie.': S. Theloall, *Digest des Briefes* (London, 1579), fol. 103.]

broughte againste J. S., the sonne of R. S., butcher, it is the father that muste be calledde butcher here & not the sonne.[81] Thys grounde faylethe *si impediatur sententia*, for allwaies an exposicion ought to be made that the sence maie be saved, and therfore, it is well said, that is an evill glose that doethe confounde the texte.[82] But what yf there be divers antecedentes goynge before, so that yt can not be knowen which is the nexte? As yf twyse in a charter mencion be made of Rycharde & it saiethe [fol. 7] in the later end *filio et heredi eiusdem Richardi*, to whome shall we in suche case make relacion? You muste herein consider the matter & make relacion to whome aptelieste it maie be made. As yf for the purpose one of those Richardes so named were an abbotte, relacion can not be made aptelye to hym, for he by presumpcion can have no sonne. And yf the sentence will aptelie suffer that the relacion be made to bothe, then let it so be made. And sure in these interpretacions it is true that is commenlye said, *res consilium dabit*, which who so of hymselfe is not hable to descerne doethe but lose his tyme & trauell in the lawe. But here is yet agayne to be noted that when an estatute doethe establyshe one thinge, makinge therof relacion unto an other, althoughe the thynge wherunto the relacion is made be not so as the statute recytethe, yet notwithstandinge the lawe shalbe taken in the case referred as the statute speakethe, and in the case wherunto the relacion ys made it shalbe as yt was at the commen

[81]*F:* T. [H.] 9 E. 4, 48, [pl. 2].
F (margin): M. 6 E. 4, 3, [pl. 10]: issint vn fuit endite per nom de J.S. fitz J.S., baker, & ale a Dieu pur ceo que nad addicion que baker referre al pere & nemy al fitz.
[M. 5 E. 4, Long Quinto, 141-42; Theloall, *op. cit.,* fol. 103.]

[82]*F:* maledicta glosa quae confundit textum.
[Plowd. 196, 288ᵛ; 2 Rep. 24; 4 Rep. 35; 8 Rep. 56ᵛ, 154ᵛ; 10 Rep. 105ᵛ; 11 Rep. 34.]

lawe, and the statute shall not be saide to make a lawe therin.[83] As the statute 7 R. 2, ca. 10, that willethe that an assyse
of rente in divers counties shalbe taken *in confinio comitatus*
as it was at the commen lawe of pasture in one countie
belonginge to lande in an other countie &c.[84] So Charta de
Foresta, ca. 4, saiethe that men shall have theire liberties in
forestes *sicut habuerunt tempore coronacionis &c.*, and what
yf they had no libertie then but by graunte afterwarde, yet
they shulde have it also. So the statute of Marlebridge, ca. 9,
that saiethe *ad huiusmodi &c.*, yet that wherunto relacion
was made was [blank][85] and so is it taken, for that it is but
an oversighte in wrytinge. So the statute of Westminster 1,
ca. 3 [40], saiethe *in breuia de possession come mordaun-
cestor, cosinage, & escheate*, yet is not the statute extended
to writtz of escheate.[86] In lyke maner the statute of Gloucester, ca. 10, recytethe the statute of Westminster 1, ca. [43],
and saieth *come est conteynus que tenauntz en commen
&c.*, & yet is it taken for jointenauntes so as it was com-
prysed within the statute of Westminster 1.[87] The statute
of Magna Charta, ca. [preamble], saieth *concessimus has liber-
tates &c.*, and yet manie thinges are graunted which are no
liberties, & good. But what yf the wordes of an estatute be
contraryant or repugnant, what is there then to be saide?
And suerelie therin we ought to make our construccion as

---

[83][Similarly *supra*, p. 114, that a preamble which recites the common
law incorrectly does not change it.]

[84][*Abridgement of the booke of Assises*, fols. 18ᵛ, 64ᵛ-65; Theloall, *op.
cit.*, fols. 110ᵛ-111; Bulwer's case, 7 Rep. 3ᵛ-4.]

[85][Magna Carta, ca. 10.]

[86][T. 4 E. 3, 33, pl. 17; 2 Inst. 241 (6).]

[87]*F* (margin): [T.] 38 E. 3, 12, [pl. 2].
[For similar blunders in other statutes, see Plucknett, *Statutes*, p. 104.]

A DISCOURSE 133

nyghe as we can in suche sorte that nothinge be repugnant;[88] yet yf [fol. 7ᵛ] yt can not be avoided but that a repugnancie must nedes be, then is the former sayenge good & the thynge repugnant voide, as we see the construccion is in dedes.[89] As the statute Westminster 1, ca. 1, saiethe, *nul prelate receue per son gree &c.*, which wordes are construed contrarie to that that went before, for the statute saiethe that by lycence a man maye enter, and therfore are the former wordes good and the later, because they make a jarre by reason of the repugnancye, shalbe omytted. So the statute of Magna Charta, ca. 8, ys taken to be repugnant by the readers, for that in the former parte yt saieth that the pledges shall not be distreined so longe as the principall ys sufficient, and after yt saieth, *aut reddere noluerit*, but suerlie I am not of that opynyon as maie appere &c.;[90] but yf it were repugnant

[88][Plowd. 196, 288ᵛ, 396; 3 Rep. 84ᵛ: '*Nota Lecteur*, loffice dun Interpreter est a faire tiel construction non solement que vn mesme author ne soit encontre luy mesme, mes auxy que resolutions ou iudgements report en vn lieur ne serra par ascun litteral interpretation expound encontre ascun resolutions ou iudgements report en ascun autre, mes que touts (*si fieri possit*) poient estoier ensemble.'; 5 Rep. 8; W. Jones 22 (H. 20 Jac.): 'Admit que cest statute de cap. 5. serra prise subsequent al auter statute tamen ceo ne fist riens, car coment le rule leges posteriores abrogant priores tenet in thesi, tamen non tenet in hypothesi, si le darrein Act nest contradictory ou contrary al primer, mes si solement diuerse & dissentanious & que per ascun construction l'vn & l'auter poient estoier ensemble ceo est auterment . . .'; 26: 'Et vn Statute doit estre expound issint tout le parts de ceo estoiera semble . . .']

[89][For the word 'repugnant,' see R. Bellewe, *Les Ans dv Roy Richard le Second* (London, 1585), pp. 102-3; M. 3 E. 4, 12, pl. 3; 1 And. 41, pl. 104; Fraunce, *The Lawiers Logike* (London, 1588), fol. 48; H. Swinburn, *A briefe Treatise of Testaments and last Willes* (London, 1590), fol. 122 (11); 1 Rep. 47: *supra*, p. 86, n. 185; 4 Rep. 3ᵛ; 6 Rep. 41, 41ᵛ; 9 Rep. 109ᵛ; 10 Rep. 31, 39; Co. Litt. 206ᵛ; Plucknett, 'Bonham's Case and Judicial Review,' *Harvard Law Rev.*, XL, 34, n. 17; Thorne, 'Dr. Bonham's Case,' *Law Quart. Rev.*, LIV, 549; *idem*, in *The Constitution Reconsidered* (New York, 1938), p. 21. Repugnancy in statutes receives little consideration prior to the late sixteenth century.]

[90][2 Inst. 20.]

it ys there declared by the readers that the later wordes shulde be of effecte, which is contrarye to the grounde that we have layde & to reason.[91] And sometymes you maie note in the statute the order of the sentence troubled & the carte sette before the horse, whiche muste be broughte unto his right order agayne by the iudgement of the reason. As Westminster 2, ca. 26 [25], saiethe *habeantur pro disseisitoribus tam feoffator quam feoffatus*, and yet it shulde be *tam feoffatus quam feoffator*, for *feoffator* was a disseisor at the commen lawe & so was not *feoffatus*.[92] So lykewyse the statute that encreasethe the atteynte,[93] saiethe yt shalbe as well in plee reall as in plee personall, where it shulde have saide in plee personall as in plee reall, for it was in plee reall at the commen lawe,[94] & not in plee personall. So upon Westminster 2, ca. 3 & 4, wordes that be placed in one parte of the statute shulde have bene placed in an other, and that ys recyted by the sence of the statute & the wordes in the same.[95] There is yet an other thinge to be noted, and that is that when a sentence maie be gathered by implicacion yt maie be gathered; howbeit yt is sometymes true & moost

[91][The position adopted by the readers was doubtless a reflection of the maxim 'Leges posteriores priores contrarias abrogant': Staunforde, *Exposicion of the Kinges Prerogatiue*, fol. 69v; 1 Rep. 25v; 8 Rep. 137v; 11 Rep. 62v; 2 Inst. 685; G. Bowyer, *Readings Delivered before the Honourable Society of the Middle Temple* (London, 1851), p. 34.]

[92][T. 19 E. 2, *Assise*, 400; T. 35 H. 6, 62, pl. 1; M. 10 E. 4, 18, pl. 22 (Y.B. 10 Edw. IV [Selden Soc.], pp. 160-62), Danby; 2 Inst. 412.]

[93][34 E. 3, ca. 7.]

[94]*F:* Westminster 1, ca. 38.

[95][Westminster 2, ca. 3, is clumsily worded, and in addition was often misprinted. Egerton noted in his copy of *Magna Charta cum Statutis* (London, 1556), fol. 45, that in Michaelmas term, 14/15 Eliz., 'Dyer dit que le liuer est misprint en cest poynt,' and that 'vel in vita vxore reddere voluerit' should be read for 'vel in vita sua respondere noluerit'; Dyer 298, pl. 28; see 2 Inst. 290; Plucknett, *Statutes*, p. 49, n. 2.]

tymes false. As Magna Charta, ca. 3, saiethe *pro terra rema-nebit in custodia*, quasi diceret pro corpore non item. And so upon the same statute, ca. 12, yt is saide *nos si extra regnum fuerimus*, as who woulde saie yf the kinge were within the realme, then he hymselfe woulde make the assignment. So upon the same statute, ca. 34, *femina non habeat appellum de morte alterius quam viri*, as who woulde saie of her hus-bands deathe [fol. 8] she shall have an appeale.[96] But this ys false in many cases. As Magna Charta, ca. 7, saiethe that the wyfe shall have her quarentyne *quousque assignetur ei dos sua*. And what when it is assigned, shall she be packinge? Naye, she shall remayne there by the space of 40 daies. So upon Westminster 2, ca. 2, the statute saiethe *quam cito attachiati fuerint*, and yet yf he appere before the attach-ment he shall answerre as the statute doeth appointe. So Westminster 2, ca. 5, saiethe *postquam heres peruenerit ad*

---

[96]F:/Vide Marlebridge, ca. 29, de breue dentre en le post &c./
[The statute reads, '. . . per tot gradus fiant quod breue illud in forma prius vsitata haberi non possit, habeat conquerens breue de recuperanda seysina sine mencione graduum,' which may be taken by implication to mean that if alienations are within the degrees, then the writ of entry in the *post* may not be used, but only the former remedies of entry in the *per* or in the *per* and *cui;* but see 2 Inst. 154 (3).]
 F (at foot): /P. 2 Eliz., Plowd. 204: Lestatut anno 33 H. 8, ca. [39], de courte de surueyors, done penaltie al officers le roy queux receiuont pur payments de pencions ou annuities ouster 4 d. pur chescun liuer, & sur ceo est pris per implicacion que puissoient prender 4 d. pur chescun liuer./
   /P. 13 Eliz., Plowd. 396[v]: Lestatut anno 27 H. 8, ca. 10, voit que femes naueroient dower ou terres fueront assure als eux pur joynture, prouiso que si terre soit assure al ascun feme puis le mariage, que donques per mort del baron el poet refuser ceo & demaunder sa dower. Et sur ceo est pris per implicacion que si terre soit issint assure deuaunt mariage el ne poit refuser &c. Anderson en le Counte de Leycesters case./ [4 Rep. 3; Co. Litt. 36[v].]
   /Staunf[orde, *Prerogatiue*, fol.] 79[v]: Statute 33 H. 8, ca. [22], que done que chescun poet suer generall liuerye de terres que nexede 5 li. per an, ne restreyne mes que generall liuerye poet estre quant le terre excede 5 li./

etatem, and yet he hathe his remedie within age.[97] But as for the statute of Improwementes,[98] it is said that those that have improwed theire landes, after seven yers shall paye tythe: upon which by implicacion it is saide that before he shall paye no tythes, for in those thinges the meanynge ys to be considered.[99] There is also in the sentence of an estatute the couplinge or severans of the same to be considered. *Et, que, atque, ac* are those that buytte the saienge together.[100]

[97] [Y.B. 16 Edw. III, 2 (Rolls Ser.), pp. 540-42, *Quare impedit*, 67; 6 Rep. 50.]

[98] [2 & 3 E. 6, ca. 13, §5.]

[99] *F:* /Vide Westminster 1, ca. 22, que done 16 ans per tender &c. pris per implicacion./
[H. 35 H. 6, 52, pl. 17 (*Select Cases in the Exchequer Chamber*, 132-43); similarly: H. 14 H. 8, 30, pl. 8: 'car ceo que lie le Roy lie chescun common person, car si ascun sera faueur, il serra faueur, mes le *Statut* veut que il plede vers le Roy, donq il plede vers chescun common person.']

[100] [4 Rep. 41ᵛ.]

E (margin): Vide les ioynt parolls en lestatute de fourger [1 H. 5, ca. 3] come ils ne sont ioyntment prise. Et nota le difference enter copu-latiue & copulatim per Lytleton, [P.] 15 E. 4, 25 [24, pl. 5: '. . . car en Logike cest conjunction (&) *aliquando sumitur copulatiue, & aliquando copulatim*, & si ceo soit pris *copulatiue* si vn forge vn fait & vn estranger proclaime meme le fait, l'accion serra meintene, mes s'il soit pris *copulatim* donque si le pier forge vn fait, & son fitz le proclaime, le party que est disturb de son possession n'auera jammes accion, pur ceo que le forger & le proclamacion couient d'estre fait tout per vn . . .' See also: *infra*, n. 131; T. 9 H. 6, 26, pl. 22, Babington, Paston; M. 9 H. 6, 50, pl. 33; M. 20 H. 6, 11, pl. 22; H. 14 E. 4, 2, pl. 5; T. 10 H. 7, 29, pl. 27: 'Vauisor dit, que *Anno 9. H. 6.* parle, que le defendant *sciens* le fait, &c. nient obstant que il ne forge, s'il proclaime & auoit notice que est faux fait, donq le brief sera maintene, mes jeo entende le *Ley* contrary a ceo jour. A que *les Serjeants agreerent.*' In the sixteenth century, these cases will be seen as examples of 'lequity de lestatut': *infra*, pp. 146-47; Plowd. 54: 'Et issint lestatute de 1 H. 5, ca. 3, done action de faux faits forge, per queux les titles et possessions dauters sont troubles. Et issint lestatute est en le copulatiue, vncore si le title solement soit disturb, il serra pris deins lequitie del statut: car le disseisee que nad que droit auera laction come est adiudge. Et issint nous veiomus ou le common ley suffre vn chose, ou done libertie a vn, que per le reason que est naturalment insite en chescun, est adiudge tort ou preiudice a auter, et statute est fayte pur redresse de ceo, que per equitie del statute semblable choses serra prise in semblable puruiew.

But *aut, vel, ve, seu, siue, nec, neque* do sever & devyde the sentence. And sometyme the statute runnethe loose, without anie coniunctyon or disioynenge, of which construccion must be made as sence will serve. As Westminster 2, ca. 41, *statuit dominus rex quod si abbates, priores, &c.* hathe no note of ioynynge or couplinge, & yet is taken disiunctyvelie, for that the sence doeth so beare yt. But yf there be but one coniunction in the later ende of the statute then yt is said that all the wordes before are coupled by that. As upon Yorke, ca. 2, *quant chartre, quyte clayme, acquitance, &c.* So upon Prerogatiua Regis, ca. 16 [18], *rex habebit catalla felonum dampnatorum, & fugitiuorum &c.*[101] But what yf there be severall sentences, shall the copulacion couple the one sentence to the others or not? As Prerogatiua [Regis], ca. 12 [13], the kinge shall have wrecke & sturgeons except &c.[102] This excepcion shall have relacion & be coupled bothe to the wrecke & sturgeon goynge before. So upon the statute of devises,[103] the wordes are that he shall devyse twoo partes, or so muche as maie amounte to twoo partes, so that yt maie be knowen in severaltie, and that hathe relacion to the whoale sentence before. So the statute Westminster 2, ca. 34, *si sponte reliquerit maritum & abierit & moretur*, where *sponte* coniunctyvelie extendethe to the three wordes.[104] And herein

---

Et tiel construction del statutes est graund aid & relief al innocent et giltlesse persons, & vn grand discomfort et correction al nocent persons et tort feasors: et issint est beneficial pur le publique bien, le quel le ley plus chifement esteme.']

[101][Staunforde, *Prerogatiue*, fols. 44ᵛ-50.]

[102][*Ibid.*, fols. 37ᵛ-38ᵛ; F. C. Hamill, 'Wreck of the Sea in Medieval England,' in *University of Michigan Historical Essays* (Ann Arbor, 1937), p. 10.]

[103][32 H. 8, ca. 1; 34 & 35 H. 8, ca. 5.]

[104]*E* (margin): [T.] 43 E. 3, [19, pl. 5].
F (margin): Perk[ins, *Profitable Book*], 70; T. 3 E. 3, [23, pl. 9], *Dower*,

the poynctinge & parenthesinge is muche materiall.[105] Yet
in bookes yt is said that yf I graunte *quoddam manerium cum
quadam insula et wrecko et wardis, releuiis, amerciamentis et
aliis infra predictum manerium emergentibus* this hathe relacion to all before.[106] [Fol. 8ᵛ] Coniunctions shall sometyme
be taken in the disiunctyve, and that, namelie, there where
twoo suche thinges so contraryant are coupled together that
they can not drawe under one yocke. As *pax & trithinga
teneatur integra* saiethe the statute of Magna Charta, ca. 35,
yet they shall not be ioyntelie houlden, but severallie, at
severall tymes. So yf twoo wordes of one significacion are
ioyned together, then they are devidedlie taken as one expoundinge the other. As Marlebridge, ca. 6, *de hiis qui feo-
fauerunt primogenitos & heredes,* it is taken *aut heredes.*[107]
So also where the statute recytethe a multitude for to take
advantage of a lawe, as *les hautes homes & lor baylyffes et
des auters* are taken upon the statute of Westminster 1, ca.
34 [35]. So upon the statute de Religiosis, *liceat nobis et aliis
immediate dominis ingredi* is taken dysiunctyvelie. So lykewyse where divers thynges are tumbled up together *lego,
empta parata &c.*; and so where they be governed of divers
verbes. Now, contrarye, havinge knowen how wordes couplinge shall be taken dysiunctyvelie, you maie also partelie

---

72; /T. 6 E. 3, [29, pl. 1], *Dower,* 119./
[2 Inst. 434; *infra,* n. 211, §7.]

[105][Plowd. 88-89; Hatton, *Treatise concerning Statutes,* p. 49.]

[106]*E* (margin): T. 9 H. 6, 27, [pl. 30; *Select Cases in the Exchequer
Chamber,* p. 58; Plowd. 12ᵛ.]

[107][2 Inst. 110 (1): '. . . this (*et*) a conjunctive, was by construction
taken for a disjunctive, *viz. qui primogenitos vel haeredes &c.*' For copulatives and disjunctives generally, see Plowd. 154, 288ᵛ-89ᵛ (many cases are
collected in the margin of the later editions, particularly the English translation of 1761); 2 Rep. 48ᵛ; 4 Rep. 10ᵛ; 5 Rep. 7ᵛ, 112; 10 Rep. 101ᵛ;
1 And. 133; there was no general rule.]

A DISCOURSE 139

knowe howe wordes severinge shall be taken ioyntelie, synce
that *contrariorum eadem sit disciplina*, as upon the statute of
forcible entrees,[108] thoughe it be in the dysiunctyve of entre
or deteynynge with force, yet yf he enter with force &
deteyne with force all ys mentenable.[109] So the statute of
Westminster 1, ca. 10 [3], that saieth *nul rien soit demande
ne prise ne leuie*, nothinge shalbe forfetted onlesse it be
levied.[110] So upon Merton, [ca. 6], *de heredibus abductis,
detentis, seu maritatis*, yet it is taken in the copulatyve.[111]

[108][8 H. 6, ca. 9.]

[109]*F* (margin): [M.] 6 H. 7, 12, [pl. 12]; 14 H. 6, 16, [pl. 53]; Fitz[her-
bert, *Natura Breuium*], 248*D*.
[See also: 14 H. 6, 1, pl. 3; M. 3 E. 4, 19, pl. 13: 'Choke: . . . car quant
ceux que fierent le statute donent punishment per le statute enuers les
disseisors, ou transgressors, que oustent ou disseisont ascun home oue force,
ou enuers tiel home que entre peaceablement & teigne oue force, issint
que appiert que le punishment est done enuers ascun que fist le force
forsque vn foits, s. sur l'entre, ou auterment apres sur le reteignment,
semble a pluis fort que l'entent de eux fuit a punisher ceux que oustent
ascun oue force & teigne oue force auxy, quant le statut de ceo fait proue
expressement, que si l'vn soit fait oue force, s'il enter ou tener, que ils
serront punies per treble damages recoueres en assise, ou en transgressione.';
M. 3 E. 4, 24, pl. 18; T. 10 E. 4, 11, pl. 6 (Y.B. 10 Edw. IV [Selden Soc.],
pp. 100-101); M. 6 H. 7, 12, pl. 12: '*Jay* semble que sur cest verdict il
n'auera Jugement: car n'est troue accorde al *Statut*, s. disseisin oue force
& reteiner oue force. Et fuit responde per le *court* que le *Statut* est in
l'disiunctiue, & si vn soit troue, le party recouera, & auxi il aura auantage
d'ambideux points in vn brief & declaracion, & si ambideux ou vn des
articles soit troue, est suffisant. Et issint ad este ajuge quand nous sumus
serjants.' In the sixteenth century, Choke's argument, based upon intent, is
usual: Plowd. 86: '. . . si les feasors del estatut voilent que home serra punie
que offende en lun point solement, *a multo fortiore* lour entent fuit a
punier eux que offende en ambideux les points.'; T. Risden's Inner Temple
reading (20 Eliz.) in *Three Learned Readings made upon three very usefull
Statutes* (London, 1648), p. 99; Fraunce, *Lawiers Logike*, fol. 79ᵛ; Jenk.
118. Similarly: 10 Rep. 81: 'Coment que lestatute soit in le disiunctiue, per
act execute ou per son volunt, vncore lentention del act fuit . . .'; Co.
Litt. 272.]

[110][2 Inst. 165.]

[111][2 Inst. 90-92.]

And so ys it allwaies when a man may gather it to be so either by force of the wordes, or by other statutes, or by the meanynge of the statute makers.[112] [Fol. 9 blank; fol. 9ᵛ]

Ca. 7. Construction de Statute per Equytye &c.

Hit hathe hitherto bene shewed for wordes & sentences in an estatute how they shulde be declared: all which matter, thoughe it be good to be knowne, yet is it nothinge so frutefull as that parte that folowethe, which concernethe the sence & meanynge of an estatute. For synce that wordes were but invented to declare the meanynge of men, we muste rather frame the wordes to the meanynge then the meanynge to the wordes.[113] Yt is therfore to be knowen that somme-tymes statutes are taken by equytye more then the wordes, sommetyme contrary to the wordes, sommetyme it is taken strayctelye accordinge to the wordes, and sommetyme, where there are no wordes in the statute and yet a case happenethe upon an estatute, the commen lawe shall make a construc-

[112][*Speech . . . touching the Post-nati*, pp. 49-50: '. . . words are taken and construed sometimes by Extension; sometimes by Restriction; sometimes by Implication; sometimes a Disiunctiue for a Copulatiue; a Copulatiue for a Disiunctiue; the present tense for the future; the future for the present; sometimes by equity out of the reach of the wordes; sometimes words taken in a contrary sence; sometimes figuratiuely, as *Continens pro contento,* and many other like: And of all these, examples be infinite, aswell in the Ciuile lawe as Common lawe.' The modern doctrine requires some circumlocution: C. K. Allen, *Law in the Making* (3d ed.; Oxford, 1939), pp. 431, 432, n. 1.]

[113][Plowd. 82, 140ᵛ; 363: *supra*, n. 132; 465; Hatton, *op. cit.,* p. 14: '*Vt verba seruiant intentioni & non intentio verbis:* which is allowable in all laws; for the words are the Image of the law, and the meaning is the substance or body of the matter; but whensoever there is departure from the words to the intent, that must be well proved that there is such meaning.'; Fraunce, *op. cit.,* fols. 46-46ᵛ, 73-73ᵛ; 5 Rep. 2ᵛ: *Sensus verborum est anima legis.*'; 10 Rep. 100: *supra*, n. 162; *supra*, pp. 59-62.]

cion.[114] For the firste, yt is necessarie to be knowne what was the commen lawe, for surelie, althoughe the opynion of some be that it forcethe not what the commen lawe was, sence it ys certen what the lawe is nowe by estatute, yet are they muche deceyved in theire opynion, for without knowledge of the auncient lawe they shall neither knowe the statute nor expounde it well, but shall, as it were, folowe theire noses & groape at yt in the darke.[115] I conclude, then, that of necessitye the commen lawe ys to be knowne. And it is knowne either by the statute itself, as the statute of Westminster 2, ca. 1, by the preamble shewethe that the statute was made for a myschieffe at the commen lawe. The statute of Westminster 2, ca. 16, by the wordes *dubitatio hucusque extitit* sheweth that at the commen lawe there were diversitye of opynions & the lawe uncerten. And, to be short, of later tyme all the statutes in theire preambles doe recyte the lawe before the statute. An other waie is by a rule which ys muche in use amonge the readers, and that ys that, yf it

[114]*F* (at foot): /Aristoteles [*Ethica Nicomachea*, V, 10.] *Equitas est correctio iuste legis qua parte deficit, quando generatim lata est.* Catlyn en Stowells Case./ [Plowd. 375, 465, 467.]

[115][Phrases such as 'adprimes est a veier si l'action gist al commen ley ou non,' or 'al comen ley deuant lestatute,' are frequent in the cases: M. 11 H. 6, 3, pl. 8; M. 3 E. 4, 14, pl. 8; M. 4 E. 4, 33, pl. 15, Nedham; M. 18 E. 4, 16, pl. 17, Pigot; H. 21 H. 7, 10, pl. 11, Frowicke; Plowd. 363: *supra*, n. 132; 7 Rep. 30ᵛ; 9 Rep. 38ᵛ: 'Ore est necessarie ascauoir 2 choses, 1. que fuit la ley deuant cest statute: et 2. quel alteration lestatute de 31 E. 3. ad fait.'; 10 Rep. 60, 73: 'Mes a concluder cest point appiert a toy, bone Lecteur, que a scauer que le ley fuit deuant lact de *28. E. 1.* come necessarie lauthorities des dits auncient liures del *Mirror des Iustices*, de *Bracton, Britton* & *Fleta* sont a discusser cest point; & coment que vn peraduenture poet scauer le ley sur les ancient statutes, vncore ils ne vnques scauer le voier reason del interpretation de eux, sil ne scauoit que fuit le ley deuant le feasanz del eux, & per ceo voier est *quod multa ignoramus quae nobis non laterent si veterum lectio fuit nobis familiaris:* (Macrobius, 6. Saturnalia.)'; 2 Inst. 308: 'To know what the common law was before the making of any statute . . . is the very lock and key to set open the windowes of the statute . . .'; 1 Chan. Rep. 70.]

be uncerten what the commen lawe was, then by entendement the commen lawe ys taken to be contrary to the
statute,[116] as rape, they gheasse, was but trespasse at the
commen [lawe], because Westminster 1, ca. 13, doeth make
it felony. But this ys an uncerten rule, for they were deceyved, as you maie easylie see in Staunforde upon that
statute.[117] And therfore the more sure waie ys that, yf it can
not be gathered by the wordes of the statute, then to see
what auncient writers, as Bracton & Glanvyle, those wor-
shippefull antiquyties of our lawe, have had wryten in theire
bookes, or, yf they be but later statutes, then in later bookes
which were yet before the makinge of the [fol. 10] statute,[118]
for the other waye of gheassinge at the commen lawe, althoughe yt be muche & almoste alltogether in use amonge
the readers, yet hathe yt caused them muche to be deceyved,
as well maie be sene upon Merton & Magna Charta, which
bothe statutes for the mooste parte did but affyrme & con-
fyrme the commen lawe & yet are taken by them to make
a lawe.[119] The commen lawe then knowne, you shall fynde

[116]E (margin): [H.] 35 H. 6, 48 [52, pl. 17; *Select Cases in the Exchequer Chamber*, p. 139], Choke ['Et auterment cel *statut* ne sera de nul
valu, mes il fuist pur vn remedy, & le contrary de meme le remedy nous
entendrons que fuit al *comon ley*.'; similarly, Needham's remarks (p.
133): '. . . quar si vn statut remedy vn chose il serra entendu que le
contrarie de le remedy de le dit estatut fuit la comen ley deuant le fesanz
de cel estatut . . .']

[117]E (margin): Staunf[orde, *Plees del Coron*], 21[ᵛ].
[See also: T. 9 E. 4, 26, pl. 35; M. 22 E. 4, 22, pl. 2; T. 6 H. 7, 5, pl. 4,
in fine; P. 11 H. 7, 22, pl. 11.]

[118][2 Inst. 25: 'Hereby it appeareth (that I may observe it once for all)
that the best expositors of this and all other statutes are our bookes and
use or experience.'; 2 Inst. 149: 'Wherein it is to be observed . . . how
necessary it is for understanding of old statutes, to reade old bookes.']

[119][8 Rep. 39ᵛ; similarly: Prerogatiua Regis: M. 43 E. 3, 22, pl. 12;
M. 7 H. 6, 11, pl. 16; P. 8 E. 4, 4, pl. 9; M. 15 E. 4, 12-13, pl. 17; M. 13 H.
7, 11, pl. 12; Plucknett, *Statutes*, p. 12, n. 8; Richardson and Sayles, in
Law Quart. Rev., L, 564; 8 Rep. 172.]

that the statute is either incresinge the commen lawe, or remedyenge a myschiefe at the commen lawe, or confyrminge the commen lawe, or makinge clere a doubte that was at the commen lawe, or abridginge the commen lawe, or else quyte takinge yt awaye. As for those statutes that come in encrese of the commen lawe, they shall be taken by all equytye, for synce the commen lawe is grounded upon commen reason yt is good reason that that which augmenteth commen reason shulde be augmented.[120] Also where lyke reason

[120][H. 14 H. 7, 17, pl. 7: 'Coningsby: . . . le *statut* . . . enlarge le *comon ley* . . . & si sic, il sera pris alarge. Et cases que sont in mesme le mischief pris per l'equite de ceo: come le *statut de Anno 4 E. 3, ca. 7*, que *Executors auront brief de transgressione de bonis asportatis in vita testatoris*, cest *statut* enlarge le *Comon Ley*, & pur ceo que administrators sont in mesme le mischief, ils auront mesme le remedy . . . Mordant: . . . car cest *statut* enlarge le *Comon Ley* . . . cest *statut* sera pris large, & ou *statut* sera pris large, ces sont beneficial, & auront construction per equitie.'; similarly: M. 7 H. 6, 10, pl. 16, Cheine: *supra*, p. 129, n. 74; M. 14 H. 7, 9, pl. 19, Fineux; H. 14 H. 7, 18, pl. 7, Wood; T. 15 H. 7, 8, pl. 2; Keilw. 96, pl. 6: *infra*, n. 152.]

E (margin): Vide [H.] 7 H. 4, 6, [pl. 1]: *eieccione firme* per equity lestatut anno 4 E. 3, ca. 6 [7], &c.

F: Vide lestatut 4 E. 3, ca. 6 [7], que done accion de transgressione per executours pur biens emportes en vie le testatour, et *eieccione firme* pris per equytie de ceo. [See also: M. 11 H. 4, 3, pl. 8; M. 18 E. 4, 16, pl. 17; *infra*, n. 135.]

E (fol. 12): Nota que lestatute de anno 8 H. 6, ca. 9, fait de forcible entrees, voiet que apres compleint fait, *les justices de peace poient &c.* Vncore coment que ne vnques compleint soit fait a eux de ascun tiel entre, vncore sils ont notice de ascun tiel entre, ils poient et de droit sont tenus de faire inquisicion; et coment que en le inquisicion nul mencion soit fait del compleint le partie, vncore il aura restitucion. M. 7 E. 4, 18, [pl. 12]. Et le dit statute done nul power a ascun de faire restitucion al partie forsque a les justices de peace, mes vncore les justices de banke le roy per equitie de mesme lestatut, quant lenquisicion est remoue deuaunt eux, ferront restitucion: M. 7 E. 4, 18, [pl. 12], M. 4 H. 7, [18, pl. 16], pur ceo que lestatut est beneficiall per cestuy que est ouste. [Note that this is not the reason given by Coke: 9 Rep. 118ᵛ.] Vide H. 8 H. 6, 27, [pl. 18], ou ceux que ont retorne des briefs doient mester lour nosmes a lour retornes per lestatut Eborac., ca. 5. Vide M. 7 H. 6, 11, [pl. 16, Paston]: *lex beneficialis rei consimili remedium praestat, odiosa autem casu quo efficitur vlterius non extendit.*

servethe, as the statute of Westminster 2, ca. 3, that gyvethe the *cui in vita*,[121] and ca. 4, that gyvethe the *quod ei deforciat*, we see by what equytie it ys taken.[122] So upon Westminster 2, ca. 26 [25], that gyvethe an assyse in more cases then yt was at the commen lawe, you maie rede how it is taken by equytie in many braunches.[123] And so are those statutes that doe confirme the commen lawe, or decyde a doubte at the commen lawe: they are, I saie, in lykewyse taken by equy-

[121][The belief that Westminster 2, ca. 3, gave the *cui in vita* was common: Plucknett, *Statutes*, pp. 10, 108; P. 7 H. 7, 13, pl. 2, Mordant.]
E (fol. 10ᵛ): *Nota*. Le statute de Westminster 2, ca. 4 [3], que done resceit per feme ou le baron & feme sont empledes de terres de lenheritance la feme, vncore si le baron & sa feme sont vouches, & apres lentre en le garrauntie ou deuaunt, le baron face defaute, le feme serra resceue, pur ceo que est en autiel mischiefe come pur quel lestatute fuit fait. M. 7 E. 3, 47 [44, pl. 3].
[H. 14 H. 7, 18, pl. 7: 'Keble: Le statut de *W. 2 c. 3.* done que feme aura *Cui in vita* del recouerie per defaut vers son baron. Et expressement est dit, *habeat suum Recuperare per breue de Ingressu*, vncore le heir per l'equite de cel *statut* aura *Formedon*, si la terre fuit tail, pur ceo que le heir est in meme le mischief apres la mort le feme, come la feme fuit . . . [Plucknett, *Statutes*, pp. 45-47]. Wood: Auxi le *statut de W. 2. c. 3*, que done *Cui in vita*, dit, que *Post mortem viri sui habeat mulier &c.*; il dit que aprez le mort le baron, vncore per l'equite de ceo, le *Cui ante diuortium* est pris viuant le baron . . .'; T. 7 H. 4, 16, pl. 7; P. 7 H. 7, 11, pl. 2; Plowd. 58, 178: 'nous veyomus lou act est fait pur remedyer ascun myschief, que a ayder choses en semblable degree vn action ad estre prise pur auter, vn chose pur auter, vn lieu pur auter, vn person pur auter, non obstant que en ascuns cases le chose est penal . . . Issint lestatute de Westminster second ca. 3 . . .'; 2 Inst. 342-46.]

[122][Plucknett, *Statutes*, p. 74; 2 Inst. 349-53.]

[123][2 Inst. 411-16.]
E (margin): Westminster 2, ca. 5, que done *quare impedit* de capellis: [H.] 17 E. 3, 12, [pl. 40; Y.B. 17 Edw. III (Rolls Ser.), pp. 196-98].
F: Issint Westminster 2, ca. 5, que done *quare impedit &c. de capellis, prebendis, vicariis, hospitalibus, abbathiis, prioratibus, & aliis domibus &c.*, et presentment a la chauntery al aultare nostre dame en lesglise de D. pris per ceo. [H.] 17 E. 3, 12. [Plucknett, *Statutes*, p. 75; similarly, in the same statute, 'oblations' are taken for 'tythes': T. 38 E. 3, 13, pl. 9.] Vide feffements &c. per lestatut 1 R. 3, [ca. 1], de grauntz per cestui que vse. [P.] 4 [14] H. 7, 8 [17, pl. 7; also: Plowd. 348-50.] /Vide *Cui in vita*, 68./

tie.[124] As the statute of Magna Charta, ca. 33, the wordes *habeant custodiam earum* are taken by equytie.[125] So the statute of Forestes, ca. 12, by the equytie of *stagna, fossatum*, he maie make all other utensyles. In lyke maner, I saie, it is of statutes that take awaie doubtes at the commen lawe. As Magna Charta, ca. 2, where reliefe ys put in certen, is taken by equytie. So is Westminster 1, ca. 35 [36], where aide pur file marier is put out of doubte. So Gloucester, ca. 11, that puttethe in certentie the diversitie of opynions that was where a recoverye was had against the lessor, whether the lessee shulde fauxyfye–that, I saie, is taken by equytie.[126] So is the statute of Westminster 1 [2], ca. 16, that puttethe in certen pryorytie of wardshippes–that ys also taken by equytie.[127] For when these doutes are determyned by Parlyament, it shalbe saide that that was the commen lawe, for so muche as it is presumed that which they doe to be upon beste reason. And yf that be so, who can denie but that which is in lyke reason ys also in lyke lawe.[128] [Fol. 10ᵛ]

[124][*Supra*, p. 57, n. 120.]

[125][*Registrum Breuium Originalium*, fols. 162ᵛ, 171ᵛ; Fitzherbert, *Nouuelle Natura Breuium*, 140D.]

[126][Plucknett, *Statutes*, pp. 77-78; 2 Inst. 322-24; Jenk. 200; *infra*, n. 140, §8.]

[127]*E* (margin): 4 E. 3, Iter Derbie, *Resceyt*, 46: Westminster 2, ca. 16, de prioritye.
[R. V. Rogers, 'Intervention at Common Law,' *Law Quart. Rev.*, LVII, 403-4, n. 19.]

[128][H. 11 H. 4, 47, pl. 20: 'Hankford: . . . & quant cel case est en semble mischiefe que cel que est remedy per statute, il est reason que il soit aide, & il n'ad nul ley que barre Formedon per vn garrauntie oue discent mes solement l'equity de le statute de Gloucester.'; H. 14 H. 4, 28, pl. 37: 'Hankford: Jeo scay bien que il n'est pas expressement en case de statute, mes il est en owell mischiefe pur que le statute fuit fait, & auxy brief *de consimili casu* n'est my done per nul statute, eins est prist sur l'equity de le statute de *Gloucester* del tenant en dower.'; M. 31 H. 6, 11, pl. 8: 'Fortescue: Vous dites verity, le *Statut* est come vous dites, mes nienobstant le proces ad este garde plusors fois illonque cy deuant; et issint

The statutes also that remedie a myschiefe are to be taken by equytie.[129] I call those statutes which remedie a myschiefe which remedie those abuses which the lawe had neither commaunded nor forbydden, but, as it were, suffered. As the statute of fourger of faux faittes[130] remediethe a myschiefe & is taken by equytie, for not onlie he that had pos-

il couient icy, car il est en egal mischief . . .'; T. 5 E. 4, Long Quinto, 44-45; M. 9 E. 4, 37, pl. 15: 'Danby: Statutes sont prises pluis largement que le ley parle souent foits, & Sir, cest case est en mesme le mischief . . .'; *infra*, n. 135.]

[129]*E* (fol. 10ᵛ): *Nota*. Si tenaunt en dower fait alienacion celui en le reuercion auera brief dentre *in casu prouiso* per lestatute de Gloucester, ca. 7, et per lequytie de mesme lestatute, si tenaunt per le curtesye ou tenaunt a terme de vie alien, celui en le reuercion auera brief dentre *in consimili casu*. T. 4 H. 6, 26, [pl. 4], per Martyn. [See also: H. 14 H. 4, 28, pl. 37, Hankford: *supra*, p. 145, n. 128; P. 5 H. 7, 31, pl. 12, Fisher; *infra*, n. 135.] 4 E. 3, Iter Derbie, *Counterplee de voucher*, 96, Herle dit quant ley est ordeigne pur mischiefe nous prendrons ceo pluis pres pur oustre le mischiefe. Et per ceo voyes [H.] 46 E. 3, 2, [pl. 3], come Westminster 1, ca. 39 [40], serra pris per equytie. [See also: M. 20 H. 7, 1, pl. 3.]

E (margin): [M.] 10 H. 6, 15, [pl. 51], Martyn; M. 11 H. 6, 5 [4, pl. 8], Neuton; En temps E. 1, *Garrauntie*, 86.

F: Quant 2 mischiefes sont en vn accion & le meinder est remedie per expresse parollz en vn statut, le greinder serra include en mesme le remedye, coment que riens soit parle de ceo, per Neuton, M. 11 H. 6, 4, [pl. 8]. [This sentence is found in *E* at the end of chapter 8; *F* inserts it again at that point. Both add the following citations:] M. 3 E. 4, 19, [pl. 13: *supra*, p. 139, n. 109]; [P.] 31 E. 3, *Champerty*, 5; [T.] 6 E. 3, [33, pl. 19], *Champerty*, 10.

E (fol. 10ᵛ): *Nota*. Nota per Martyn, T. 4 H. 6, 26, [pl. 4], quant vn estatute est fait que remedie vn mischief al commen ley, toutz choses que puissent este pris semble a le mischiefe pur cause de quel lestatute fuit fait serrount aides per lequitie de mesme lestatute nient obstant quil ne soit deins les expresse parollz de lestatute; Temps E. 1, *Garde*, 133; [H.] 3 E. 2, [Y.B. 2-3 Edw. II (Selden Soc.), pp. 157-63], *Garde*, 6; M. 31 E. 1, [*Briefe*], 874; M. 19 H. 6, fo. 5, pl. 9 [10]; H. 3 E. 2, [Y.B. 3 Edw. II (Selden Soc.), pp. 16-19; Plucknett, *Statutes*, pp. 176-77], *Entre*, 7 & 8; M. 16 E. 3, [Y.B. 16 Edw. III (Rolls Ser.), pp. 277-85], *Quare impedit*, 147; Temps E. 1, *Garrauntie*, 86. [See also: H. 14 H. 7, 13, pl. 2, Tremaile; *supra*, p. 55, n. 112.]

[130][1 H. 5, ca. 3.]

A DISCOURSE 147

session, but also he that hathe righte, ys houlpen by that.[131]
So is the statute of Marlebridge, ca. 6, a remedie of the
myschiefe at the commen lawe, & by equytie of the worde
custodia, releuium ys there taken. So ys the statute of Magna
Charta, ca. 5, taken by equytie. And so is the statute of
Marlebridge, ca. 28.[132] In these statutes that are taken by
equytie, which of their owne nature for theire reasonableness that is in them maie be extended, you muste not take
everye thinge by equytie, as thynges farre unlyke, but such
thinges as are in the lyke reason, for the reason of the lawe
is the soule & pythe of the lawe, yea, the verie lawe itselfe.[133]
And in this the statute of Westminster 2, ca. 24, gyvethe
us an excellent grounde, sayenge: *Quotienscunque de caetero*
euenerit in cancellaria quod in vno casu reperitur breue et
in simili casu cadente sub eodem iure & simili indigente
remedio, concordent clerici in breui faciendo. Whiche wordes,
thoughe some have only understanded concerninge the makinge of writtes, yet, notwithstandinge, reason woulde that
plees shulde be taken by equytie.[134] So that hereof hathe the
grounde rysen that those that are in lyke myschiefe are in
lyke lawe.[135] [Fol. 11]

[131]*F* (margin): T. 4 H. 6, 25, [pl. 4]; P. 33 H. 6, 22, [pl. 23]; P. 15 E.
4, 24, [pl. 5; *supra*, p. 136, n. 100].
[Plowd. 54: *supra*, p. 136, n. 100.]

[132][En temps E. 1, *Trespass*, 242; P. 4 E. 4, 7, pl. 8; M. 18 E. 4, 15-16,
pl. 17; M. 2 R. 3, 2, pl. 6.]

[133][Hatton, *op. cit.*, pp. 36-37: 'But in all Expositions by Equity, there
must be parity or minority of Reason, and good judgement of evident
utility publick, and necessity for supplying defects in the Law; and it would
be utility or necessity proved otherwise than by circuit of argument, or
far borrowed circumstance, that is to say, plain and evident.']

[134][Bulwer's case, 7 Rep. 4; [Egerton], *Speech . . . touching the Post-*
nati, pp. 39-41.]

[135]*F* (at foot): /H. 14 H. 7, 14, [pl. 2]: Ascuns foitz choses en mesme
mischiefe serront pris per lequitye, mes ceo est ou si ne soit pris per

A DISCOURSE

And those that are out of the myschiefe of an estatute are lykewyse out of the compasse of the statute. As upon Charta de Foresta, ca. 7, those that levyed scottalls by the good willes of men were not punyshed—for such scottals the statute was [not] provided. So upon Westminster 1, ca. 1, yf the founders had soiorned in abbeyes, they had not offended the statute, for the mischiefe of the statute was onlie for those which soiourned there by wronge & without title.¹³⁶ Agayne, those that affirme this rule saie that, when the mischiefe & cause why an estatute was made doeth faile, there doeth the lawe ytselfe faile, layenge for a grounde, *cessante ratione legis, cessat probatio legis*.¹³⁷ And therfore they saie that the statute of Westminster 2, ca. 22, ys taken away by the statute of 32 H. 8, [ca. 32], for, synce the myschief of that statute was that the jointenaunt coulde have no writte of particion, now, since a writte of particion

---

equitye le partie naueroit ascun remedye de tiel tort. Come lestatut 4 E. 3, ca. 7, done que executours auront transgression de biens pris en la vie lour testatour, administratours serront pris per equitye, car est mesme mischiefe, & sils ne serront aides per lequitye, les administratours naueroient ascun remedie de ceo. Sic la *casu prouiso* est done per Gloucester, ca. 7, sur alienacion le tenaunt en dower, et sur ceo tenaunts pur vie ou curtesye sont pris per lequitye, car auterment ils naueroient ascun remedie./
[See also: M. 9 E. 4, 38, pl. 16, Danby; H. 14 H. 7, 18, pl. 7, Wood; Keilw. 96, pl. 6: *infra*, n. 152; 101ᵛ; Plowd. 36: '. . . car chescun estatute est penal vers ascun home. Mes entant que le prisel de ceo per equitie serra pluis benefitial que preiuditial al greinder number del gents, ceo est le reason que poit este extende per equitie per les rules de ley . . . Et issint lestatute que dit que lexecutor que primes vyent per distres respondera, est extend per equitie as administrators . . .'; 178-178ᵛ: *supra*, p. 144, n. 121; Jenk. 78: 'Vbi eadem ratio est, ibi eadem lex'; *supra*, pp. 143-46, nn. 120, 121, 128, 129.]

¹³⁶[The statute reads: '. . . perveu est que nuly vengne manger, herbiger, ne giser, en meson de Religion de autri avoeson que de la sone . . .']

¹³⁷[Hatton, *op. cit.*, p. 53: '. . . and Civilians say, that *Cessante statuti prooemio, cessat ipsum statutum;* Cases sur lestatute de 13. Ed. 1. de Winchester, 7 Rep. 7: 'ratio legis est anima legis, & mutata legis ratione mutatur & lex.'; 2 Inst. 11: 'Cessante ratione legis cessat ipsa lex.'; *supra*, p. 58, n. 123.]

is gyven, the reason of the statute failethe.[138] And so the statute of Magna Charta, ca. 36 [32], is taken awaie by Westminster 3, ca. 1.[139] Further, it is commenlie to be sene that, not onlie those thinges that were *in esse* at the tyme of a statute made shall be taken by equytie, but those thinges also that growe synce the statute shall be taken by an equytie before.[140] As the statute that gave collucion in wardeshippe

[138][2 Inst. 403-4.]

[139][Both chapters of Magna Carta were rendered obsolete by Westminster 3, ca. 1; ca. 32 seems more probable.]

[140]*E* (fol. 11): *Nota.* Vide H. 40 E. 3, 1, [pl. 3], lou fuit done per lestatut 9 E. 3, [st. 1], ca. 3, que celuy [of several executors] que vient primes per distres respondera, & apres per estatut 25 E. 3, [st. 5], ca. [17], proces dutlagarie est done en dette, & cest statute est pris per equitie dauter, issint que celuy que primes vient per *capias* respondera.
F: M. 1 E. 4, 1, [pl. 4]. [See also: H. 7 H. 4, 10, pl. 18; P. 11 H. 4, 56, pl. 2; M. 11 H. 6, 3, pl. 8, Fulthorpe; H. 39 H. 6, 45, pl. 9; Keilw, 22ᵛ; cf. T. 8 E. 4, 5, pl. 1 (Chancery); *supra*, p. 52, n. 107.]
E: Auxi P. 27 H. 8, [9], pl. 22, Pollarde dit que lestatute de 4 H. 7, [ca. 17], de vses, serra pris per lequitie de lestatute de Marlebridge, [ca. 6], de collucion. [See: 4 Rep. 4-4ᵛ.] Sicome est dit que garrauntie oue assettz est barre en formedon, et vncore ceo est per Gloucester, [ca. 3], & le formedon fuit done per Westminster 2, ca. 1. [See: Plowd. 127; 4 Rep. 4ᵛ; W. H. Loyd, 'The Equity of a Statute,' *Univ. of Penn. Law Rev.,* LVIII, 84, n. 25.]
F: Issint lestatut anno 31 E. 3, [st. 1], ca. [11], done accion de dette vers admynistratours, & per lequytie de 9 E. 3, [st. 1, ca. 3], celuy de eux que primes vient respondera.
Gloucester, ca. 3, done que garrauntie le tenaunt per le curtesye & assets descende barre le heire, et per lequytie de ceo, si tenaunt en taile, que fuit create per Westminster 2, ca. 1, alien oue garrauntie et assets descende, est barre le heire. [H.] 14 H. 4, 28, [pl. 37]; [M.] 21 E. 3, 28, [pl. 4]; [P.] 27 H. 8, 9, [pl. 22]; [M.] 38 E. 3, 23 [24, pl. 20].
Westminster 2, ca. 4, done *quod ei deforciat* sur recouery [per] defaut, & pur equytie de ceo, *quod ei deforciat* gist sur recouery per defaut en *cessauit*, que fuit done per Westminster 2, ca. 21, puis: Fitz[herbert, *Natura Breuium*], 156A; H. 5 E. 3; M. 6 E. 3, 35, [pl. 27].
Merton, ca. 6, done forfeture de mariage, & per lequytie de ceo le seignior auera forfeture de mariage vers le heire de cestui a que vse, que gardshippe est per lestatut de anno 4 H. 7, ca. [17]: P. 27 H. 8, 4, [pl. 11].
Vide diuersity quant le premier statut vae per speciall parollz & quant

was Marlebridge, [ca. 6], and the statute that gave the wardeshippe of cestuy a que use was 4 H. 7, ca. [17], and yet was that statute taken by equytie of Marlebridge, ca. 6. So, lykewyse, Westminster 2, ca. 25, that gyvethe an assyse of estovers, is taken by the equytie of the statute of Magna Charta, ca. 12, & shall not be taken out of his owne counties. So tenaunt by elegit that came not to have an assyse tylle Westminster 2, ca. [18], shall have a redisseisin upon Merton, ca. [3]¹⁴¹—which cases maie answere the doubtes that are commenlie put, whether a man may have a *quod ei deforciat* upon a *quod ei deforciat*. The reason of the doubte

---

en generaltye, quar quant est speciall donques chose accrue apres ne serra remedy per ceo, come Gloucester, ca. [5], done accion de wast vers lesse per ans, vncore ceo nextende al tenaunt per statute merchant ou staple, que fueront done apres per [Statutum de Mercatoribus &c.]; mes quant est generalle auterment, come Gloucester, ca. [11], done que le termor serra resceiue &c. sur defaut cestui en reuercion, & per lequytie de ceo, tenaunt per statut merchant &c. serra auxi resceiue, quar termor est generall parolle: [T.] 9 E. 4, [30, pl. 45]. [*Infra*, Appendix III.]

P. 8 Eliz.: Accion sur lestatut de anno 1 et 2 P. & M., [ca. 12], de destres enchace ouster troys myles del lieu ou &c. Si le pleintiffe soit nonsue le defendaunt nauera ses costes per lestatut 23 H. 8, ca. 15, per Dyer, Brown, & Weston, entant que ne fuit ascun tiel accion en esse al temps de fesans de lestatut, mes Dyer dit que si soit done per darrein statut que accion que fuit al commen ley deuaunt gyrra en plusiors cases quil poit per le commen ley, de ceo auterment serra, come en case daccompt, [H.] 14 H. 4, 20, [pl. 25]. [See also: M. 8 H. 6, 9, pl. 21, Martin; M. 22 E. 4, 23, pl. 2, Fairfax.]

Staunf[orde, *Plees del Coron*], 168*b:* en lestatut Westminster 2, ca. 12, que done damages per le defendant en appelles, *felonia* extendera al auter felonyes fait pres, come al rape, come H. 12 E. 2, *Corone*, 181 [381].

M. 18 E. 3, 51, [pl. 59; Y.B. 18-19 Edw. III (Rolls Ser.), p. 259:] mordancestor: si tenaunt per resceit vouche, il nest counterplee que cestui que &c. ou son auncestor fuit le primer que abate &c., quar counterplee est done per Westminster 1, ca. 39 [40], et le resceit per Westminster 2, ca. 3, longe temps puis. [Plucknett, *Statutes*, pp. 100-101.]

¹⁴¹[Similarly upon the statute 7 R. 2, ca. 10; 4 Rep. 4ᵛ: 'Issint lestatute de 7. R. 2. done Assise *in confinio Comitatus* et *Redisseisin* prise per equity del statute de *Merton cap. 3.* fait *20 H. 3*.']

ys because this *quod ei deforciat* was not *in esse* at the tyme
of the statute makeinge; howbeit, yf those that come after
shalbe taken by equytie, muche more they shall that were
in esse *eo ipso instante*.[142] [Fol. 11ᵛ]

The seconde case whereby the statute shall be taken is
ex mente legislatorum,[143] for that is chiefe to be considered,
which, althoughe it varie in so muche that in maner so manie
heades as there were, so many wittes; so manie statute makers,
so many myndes; yet, notwithstandinge, certen notes there
are by which a man maie knowe what it was. And this help-
ethe, not onlie to knowe where a statute shall be taken by
equytie, but also where it shall be taken straightelie accordinge to the naked & bare letter. Fyrste, yt is knowne of them
selves & by theire lyvinge voice, as Frowycke saieth that
upon the statute of Westminster 2, ca. 1, it was demaunded
of the statute makers whether a warrantie with assettz shulde
be a barre, & they answered that it shulde.[144] And so, in our
dayes, have those that were the penners & devisors of statutes

---

[142][13 E. 1, *Vowcher*, 286; 2 Inst. 351 (4); similarly an *elegit* on an
elegit: Brooke, *Elegit,* 11.]

[143][M. 14 E. 4, 1, pl. 1: 'Littleton: . . . car l'act serra construe solonque
l'entent &c. Et il ne poit este suppose que les fesors del act entendront
auterment mes que il auera general breue . . . [mes] touts les Justices
forsque *Littleton* [fueront de lopinion] que le brief ne fuit bon' [for the
remainder of the case: *infra*, n. 174]; T. 4 H. 7, 11, pl. 6: 'Jay: . . . en
ceo *Act de Parliament* nous couient aller a les *minds* de les feasors de mesme
le *Act* &c.'; T. 12 H. 7, 20, pl. 1: 'Mordant: . . . car quand vn *Statut* est
fait, le *Statut* serra construe solonque l'entent de ceux que firent le *Statut*,
nient touts foits apres les parolz del estatut.'; M. 15 H. 7, 13, pl. 1:
'Frowike: . . . Et al fesance de le *Statut* le grande part del terre *d'Angleterre*
fuit in feoffements sur confidence, & pur ceo l'entent de eux que firent le
Statut ne fuit . . . Et coment que cest construction est encounter les parols
del *Statut*, vncore nous deuons admetter ceo, pur ceo que cest fuit l'entent
des fesors. Et sont diuers *Statuts* que sont construis in auter forme que
les parols sont . . .'; T. 27 H. 8, 13, pl. 1: 'Fitzherbert: . . . car nous deuons
grandment considerer l'entent del faisors del *statut* . . .'; *supra*, pp. 59-62.]

[144][Keilw. 79; H. 21 H. 7, 10-11, pl. 11.]

bene the grettest lighte for exposicion of statutes.[145] If they have not gyven anie declaracion of theire myndes, then is to be sene howe the statute hathe bene put in use, & theire authoritye muste persuade us that were mooste neerest the statute, and that we do see muche receyved & leaned unto in bookes.[146] But a sure waie herein is to gather lyghte of

[145][See (on the statute of 14 E. 3, st. 1, ca. 6): M. 39 E. 3, 21, pl. 8: 'Thorpe: . . . il y auoit diuersity de surnom en vn brief que fuit porte en Parliament pur mesme le cause. Et les Seignors que firent le *statut* disoient que lour entencion fuit que en toutz ceux cases le proces seroit amende, &c.'; T. 40 E. 3, 34, pl. 18: 'Thorpe: Il fuit auterfoits debate ciens deuant nous, que si vn parol faile en le record, sil purra estre amende, auxibien come il failist forsque vn sillable, ou letter, & *Sir Hugh Green*, & moy al ascuns [alamous] ensemble a le counsel, & ils fueront bien xxiiii deuesque, & de counties, & nous demandomus de ceux que fieront l'statute si le record poit estre amende, & larcheuesque ou metropolitan dit, que ceo estoit vn nice demande, & vaine question de eux, sil purroit estre amende ou non, car il dit que auxibien poit estre amende en cest case come il fuit forsque vn letter . . .' The tale is repeated in T. 11 H. 4, 11, pl. 4, though there Thorpe 'ala al Chancellor adonque, & mira le matter a luy'; Crompton, *L'Avthoritie . . . des Covrts*, fol. 21ᵛ. Coke (8 Rep. 158) repeats the E. 3 cases noted, disregards the H. 4 case, and adds the characteristic note: '*Nota* ou est dit en *40 E. 3* que les justices alont al counsell, appiert per *39 E. 3* que ils alount al Parliament a scauer lopinion de ceux que fierent la ley.': he had identified Council with Parliament earlier in a similar instance: *supra*, p. 105, n. 5; 10 Rep. 38ᵛ; [Egerton], *Speech . . . touching the Post-nati*, pp. 51-53; Plucknett, *Concise History*, pp. 293-94. Earlier cases in which the intention of the legislature was ascertained, either directly or through professional tradition, are collected in Plucknett, *Statutes*, pp. 21, 49-53.]

[146][Y.B. 18-19 Edw. III (Rolls Ser.), p. 322, Pole; M. 8 H. 4, 10, pl. 12: 'Thirning: Si home voudra entender le statute solonque le letter (*virtute sermonis*) lou le statute parle de fine . . . mes nous deuoms entendre le statute solonque ceux que fueront auncient sages pluis que nous sumus a ore, & queux fueront al fesans del statute, ont mis le statute en vre, & tout temps apres le fesans d'icel statute nient contristeant ceux parollz . . .'; M. 31 H. 6, 11, pl. 8, Fortescue; M. 3 E. 4, 11, pl. 3; H. 14 H. 7, 14, pl. 2: 'Brian: . . . Et a ma entent nient plus sera pris per l'equite de cel, & ceo per 2 reasons: vne, pur ceo que est penal, & sur chose penal semble que rien sera pris per l'equite come *Hody* ad dit; autre, pur ceo que sur touts *statuts* que donent *Atteints*, vous ne scauez trouer ou rien ad este pris per l'equite; car quand il fuit done in ple real, ceo fuit pur cause d'faux verdict passe en le primer action, & ceo fuit le mischief, & mesme

the wordes of the statute either goynge before or folowinge, as yf those wordes *et similibus* be in; thys openethe a gappe to all equytye, & shewethe that theire myndes were that it shulde extende to lyke cases. So the statute of Magna Charta, ca. 3, *heres* is taken for an heire male, because that the wordes are after *quod si ipse fiat miles.*[147] So upon Merton, ca. [1], *expelluntur* ys taken for *deforciantur*, because the statute saieth in an other place *de iniusto deforciamento*. So it is taken upon Marlebridge, ca. 13, that the statute is taken in personall plees, because the words are *inquisitio capiatur per eius defaltam*, which can not be in plees realls.[148] And this is a sure rule, as may be, to knowe not onlie where they shalbe taken by equytye but also to knowe howe they shalbe taken straightelye, & when the wordes shalbe taken properlie or improperlie, & when the sense shalbe againste the sentence, and howe relacion shall be made, and, to be short, it availethe to the understandinge of every rule that is geven upon

le mischief fuit pur faux verdict done in ple personel, & vncore il ne fuit pris en mesme le manier per cause del equite que *Atteint* gesira in ceux tanque apres que ceo fuit fait per vn nouel *statut* in 5 E. 3, ca. 7 . . . Fineux: . . . Donque quand ceux qui furent plus procheins al fesance del *Statut*, & ascuns de eux in vie que firent le *Statut*, ne vouloient ceo prendre per l'equite de cel, . . . per quel reason prendrons nous ceo per l'equite . . . ?'; 10 Rep. 37ᵛ, 38ᵛ; Co. Litt. 272 (Prof. De Sloovère ['The Equity and Reason of a Statute,' *Cornell Law Quart.*, XXI, 592, n. 6] misunderstands this passage); 2 Inst. 11: '*Contemporanea expositio est fortissima in lege.*'; Jenk. 281 in fine; W. Jones 49-50 (M. 22 Jac.): 'Le rule per equity de ancient statute est, come moy semble, que si ne fuit prise per equity deins conuenient temps apres le statute il ne serra omnino, car eux que fueront pluis prochein al statute sciont melior le entention del statut & mischief entend destre relieue quam nous, & come Littleton dit del statute de Merton [*supra*, p. 119, n. 41] si action voilt giser pur le heir pur disparagement il ad estre port deuant ore . . .']

[147][H. 35 H. 6, 40, pl. 2 (*Select Cases in the Exchequer Chamber*, p. 140, Prisot); H. 35 H. 6, 52, pl. 17.]

[148][14 H. 6, 19, pl. 59; 2 Inst. 126-27 (3); similarly: T. 3 E. 4, 8, pl. 1, Laicon.]

statutes. And here you muste note that when a statute doeth make a conference of lawe betwene twooe cases, sayenge that suche lawe shall be in the one as in the other, then therein you must consider the meanynge of them, & see in what poynt they did compare it, & so construe it to be lyke in that poynte, for els you maie manye tymes straye verie farre from reason. As the statute of Magna Charta, ca. [31], that saiethe *et nos eodem modo tenebimus &c.*, it muste be understanded in nothinge but in the [fol. 12] prerogative of the tenure, for in all other thinges there is varyans. So upon the statute De coniunctim feoffatis,[149] that saieth *eodem modo statutum est quod in assisis &c.*, yet it muste not be taken so in all poyntes.[150] So is it upon the statute of Gloucester, ca. 1 & 2, upon Merton, ca. 3, upon Charta de Foresta, ca. 4.[151] So is it allwaies to be had in mynde that the mynde of the statute makers either maketh or marrethe the markette. [Fol. 12ᵛ blank; fol. 13]

Ca. 8.   Construction de Statute Stricte &c.

Althoughe that the nature of an estatute be suche as ys shewed before, that is, that it maie be bothe for the reason & the commen lawe taken by equytie, yet shall it be sometymes taken straightelie, & the groundes gyven before in speciall cases shall faile. And, firste, it is then when the lawe is penall,[152] for in those it is true that Paston saiethe, *Poenas*

149[34 E. 1.]

150[Bulwer's case: *supra*, p. 132, n. 84; cf. 'eodem modo' in Westminster 2, ca. 35: M. 3 E. 3, 40, pl. 17, Willoughby.]

151*F*: [T.] 21 E. 3, 24, [pl. 17], Shard. [Shareshulle:] En cesser de seruices le tenaunt [poit] tender damages &c. Vncore Westminster 2, ca. 21, ne parle de damages mes referre a Gloucester, ca. 4, de fee ferme, viz. *eodem modo &c.*, ou damages sont expresse. [M.] 17 E. 3, 57, [pl. 41; Y.B. 17-18 Edw. III (Rolls Ser.), pp. 232-34; Plucknett, *Statutes*, p. 79].

152[M. 9 H. 4, 6, pl. 19: 'Tremaile: Quant vn statute est ordein pur

interpretatione augeri non debere: for the lawe alwaies favoureth hym that goeth to wracke, nor it will not pulle hym on his nose that is on his knees. Pains I doe call amercyamentes, fynes, raunsoms, damages, imprisonment, pyllorye, abiuracion, relegacion, forfaicture of landes, goodes, or lyfe. Therfore, upon the statute of Westminster 1, ca. 12, *mester en enquestes* is taken straightelie & extendethe not to tryall by battell.[153] So is also, there, *suyte le roy* straightelie taken, & doeth not extende to an appeale at the parties suyte.[154] So upon Westminster 1, ca. 20, *de misfesours en parkes,* are not extended to mysfesours in forestes or chases.[155] So by the statute of Westminster 1, ca. 33 [34], the teller of false tales & rumors was punyshed, but a messynger was not punyshed tylle the statute made in the tyme of Quene Marye.[156] And here it maie evidentlie appere that Scrope his opynion can

---

emprisoner, ou chose penable, il serra entendu *Stricti juris,* & nul emprison sinon que il soit expressement en case de statute . . .'; T. 11 H. 4, 76, pl. 17: 'Horton: Il n'est my doubt que cest case n'est mye expressement en case de statute, & sur l'equite de le statute il ne serra my comprise, pur ceo que vn penal statute come le statute de Prouisoribus & huiusmodi serra pris *ex stricto jure,* mes vn statute fait pur common remedie sur general mischiefe en le case puit este pris ensemble case pur l'equitie.' M. 7 H. 6, 10, pl. 16, Cheine: *supra,* p. 129, n. 74, and Paston: *supra,* p. 143, n. 120, §4; H. 14 H. 7, 14, pl. 2, Hody, Brian: *supra,* p. 152, n. 146; M. 21 H. 7, 36, pl. 45, Eliot; Keilw. 96, pl. 6: 'Nota que fuit dit que chescun estatute que est penal, & queux alont en derogation del comon ley serra prise strict, & ceo est le common dit, & estatute penal est tiel estatute que done a vn home corporal paine come emprisonment ou forfeture de mony, & ceux estatutes queux donont remedy quel ne fuit per le comon ley serra prises per equitie . . .'; Plowd. 17, 47, 59; Hatton, *Treatise concerning Statutes,* pp. 76-77; 8 Rep. 120; *supra,* pp. 48-54.]

[153][Staunforde, *Plees del Coron,* fol. 150.]

[154][*Ibid.,* but note the diversity; 2 Inst. 179.]

[155]*E* (margin): P. 21 H. 7, 21, [pl. 8].
[See also: Plowd. 124; Hatton, *op. cit.,* p. 79; 2 Inst. 199 (1); Thorne, in *Ill. Law Rev.,* XXXI, 205-6.]

[156]*E* (margin): Anno 1 & 2 P. & M., ca. 3.

not be lawe, which saiethe that upon the statute of 14 E. 3,
[st. 1], ca. 9 [10], that willethe that the gaylour which *per
graunde dures & payne procura &c.* shall have iudgement
of lyfe & member, that, thoughe the procurement be without grette duresse &c., that yet he shall have iudgement
&c.[157] Naye, further, these penall statutes are not onlie
taken straightelie, but also sommetymes they are taken more
straightelie then the wordes are. As divers tymes in these
statutes, where the statute speaketh of raunsoms, they are
taken for fynes.[158] And upon this reason is yt that, where a
man doeth recover treble dammages by a statute, there he
shall not recover his costages at the commen lawe.[159] But this
that I have spoken of penall statutes deceyveth us in divers
cases. And, first, where the penall statute ys but a declaracion
of the commen lawe & doeth not declare the same fullye,
then the cases that are omytted shall be taken by equytie.
As what can be a more penall statute than the statute *de
prodicionibus,* 25 E. 3, [st. 5], ca. [2]? yea, & that, further,
is the same statute [that] willethe in the ende that no case
shall be taken by equytie onlesse it be a[d]iudged by Parlemente; and yet, notwithstandinge, by the equytie of the
wordes, *yf the servaunt kylle the maister,* it is taken, yf the
mayde kille the mystres, that shalbe petit treason.[160] So yf it

[157]*E* (margin): 18 E. 3, *Corone,* 272; Staunf[orde, *Plees del Coron*],
36[v].

[158]*E* (margin): M. 35 H. 6, 6, [pl. 9], Litelton.

[159]*E* (margin): P. 2 H. 4, 17, [pl. 1].
[See also: H. 9 H. 6, 66, pl. 11, Babington; 14 H. 6, 13, pl. 44; M. 19
H. 6, 32, pl. 62 (60); T. 27 H. 6, 10, pl. 7; Brooke, *Ascvns nouell cases*
(London, 1587), fol. 3; Keilw. 26, pl. 2. The cases are examined and
aligned in 10 Rep. 116-116v, but note that the explanation supplied by the
Discourse—namely, that the statutes are penal and thus strictly construed—
is found neither in Coke nor in the cases themselves; but see: H. 43 E.
3, 2, pl. 5.]

[160]*E* (margin): M. 19 H. 6, 47, [pl. 102 (100)].

maie be expresselye [fol. 13ᵛ] gathered to be the meanynge
of the statute makers, as Westminster 1, ca. 15, by the
equytye of the *constable*, the *justice of peace* is taken, by
reason of the wordes, *ou autre bayliffe de fee.*[161] And sommetyme yf they have bene put so in ure, as upon Westminster
2, ca. 11, by eschapes of the accomptant in pryson all other
eschapes are taken, & the gardeyn of the pryson chargeable.[162]
Yt faileth also when the payne is iuste & not put *in terrorem*,
as upon Westminster 1 [2], ca. 24, assize of nusaunce is taken
by equytie.[163] So upon Westminster 2, ca. 53 [23] & 26.[164]
Yt faileth also when there is gretter reason in the case to be
taken by equytie then there is in the case conteyned within
thestatute, and that more conteynethe under it the lesse.
As the paine that is gyven *in secunda superoneratione* by
Westminster 2, ca. 8, is gyven *in tertia superoneratione.*[165]
So it is upon Westminster 1, ca. 25, & Westminster 1, ca. 3,
for in these is the sayenge true, *bonis nocet quicunque parcet*

[But it is doubtful whether, in view of the penal character of this case,
contemporaries would have been in complete agreement upon the *Discourse*'s interpretation of it: Plowd. 86ᵛ: 'Et la il nest prise deins le equity
del estatute, que parle solement de tuer del Master, mes est deyns les
parols pluis toft, car Master & Mistresse sount dun effect.'; *supra*, pp. 128-29;
Staunforde, *Plees del Coron*, fol. 10ᵛ; Jenk. 101; Hatton, *op. cit.*, pp. 72-73;
3 Inst. 20.]

[161][Lambard, *Eirenarcha* (London, 1581), pp. 250-54; Crompton, *Loffice
et aucthoritie de Iustices de peace* (London, 1583), fol. 103ᵛ; Coke, *A little
treatise of Baile and Maineprize* (London, 1635), chap. 6.]

[162][H. 15 E. 4, 20, pl. 8, Choke; Plowd. 37, 178; Hatton, *op. cit.*, pp. 35-36;
2 Inst. 382 (18); *supra*, pp. 52, 152, nn. 107, 146.]

[163][2 Inst. 405 ff.; Hatton, *op. cit.*, pp. 65-66: 'Moreover Pains and Penalties inflicted for Transgression, are chiefly for Example sake; *Vt poena
vnius sit metus multorum;* the harm and damage done being many times
irreparable; in which case, it were great folly to propose for terror any
to punishment, whom the Beholders should pity for that cause to be
afflicted.']

[164][Perhaps Westminster 1, ca. 23 & 26.]

[165][*Supra*, p. 139, n. 109, and p. 146, n. 129, §3.]

improbis.[166] That also that hathe bene saide for takinge statutes by equytie faileth also there, when there is a certen
fourme prescribed within the statute, for therein the grounde
is true: he that will take an advantage of an estatute muste
straightelie observe the wordes of the statute.[167] As the statute
of Westminster 2, ca. [11], that gyvethe auditors authoritie
to commytte the accomptant to the nexte gayle, yf so be
that they folowe not the wordes, all that they doe is without
warrante.[168] So upon the statute of Merton of improve-
mentes,[169] yf they improve more then they shulde doe, all
is without warrante.[170] So is it upon Westminster 2, ca. 1;

[166][The reference may be to Westminster 1, ca. 33 [34], or Westminster 2, ca. 3.]

[167][P. 42 E. 3, 13, pl. 20; 14 H. 6, 1, pl. 3: 'Juin: Car ou vn action sera
done per *Statut* il luy couient prendre l'action accordant al *Statut*, ou auterment il ne prendra auantage per le *Statut.*;' T. 21 H. 7, 28, pl. 8: 'Rede:
Seme que il ne puit varier. Car quand le *Statut* luy done cest breue, il est
reason que il pursuira l'effect del *Statut*, & face accord a ceo . . .'; Brooke,
Ascvns nouell cases, fol. 51 (misnumbered 52): 'Nota si home en action
ou pleading alledge statute & ceo misrecite in matter, ou in an, iour, ou
lieu, lauter poet demurrer generalment, car la est nul tiel statute, & donque
est nul tiel ley, car chescun que medle oue ceo doit mire la ley veraciter.';
this argument is very common in the cases.]

[168][H. 27 H. 6, 8, pl. 7, Prisot; Plowd. 206ᵛ; Hatton, *op. cit.*, pp. 81-82:
'All Statutes appointing a thing to be done in a form must be strictly
taken touching the observance of the Forn and circumstances specified, and
therefore the Statute that giveth power to Auditors to commit to the
next Gaol Accomptants found before them in Arrerages, saying, *Per tes-
timonium Auditorum mittantur proximae Gaolae*, is strictly taken both
in the number, so that one Auditor cannot commit; and in the Gaol, for
that he must be sent unto the next Gaol, though it be in another County.';
similarly: *supra*, p. 128, n. 69; 8 Rep. 119ᵛ: 'ils duissoient auer commit le
plaintif maintenant per construction del ley coment que nul temps soit
limitte en lact, come en lestatute de *W. 2. c. 12* [11] . . . en cest case
coment que nul temps soit limitte quaunt le accountant serra imprison,
vncore ceo doit este fait maintenant come est tenus en *27. H. 6. 8.* & le
reason de ceo est rendue . . . que le generalty del temps serra restraine al
present temps pur le benefit de cesty sur que le peine serra inflict . . .']

[169][Merton, ca. 4.]

[170][2 Inst. 87.]

Gloucester, ca. 1 & 4 & 13; Westminster 2, ca. 3; Westminster 1, ca. 20; Marlebridge, ca. 7.[171] And unto this
grounde it apperteyneth that, yf dammages be gyven me by
an estatute, that I shall recover no dammages in my wrytte,
onlesse I make mencion of the statute.[172] Howbeit, yt is not
taken therein where the statute in yt selfe recitethe my
writte, that there my wrytte shall recyte the statute.[173] Yt
faileth also yf anie thinge be speciallye gyven in favoure of the
person, for it is said, *quae specialiter collata sunt personam
non transgrediuntur*.[174] Yf it be so that the statute abridgethe
the commen lawe, then by the same reason that an estatute
encreasinge the commen lawe shalbe taken by equytie, by
the same reason shall this statute abridginge commen reason

[171][See also: M. 7 H. 7, 4, pl. 4, Brooke, *Parlement & Statutes*, 95:
'Statute de Marton, ca. 4, est que vicount in redisseisin alera al terre, &
la ferra inquisicion, & ideo sil ne veigne in person & returne accordant tout
est void, pur ceo que il ne ensua lestatute quar stricte &c.'; 4 Rep. 65ᵛ.]

[172][Theloall, *Digest des Briefes*, fol. 210ᵛ: 'Quant vn action fuit a le
comen ley, & puis pluis graunde peine est done en cel action per vn statut,
si le pleintiffe ne vsa son brief sur le statut, il nauera plus graunde auantage
que il ne auera per la comune ley. P. 9 H. 6, 2, [pl. 5].'; *infra*, n. 204.]

[173][Plucknett, *Statutes*, pp. 145-48; Brooke, *Parlement & Statutes*, 75:
'Nota ou statute done brief, & ordeigne le forme del brief certen, la le
partie ne sera passe mencion del statute in son brief ne counte, vt in
formedon in discender, Quod ei deforciat, & huiusmodi, & econtra in
transgressione sur lestatute 5 R. 2, [st. 1, ca. 7] & 8 H. 6, [ca. 9] & de
malefactoribus in parcis, Westminster 1, ca. 20, lestatute serra rehearce in
le brief, quar lestatute est in laffirmatiue, & sauns rehersall non patet sil
vse laccion per le comen ley sicut potest, vel laccion sur lestatute, mes in
dette per administrators, vel per executors de bonis asportatis in vita
testatoris, il ne rehearce le statute, quar accion de dette & trespas fueront
al comen ley deuant in auters cases, & per Mordant [P. 5 H. 7, 17, pl. 10]
in waste vers tenant pur vie ou ans, lestatute serra rehearce, quar ne fuit
auter accion ne prohibicion al comen ley, contrary in wast vers Garden,
ou tenant in dower, quar fuit prohibicion de waste vers eux al comen
ley.'; Brooke, *Surmise & suggestion*, 27.]

[174][M. 14 E. 4, 1, pl. 1: 'L'opinion de la Chancellor, & touts les Justices
forsque Littleton . . . quant vn act est fait pur le comen profit de realme,
ceo serra interpretate largement, mes vn particuler act serra interpretate
stricte.'; Chrimes, *op. cit.*, pp. 262-64; Hatton, *op. cit.*, p. 80.]

be taken strycte.[175] And therfore Westminster 2, ca. 40, because the statute abridgethe the commen lawe, as in taking awaie his age, it shalbe taken all throughe straightelie.[176] So shall it be upon Westminster 1, ca. 46 [47], where it is said that the parolle shall not staye for nonage of the one nor the other.[177] But yf it take [fol. 14] awaye a commen lawe that was penalle, then it is otherwyse, as maie appere upon

[175][M. 18 E. 4, 16, pl. 18: *infra*, n. 176; M. 5 H. 7, 6, pl. 11: 'Dauers: . . . car le *statut* sera pris *stricti juris*, pur ceo que est enconter *Comon Ley*.'; H. 14 H. 7, 14, pl. 2: *supra*, p. 152, n. 146; H. 14 H. 7, 17, pl. 7; H. 21 H. 7, 17, pl. 28: 'Rede dit que nul equite peut este pris de tiels *statuts* que sont in abrigement de l'*Common Ley;* come *Forcible entre* est done per *statut* de terre, mes il n'est issint de rent: issint tiel *Forcible entre* in rent ne peut este pris per l'equite, pur ceo que le *statut* est in abrigement del *Common Ley*.'; Keilw. 96, pl. 6: *supra*, p. 155, n. 152; *supra*, pp. 48-51.]
E (fol. 14): *Nota*. Lestatut de anno 2 H. 4, ca. 7, que voile que ou vn verdit passe enconter le pleintiffe, que le pleintiffe ne serra nonsue apres; vncore si le court escrie al euesque que certifie conter le pleintiffe, il est nonsue quar ceo est en abridgement de commen [ley] & pur ceo pris stricte. M. 3 E. 4, 11, [pl. 2; Brooke, *Nonsuite*, 44].

[176][Plucknett, *Statutes*, p. 59; M. 18 E. 4, 16, pl. 18: 'Hussey: Il est ajudge *anno 28 H. 6.* que en vn formedon le tenant mire que son pier enfeoffa vn tiel, le quel done mesme le terre en le tail, & puis son pier morust, & il vouche l'heir le donor, & pur ceo que il est deins age, il pria que le parol demurre, & ajudge que il fuit hors de case de le statut, car le statut est *caveat emptor*, le quel n'extend ouster, car cest statut restreint le commen ley, le quel serra pris *stricti juris*. Et puis par agard del court le plee fuit mis sans jour pur le nonage l'enfant, &c.'; H. 14 H. 7, 18-19, pl. 7 (note especially Vavisor: 'Et auxi le *statut* limite que en *cui in vita* vers alienee le baron, *le parol ne demeure* pur le nonage le heir le baron, *Sed expectet emptor*. Vncore si alienee son baron meurt, issint que son heir est einz per descent, or le *parol demeure* per le nonage le heir le baron, & vncore mesme le mischief est al feme ou le alienee vouchera ou son heir vouchera, mez pur ceo que est enconter Common droit que ou vn enfant est vouche per le fait son ancestor, que il n'aura son age, purque il est pris *stricte*.'); Plowd. 17[v] ('le parol demurre, eo que le dit estatut est penal al voucher, & les parollz generals, s. per l'nonage le heire, sont restraine & abridge & straite del generalty . . .'); 47 ('statute que est penall . . . ceo nextende as auters persones'); 1 Rep. 15 ('coment que les parols del statute sont general, vncore ils sont intende . . .'); 6 Rep. 5; 2 Inst. 455.]

[177][Plucknett, *Statutes*, p. 85; M. 27 H. 6, 1, pl. 3; M. 12 E. 4, 17, pl. 20; 6 Rep. 4[v].]

Magna Charta, ca. 14, *si inciderit in misericordiam nostram—*
yt is also taken *si inciderit in misericordiam alterius.* So yf it
take awaie a commen lawe that was slavyshe & coulde not be
defended by reason, as that of Magna Charta, ca. 18, that
takethe awaie the commen lawe that dyd forbidde a man to
devise his goodes.[178] And as this grounde ys for statutes
abridginge commen lawe, so is it for those statutes that doe
abridge the kynges prerogative. Magna Charta, ca. 27 & 31.[179]
[Fol. 14ᵛ blank; fol. 15]

Ca. 9.   Construction de Statute Conter les Parollz &c.

It hathe bene spoken before howe statutes shall be taken
by equytie & howe strayghtelie, & that partelie by the knowledge of the commen lawe, partlie by other circumstances

[178][2 Inst. 32-33.]

[179]*F:* Nota per Wray, lectura sua 2, 9 Eliz., que lestatute anno 2 [& 3]
E. 6, ca. 8, de offices, &c., serra pris stricte & nemy per equytie, pur ceo
que il vae dabridger le prerogatiue le roy. Et lopinion de eux en court
de Wardes en vn case ou le tenaunt le roy graunt rent charge & pres
lessa le terre a le grauntie per ans & deuie & apres sa mort fuit trouue per
office que il deuie seisie de cest terme mes le graunt de le rent ne fuit
trouue, fuit que en cest case le grauntie nad ascun remedie per le dit statute,
entant que le rent fuit en suspens al temps doffice trouue, quar pur ceo il
nest deins les parollz destatute, *hauinge any suche rent &c.* Mesme le ley
est si tenaunt le roy fist lese per ans de commencer 10 ans apres, il nest
remedie per ceo statute, pur ceo que il nauera lese en esse &c.

[Brooke, *Parlement & Statutes,* 77; Crompton, *L'Avthoritie . . . des
Covrts,* fol. 17; the prerogative is here still within private law: there is
as yet no distinction between the prerogative *regale* and *legale* (C. H.
McIlwain, *Constitutionalism & the Changing World* [New York, 1939],
p. 256; idem, *Constitutionalism Ancient and Modern* [Ithaca, 1940], p. 138;
F. D. Wormuth, *The Royal Prerogative, 1603-1649* [Ithaca, 1939], pp. 54-57),
though there are anticipations of it in Plowden and Crompton (*supra,* n. 3;
W. S. Holdsworth, *A History of English Law,* IV [1924], 207). Staunforde's *Exposicion* similarly, as has been recently noted with some sur-
prise, 'does not so much as mention . . . the king's prerogatives as national
sovereign, much less does he attribute to the king a power above the law.':
Baumer, *Early Tudor Theory of Kingship,* p. 186.]

comprised within the statute. Yt shall be now shewed where an estatute shalbe taken contrarie to the wordes of the statute. And that is, first, *ex necessitate*, as when yt can not otherwyse happen, & therfore the rule is true that saiethe *necessitas exlex*.[180] As the statute of Magna Charta, ca. 5, willethe that the gardeyn shall repaire thenfantes howses of the issues of the lande. Yf the issues be so smalle that he can not bothe meynteyne the heire & fynde reparacions, he is excused thoughe no reparacion be done. So the same statute, ca. 7, saiethe that the wyffe shall have her quarentyne *nisi domus illa sit castrum*, yet yf so be that he have none other howse but a castle she shall have her quarentyne of that.[181] So upon Marlebridge, ca. 21, that willethe that the beastes distreyned shall be delivered *sine impedimento*, yet yf the beastes be deade that is *impedimentum*. So the statute of Marlebridge, ca. 22, willethe that the lorde shall not sweare his free tenauntes, and yet yf he have none but free tenauntes they shalbe sworne.[182] The seconde case wherein an estatute shalbe taken against the wordes is *vt euitetur iniquum*, for statutes come to stablyshe lawes, & yf anie iniquitye shulde be gathered of them they doe not so muche as deserve the name of lawes.[183] And therfore the statute of 4 [1] E. 4, [ca. 2], that

---

[180][6 Rep. 21ᵛ; 10 Rep. 139ᵛ; Fraunce, *Lawiers Logike*, fol. 13; Allen, *op. cit.*, pp. 384-85.]

[181][Cf. Co. Litt. 31ᵛ, 165; J. H. Round, *Peerage and Pedigree* (London, 1910), I, 113-28.]

[182][M. 39 E. 3, 35, pl. (41); 2 Inst. 143.]

[183]*E* (fol. 16ᵛ): /*Nota*. Lestatute de anno 21 H. 8, ca. 15, que done que toutz termors poient fauxer recoueries ewe vers lour lessours sur faux & feynt titles &c. Vncore T. 26 H. 8, 2, [pl. 3], le parson dun esglise fist lese per [ans] & *quare impedit* fuit port vers le patron & lencumbent & ils pledent feyntement per colucion &c., & teigne la que le termor ne poit fauxer, quar son terme nest bon pluis longe que le parson demeure parson, & sil resigne, le lese vst estre determyne, & per mesme le reson icy, quar appiert per recorde que son volunte fuit a departer oue lesglise.

willeth that the shyreffe shall remove all presentmentes had
before hym before the justices of peace, you muste take it
that it meante all suche presentmentes wherof he mighte
lawfullye houlde plee.¹⁸⁴ So the statute of Gloucester, ca. [3],
dount nul fyne est leuie en courte le roy, is understanded
wherof no fyne ys lawfullye levied in the kinges courte.¹⁸⁵
So the statute of Magna Charta, ca. 30, that confyrmethe
all customes, doethe not confirme ylle customes & such as
coulde not have a reasonable begynnynge. So the statute of
Magna Charta, ca. 7, *nec aliquid det*, ys yet allso true for
thinges due of commen righte she shall & oughte to houlde
charged. So the statute of 4 H. 7, ca. [17], that saiethe the

---

Vncore les parollz sont generall, de toutz termors, sed nota *vt euitetur
iniquum.*/ [Jenk. 200.]
    E (margin): [H.] 35 H. 6, 47, [53, pl. 17; *Select Cases in the Exchequer
Chamber*, pp. 141-43], Fortescue.

¹⁸⁴*E* (margin): M. 4 E. 4, 31, [pl. 12].
    [Staunforde, *Plees del Coron*, fols. 85ᵛ-87ᵛ: '. . . mes cel statute serra
entendue de tielx matters queux le Viscount par le comen ley, ou per ascun
statute, ad poar d'enquirer &c.'; Brooke, *Presentement in courts*, 16: '. . .
car le Statute est intend de tiels choses dont le vicount per le comen
ley ad auctoritye denquere.'; 5 Rep. 112ᵛ: '. . . [act] est entende de loyal
& sufficient presentments en ley, & nemy en presentments que le vicont
ne poit prendre per le common ley.'; Co. Litt. 381ᵛ: '. . . construction
made in suppression of mischiefe and in advancement of the remedie.']

¹⁸⁵[Litt. §731: 'Mes ils ont dit, que le statute serra entend . . . dont vne
loial fine est droiturelment levy en la court le roy.'; Plowd. 57ᵛ: 'Et lestatute
de Gloucester, cap. 3 dit . . . mes le entendement de eux est dont nul fine
est leuy per le baron & feme, car fines poyent este bien leuies per eux,
et tiel ad este le exposition tout temps puis, per lentent del feasors.'; 82ᵛ:
'Et issint lestatute de Gloucester, cap. 3 est . . . vncore si le pere solement
leuy le fine, il [le heire] serra receiue a demaunder le terre encounter ceo
fine, & issint les expositors del ley ount ceo prise, mes ount expounde
lentent del estatute deste, dont nul loyall fine est leuy, cestassauoir, per le
pere & mere. Et issint le efficacy del estatutes nest solement en les parols
del estatutes, mes en lentent del estatutes . . .'; Dav. 75ᵛ; Hatton, *op. cit.*,
pp. 60, 78-79 (statute penal, therefore strictly construed); 9 Rep. 26ᵛ: '. . .
extend solement per construction del ley al proceding sur loyal & sufficient
endictments, & ne fait ascun insufficient indictment bone . . .']

kynge shall have the wardeshippe of the lande wherof there
is no wille declared, ys taken for a lawfull wille & not a
wille by collucion.[186] So the statute of Marlebridge, ca. 6,
that gyvethe that the lordes can not enter upon the [fol. 15ᵛ]
feoffes,[187] yet yf the villen be tenaunt & the lorde gardein
he shall enter upon hym, for els he shulde loose his villen by
bringinge an accion againste hym.[188] And here is also to be
noted that, by generall wordes in a statute, pryvate mens
interestes be not taken awaie, notwithstandinge that which
is commenlye sayde, that everye man ys partie & privie to
an acte of Parlemente.[189] As thestatute of Westminster 2,
ca. 1, that gyvethe the formedon doeth not take awaie the
writte of righte in London.[190] The statute of Westminster 1,
ca. 1, that saieth no man shall enter a howse &c., doeth not
take awaie the custome that they have in London, by which
the constable doethe enter to see bawdrye punyshed.[191]

[186]E (margin): P. 27 H. 8, 9, [pl. 22], Poll[arde].
[Hatton, op. cit., pp. 71-72.]

[187]F: mes auera son breue de garde.

[188][9 Rep. 73: 'Issint sur lestatute de *Marlebridge, Non liceat huiusmodi
feoffatos expellere*, si le villeine del Seigniour soit infeoffe, le Seigniour
expellera luy, car le general ley ne voet faire tort, cestassauoir, a enabler le
villein enconter le Seignior.'; 11 Rep. 77ᵛ: '. . . car les generall parols del
act ne enablera le villein . . .'; 2 Inst. 112: *supra*, p. 27, n. 51.]

[189][*Supra*, pp. 26-28.]

[190]E (margin): T. 8 H. 6, 4, pl. 9.
[See also: P. 19 H. 6, 64, pl. 1, Fortescue: *supra*, p. 20, n. 35, and the
confusion between his words and those of Newton (P. 7 H. 6, 35, pl. 39)
in Dyer 373; Plowd. 59: *supra*, p. 26, n. 49; 1 And. 71: *supra*, p. 24, n. 42;
Crompton, *op. cit.*, fols. 13ᵛ-14: *supra*, p. 30, n. 54; 3 Rep. 35: 'Et quant
al case *4 & 5 Phillip & Mar. Dyer 155* que si terres en Londres, ou terres
sont deuisable per custome, sont tenus *in capite*, vncore tout poit este
deuise: A ceo fuit responde, que ceo ne fuyt per force del statute, mes
pur ceo que les terres fuerunt deuisable per custome deuaunt lestatute, et
lestatute est en laffirmatiue et ne tolle ascun custome.'; *supra*, pp. 39-41.]

[191][For the custom see: M. 2 H. 4, 12, pl. 51; H. 1 H. 7, 6, pl. 3; *Vn
Abridgement de touts les ans del roy Henrie le sept* (London, 1614), fol.

Neither doethe the statute of Marlebridge, ca. 20, take awaye
the iurisdiccions that have conusans of plee.[192] Neither did
the statute[193] that gave thenheritance of the crowne, with
all franchesses & prerogatives, gyve awaie private mens interests.[194] Neither doeth yt annie thinge make againste this
purpose the case that ys commenlye put—that is to saye,
that by graunte of dysmes by convocacion howse he that
had a graunt to be discharged of dysmes shulde, notwithstandinge that, be charged, for in those bookes the statute
wente by expresse wordes, *non obstante aliquo priuilegio,*
to which when the partye said nothinge he semed to yielde,
accordinge to that the Lorde Chauncellour there recytethe
qui tacet consentire videtur.[195] The thirde case *temporis
longinquitate.* For althoughe the force of statutes be suche
that no contynuaunce of tyme can gayne anie prescripcion
against them, as maie appere upon Magna Charta, ca. 30, yet,
notwithstandinge as yt devoureth all thinges, so hathe it in
some poyntes enfeebled the strengthe of our statutes. For

Aiiiᵛ; 8 Rep. 126: 'Sont diuers customes in Londres, que sont encounter
common droit & le rule del common ley, & vncore sont allowe en nostre
liures, & *eo potius* pur ceo que sont auxi support & fortifie per authoritie
de parliament . . . Ils ount custom de enter en la meason dun auter que
est son Castle: & pur ceo le custom de Londres est, que quant vn Chaplein
ou priest ad femme en son mese & chambre, & ascun sur ceo ad male
suspition, que il que ad tiel suspition viendra al constable del garde, ou
bedell, et oue luy poet enter en le mease & Chamber del Chapleine ou
priest & committer loffender al prison.'; 129.]

[192][2 Inst. 138.]

[193][1 H. 7; also 7 H. 4, ca. 2.]

[194]*E* (margin): H. 1 H. 7, [12], pl. 15 [25].
[1 And. 71-72; Crompton, *op. cit.,* fol. 16-16ᵛ.]

[195]*E* (margin): P. 19 H. 6, 62, [pl. 1]; M. 20 H. 6, 12, [pl. 25; *Select Cases
in the Exchequer Chamber*, pp. 84-95]; [M.] 21 E. 4, 44, [pl. 6].
[Plucknett, 'The Lancastrian Constitution,' in *Tudor Studies* (London,
1924), pp. 161-81; *supra*, pp. 18 *et seq.*]

in these it is true that Livie saiethe, that lawes are mortall
as men be, and a lawe that was made in peace may be unmete
in warre, and that which was ordeyned to restreyne & bry-
dell the eville doinges of men shall waxe out of season then
when men have reformed theire manners.[196] And therfore
the statute of Magna Charta had the force of a statute, yea
& althoughe by 40 [42] E. 3, that no authoritie of Parlyament
hereafter to come shulde be of power to take awaie that
statute, yet hathe age, which all can frette & byte, taken it
awaie in many thynges. As the same statute, ca. 3, that willeth
that the lorde shall not have the wardeshippe *antequam
homagium eius acceperit*, yet, notwithstandinge yf at this
daie he shulde take the homage of hym, he shulde be concluded of the wardeshippe.[197] So the same statute, ca. 7 [8],
ita tamen quod se non maritabit &c: this was a lawe that
was made in warre, & in tyme of peace decayed agayne, so
that at this daie nothinge ys more commen then wydowes
to marry [fol. 16] without the assente of theire lordes. So the
statute of Magna Charta, ca. 12, & Westminster 2, ca. 26
[30], that willethe assyses to be taken thryse by the yere,
yet at this daie they are houlden but twyse. So upon Magna

[196][Egerton, *Speech . . . touching the Post-nati*, p. 47: 'Vpon this reason
it is, that some lawes as well Statute Lawe, as common Law, are obsolete
and worne out of vse: for all humane lawes are but *Leges temporis:* And
the wisedome of the Iudges found them to bee vnmeete for the time they
liued in, although very good and necessarie for the time wherein they
were made. And therefore it is saide, *Leges humanae nascuntur, vigent,
& moriuntur, & habent ortum, statum, & occasum.*' The quotation is from
Joachim Hopper, *Sedvardus, sive de vera jurisprudentia* (Antwerp, 1590):
see Huntington Library MS EL. 2755. It is repeated in Calvin's case, 7 Rep.
25; F. Bacon, *The Essayes or Counsels, Ciuill and Morall* (London, 1625),
p. 319: '. . . *penall lawes*, if they haue beene Sleepers of long, or if they be
growne vnfit for the present Time, [should] be by Wise *Iudges*, confined in
the Execution.'; W. M. Graham-Harrison, 'Criticisms of the Statute Book,'
Journal of the Society of Public Teachers of Law, 1935, p. 10; Allen, *op.
cit.*, pp. 393-96.]

[197][2 Inst. 11, 111 (9).]

Charta, ca. 8, the wordes *nos non seisiemus* are voyde, & so upon Magna Charta, ca. 14. So Marlebridge, ca. 2, it hathe not bene sene any accion to have bene broughte upon yt. But yet, notwithstandinge thoughe an estatute have not bene put in use, it loosethe not the force of an estatute.[198] Looke for these matters: Merton, ca. 2 [6]; Marlebridge, ca. 22; Westminster 1, ca. 1 & 22; Gloucester, ca. 8.[199] Another case where statutes shall be taken againste the wordes is where the wordes seme to have escaped idellye & were put in of no purpose of them that were the statute makers. So upon the statute of Marlebridge, ca. 21, this worde *iniuste* seemethe to have crepte in, for, were it iustelie or uniustelie, all is one. And so semeth this worde *recenter* upon the statute of Marlebridge, ca. 28.[200] So upon Westminster 2, ca. 5, the wordes *de vicina parochia* are not of effecte.[201] So upon the same statute, *annuatim* is to no effecte. The statute shall also be taken contrarie to the wordes yf the partie whose

[198]Y.B. 19 Edw. III (Rolls Ser.), p. 170: see Plucknett, '*Execrabilis* in the Common Pleas,' *Cambridge Law Jour.*, I, 64, n. 1; *idem, Statutes*, p. 143; M. 11 H. 4, 8, pl. 20: 'Hankford: Coment que le statute ne fuit my mis en vre vnques enconter le Roy, vncore le statute demurt tout temps en son force.'; M. 11 H. 4, 39, pl. 67: 'Thirning dit, Que en le *Quare impedit* que le Roy port vers Sir R. Westwood [M. 11 H. 4, 7, pl. 20], vn statute fuit plede, que ne fuit mis en vre plusors ans auant, vncore pur ceo que il fuit vn statute fait, & ne fuit vnques repeal il est assets bon.'; P. 4 E. 4, 4, pl. 4: 'Et l'opinion de *Choke, Illingworth & Yelverton* fuit . . . et coment que cel statute icy n'ad pas este mis in vre, ceo ne fait matter, car si sont en les liueres del statutes multes articules, queux ne ont my este mis en vre, mes ceo ne fait matter, car vncore ils sont ley, & poient este execute per chescun home que est greue contrary a eux.'; Crompton, *op. cit.*, fols. 11ᵛ-12 (misnumbered 13); Plucknett, *Concise History*, pp. 301-3; *supra*, p. 119, n. 41.]

[199][For Gloucester, ca. 3, see: *Chester County Court Rolls* (Chetham Soc., 1925), pp. 75-76, and the comments upon it by Plucknett, in *Harvard Law Rev.*, XL, 57, n. 75; *idem*, 'New Light on the Old County Court,' *ibid.*, XLII, 658-61.]

[200][Y.B. 16 Edw. III, 2 (Rolls Ser.), pp. 244-46; 2 Inst. 152 (6).]

[201][2 Inst. 364 (34).]

benefyte lyethe therby will despence therwithall, accordinge
to the sayinge of Westminster 2, ca. [46], *conuentio legi
derogat.*[202] As the statute of Religiosis, yf the partie will he
maie dispence with it. So maie he with the statute of Westminster 3, ca. 1.[203] And those statutes which gave hym a
remedie he maie chose whether he will take it or not. *Com-
modum nemini obtruditur.*[204] And here it myghte aptelie be
shewed howe the kinge shall dispence with statutes, for he
is above his lawes & maie dispence with his lawes. But that
is true in suche thinges that are *mala prohibita,* as for the
caryenge of wolles &c.,[205] for havinge of tennys courtes, for

[202]*E* (margin): P. 11 H. 6, 30 [31, pl. 17], Rolfe.
[See also: 5 Rep. 36ᵛ, 40ᵛ; 10 Rep. 101: 'Quilibet potest renunciare juri
pro se introducto.'; 2 Inst. 183; Co. Litt. 166: '*Modus et conuentio vincunt
legem. Pacto aliquid licitum est, quod sine pacto non admittitur. Quilibet
potest renunciare juri pro se introducto.* But with this limitation that these
rules extend not to any thing, that is against the commonwealth or common right. For *conuentio priuatorum non potest publico juri derogare.*'
For this last see: *Abridgement of the booke of Assises,* fol. 68ᵛ; Clark's
case, 5 Rep. 64: 'Car cest ordinance est encounter lestatute *de Magna Charta
ca. 29. Nullus liber homo imprisonetur:* Quel act ad estre confirme, &
establie oustre *30* foits, & lassent le pleintif ne poit alter le ley en tiel
case.'; 9 Rep. 141ᵛ.]

[203][M. 27 H. 8, 26, pl. 5; 5 Rep. 40ᵛ; 2 Inst. 501 (5).]

[204][M. 47 E. 3, 10, pl. 7: 'Finchden: Ceo action est done per le comen
ley, & coment que le statute done que home recouera greindre damages,
s'il voillet suer per le statute, vncore ceo ne oustra pas home de suer per
breue al comen ley, s'il voile . . .'; P. 9 H. 6, 2, pl. 5; M. 3 E. 4, 27,
pl. 24: 'Genney: . . . mes jeo entende que il poit auer a son eleccion breue
de Det al comen ley, ou autrement le remedy per le statut.'; 5 Rep. 36ᵛ,
40ᵛ: '11 H. 6. 13 [23, pl. 22]: Le court en *Quare impedit* per consent poit
done pluis longe iour que est limitte per lestatute de Marlebridge, [ca. 12];
11 H. 4. [78, pl. 18 (17)]: Lestatute de 2 E. 3, [ca. 8] & 20 E. 3,
[ca. 1] prouide, que neque pur le graund seale, ou petit seale, Justice ne
serra delay; vncore quant le matter concerne le Roy solement, sil com-
maunde ceo, poit estre stay; Fitz. *Nat. Br. 21b.* [210] 27 H. 8: Tenure
poit estre create a cest iour per consent de touts, nient obstant lestatute
de Quia emptores terrarum . . . Et plusors auters cases fueront mys, ou
consent des parties altera le forme et course del ley.']

[205][M. 2 R. 3, 11-12, pl. 26; M. 1 H. 7, 2-3, pl. 2; M. 11 H. 7, 11-12,

bowlinge, or suche lyke. But for suche statutes that have
the force of a lawe & bynde men generallye & everye man
speciallye, as the statutes of *quod ei deforciat*,[206] of collaterall
warranties,[207] &c., that are made, as you woulde saie, for a
commenwealthe, with suche thinges he can not dispence.[208]
The last case where a statute shall be taken againste the wordes
ys there where an absurditye or contrarietye shulde folowe—
for generallie in expoundinge of statutes yt ys gyven in
precepte, *ne quid absurdum, ne quid repugnans aut contrarium
ne quid nugatorium elusoriumue admittatis.*[209] As upon Merton, ca. 7, *siue se voluerit maritare siue non*, you muste take
it ayllours, for yf you shulde take it at the lordes tender it
were absurde. So the statute of Westminster 1, ca. 9, *de
arrester & persuer*, it is taken also *et de amesner*, for els the
statute were to smalle purpose. So upon the [fol. 16ᵛ] same

---

pl. 35: 'Diuersite entre *malum prohibitum & malum per se.* Car *malum prohibitum* est ou le *Statut* prohibite que on ne fera monnoie, & s'il face, que
il sera pendu; ceo est *malum prohibitum*: car deuant le dit *Statut* fuit loyal
acte, faire monnoie, mes or nient: & pur cest mal le Roy poit dispenser.
Issint si on eskippe laine in autre lieu que al *Calice*, ceo est *malum prohibitum*: car est prohibite per *Statute*, & pur cest *malum* le Roy poit
dispenser . . . Mes *malum in se* le Roy ne nul autre poit dispenser. Sicome
Roy veut pardon a occire vn autre, ou luy licence a faire nusance in le
haut-chemin, ceo est void; . . . *Quod Nota per Fineux Chief Justice.*'; Brooke,
Charter de pardon, 76, *Licenses grauntes*, 24, *Recognisans*, 22.]

²⁰⁶[Westminster 2, ca. 4.]

²⁰⁷[Gloucester, ca. 3.]

²⁰⁸[*Infra*, Appendix II; Plowd. 235-238; 7 Rep. 37 (36); 11 Rep. 88;
[Egerton], *Certaine Observations concerning the Office of the Lord Chan-
cellor* (London, 1651), p. 7; Jenk. 307; Birdsall, in *Essays . . . in Honor of
Charles Howard McIlwain*, pp. 37-76; Chrimes, *op. cit.*, pp. 55, 279-83; D. O.
Wagner, 'Coke and the Rise of Economic Liberalism,' *Economic History
Rev.*, VI, 41; *supra*, p. 110, n. 15.]

²⁰⁹[*Speech . . . touching the Post-nati*, p. 100: '. . . and for that, I wil
remember one rule more which is certen and faileth not, and ought to be
obserued in all Interpretation of Lawes; and that is, *Ne quid absurdum,
ne quid illusorium admittatur.*']

estatute [ca. 36], *soient dones xx s.*, it is taken for the oulde
rente, for els were the statute in vayne & to no purpose, for
aide par file marier shulde els be everye daie more uncerten
then other.[210] So upon Westminster 2, ca. 55 [5], the wordes
are *jus non habens praesentandi*, but, yf we woulde turne the
wordes & saie that he that had righte to presente shulde have
possession, yt were but a meere absurditie & cavillacion. And
so is it upon the wordes *arte vel ingenio* upon the statute de
Religiosis.[211] [Fol. 17 blank; fol. 17ᵛ]

[210][2 Inst. 233, 596-597.]

[211][M. 41 E. 3, 21, pl. 8; M. 3 E. 4, 14, pl. 8.]
F: /P. 14 E. 3, [Y.B. 14 Edw. III (Rolls Ser.), p. 123], *Quare impedit*, 53,
lestatute de anno 14 E. 3, [st. 4], ca. 2, de clero./
    Westminster 2, ca. 21, *habeat ille qui dimisit & eius heres &c.* cessauit,
et vncore le heire ne poit suer ceo de cesser en temps son pere [*Vieux*]
Natura Breuium, 138[ᵛ], 141. /P. 6 E. 6, Plowd. 110, Bromley./ [See: 8 Rep.
118; 2 Inst. 402, 460 (13); C. H. McIlwain, *The High Court of Parliament*
(New Haven, 1910), p. 297; Plucknett, *Statutes*, p. 66; *idem*, in *Harvard
Law Rev.*, XL, 35-36; Thorne, in *Law Quart. Rev.*, LIV, 550.]
    Staunf[orde, *Plees del Coron*], 57b: Les justices de assises poient de-
liuer les gaoles sans auter commission per lestatute 27 E. 1, [ca. 3], *de
finibus*, et les parollz sont generall *de prisonibus quibuscunque*, et vncore
pur ceo lour authoritie nextende a deliuerer le gaole de auters forsque
ceux queux fueront pres pur felony &c. ['car sils purroient, donque fuit
lestatute de anno 3 H. 5, stat. 2, cap. 7, fait en vaine . . .'].
    Lestatute de anno 25 E. 3, ca. 16, voet que per lexcepcion de nontenure
de parcell nul breue abatera forsque pur le quantytye de le nontenure
que est alledge. Vncore en *praecipe quod reddat* dun manor pur nontenure de parcell, tout le breue abatera: [P.] 21 E. 4, 25, [pl. 13]. /P. 6 E. 6,
Plowd. 109b, Bromley./ [See also: M. 19 H. 6, 13, pl. 33 (31); 36 H. 6, 6, pl.
3, Prisot; M. 4 E. 4, 32-34, pl. 15; M. 5 H. 7, 7, pl. 16; *Abridgement of the
booke of Assises*, fol. 136ᵛ; Dyer 291, pl. 67; Theloall, *Digest des Briefes*,
fol. 132-132ᵛ, pl. 23; 1 And. 111; Plowd. 205; Hatton, *op. cit.*, pp. 44-45.]
    Lestatute Westminster 1, ca. 42 [43], voet que en accion vers plusiours
jointenauntes ou parceners, ils ne serront essoyne forsque a vn iour ne nient
pluis que vn sole tenaunt, le quel est dentender apres que chescun de eux
ad este vn foitz essoyne aperluy, quar en apres ils ne serront forsque
come vn sole tenaunt, quar clerement chescun auera vn essoyne: [M.]
21 [2] E. 4, 21, [pl. 17].
    Westminster 2, ca. 34, est *vxor si sponte abijerit & moretur &c.* Vncore
P. [T.] 43 E. 3, 19, [pl. 5], feme fuit rauyshe & pres demurre oue le

Ca. 10. Statute Extende al Cases Dont Ne Sont Ascun Parollz &c.

The laste matter to be seene ys to knowe where a statute shall be extended to cases wherof there is no wordes. And it is saide that the statute is expounded by the commen lawe. As the statute of Waste[212] shewethe not what is waste, and therfore upon Magna Charta, ca. 3, in the case of the gardeyn xx d. is adiudged waste, and upon Gloucester, ca. 5, iij s. iiij d. ys a[d]iudged waste. So Gloucester, ca. 4, sheweth not who shall have a *cessauit*, nor againste whome it lyethe, nor what plees or what processe shall be in yt, yet all that

---

rauyshour de bon gree, & pur ceo el perdre sa dower. [*Supra*, p. 137, n. 104.]

Westminster 2, ca. 4, voet *quod si vir reddat tenementum aduersario suo de plano &c.*, que pres le mort le baron le feme auera sa dower, mes ceo ne poet estre entende solonque les parollz, mes doit estre entende lou le baron auoit droit & cesty que recouer nul droit, per Fortescue: [T.] 36 H. 6, *Fauxer de recouery*, 27.

/P. 27 H. 6: Lestatute de Carlyle, anno 35 E. 1 (in Magna Charta, fo. 26 parte 2), voit que lorders de Cystercians & Austens que ount commen seale, que le seale ne serra en garde labbe mes en garde le prior & 4 auters, les pluis sages del meson, & que chescun fait enseale oue le commen seale que nest issint garde serra voyde. Et per curiam cest statute est voide quar est impertinent destre obserue, quar esteant le seale en lour garde, labbe ne poet riens enseailer oue ceo; et quant est en les maynes labbe, il est hors de lour garde *ipso facto*. Et si lestatut serra obserue chescun commen seale serra defete per vn symple surmyse, que ne poit estre trye: *Annuitie*, 41./ [See: 8 Rep. 118; 2 Inst. 587-88; McIlwain, *op. cit.*, pp. 273-77; Plucknett, in *Harvard Law Rev.*, XL, 36-41; Thorne, in *Law Quart. Rev.*, LIV, 551.]

/Westminster 2, ca. 39, sur auerrment de trop petit issues *venire facias* agarde retourne deuant mesme les justices: [T.] 22 E. 3, 20, [pl. 91]./ [See also: H. 2 H. 4, 14, pl. 9; M. 8 H. 6, 12, pl. 30; Jenk. 143.]

Staunf[orde], Pr[erogatiue], 33: Prerogatiua Regis, ca. 8 [10], que voit que *nullum tempus occurrit regi, dum tamen rex presentauerit infra tempus 6 mensium*. Vncore laps non curre vers le roy coment que il ne present deins les 6 moys./ [Plowd. 243; *Table Talk of John Selden*, ed. Sir F. Pollock (Selden Soc., 1927), p. 112.]

[212][20 E. 1.]

ys construed by the commen lawe. And so it is par aide per file marier upon Westminster 2 [1], ca. 35 [36]. This matter is muche in use amonge our readers at this daie, and in maner their whoale readinges consyste in shewinge who shall have the remedie, againste whome, in what courte, & all that geare; where they please themselves muche yf they can plante theire cases in to that square difference that ys lyke a square battelle. As to shewe where the heyre shall be in warde & paie reliefe, where he shall neither be in warde nor paie reliefe, where he shall paie reliefe & not be in warde, where he shall be in warde & not paie reliefe, and where he shall paie twooe relieffes or be twyse in warde. Those cases that hereupon maie be multiplied, althoughe they be infynite whereof there is no knowledge, yet for the mooste parte they consyste of these predicamentes: *Res*, as to shewe the nature of the thinge; *Persona*, who & againste whom; *Locus*, where, in what court, before whome; *Tempus, Quantitas*, and *Qualitas*,[213] & suche, of which, as I have saide, for the mooste parte the readers differences doe stande & consyste. [Fol. 18]

Ca. 11. Provisoes

The provisoes in statutes are the laste parte,[214] and they make a lawe, for in them commenlye the wordes are by

---

[213][Joachim Hopper, 'De Iuris Arte,' in *Tractatus Vniversi Juris* . . . (Venice, 1584), I, 95.]

[214][Bacon, *Reading upon the Statute of Uses*, p. 27: 'The Preamble setteth forth the inconveniences, the Body of the Law giveth the Remedy, and the savings and Provisoes take away the inconveniences of the remedy; for new Laws are like the Apothecaries Druggs, though they remedy the Disease, yet they trouble the body, and therefore they use to correct with Spices, so it is not possible to find a Remedy for any mischiefe in the Common Wealth but it will beget some new mischiefe, and therefore they spice their Lawes with Provisoes to correct and qualifie them.']

A DISCOURSE 173

aucthorytie before sayde. Of these statutes, yf any be to take advauntage, he muste shewe that he is not conteyned wythin the provisoes, yf they be to his disadvantage. As yf the statute be a pardon, & by the provisoes certen are exempte, he muste shewe he ys none of them &c.[215]

---

[215]*F* (margin): P. 34 H. 6, 34, [pl. 1].

F: M. 8 E. 4, 7, [pl. 1]; P. 4 H. 7, 8, [pl. 9].

F: /P. 6 E. 6, Plowd. 105: Si home en pleder puist auaile de lestatute fait per abbe &c. deins an deuant le surrender del meson, accorde al tenore del prouiso en lestatut anno 31 H. 8, ca. [13], il doit mirer que tiel rent est reserue sur ceo & auerre que ceo est launcient rent, quar les parollz del prouiso sont issint, que launcient rent soit reserue. Fulmerstons Case./

Appendixes

APPENDIX I

Nota ou statute sera construe enconte<r les parollz>[1]

Lestatut Westminster 2, ca. 21, est *quod habeat illi qui dimisit & eius here<s &c.> cessauit &c.*, & vncore le heyre ne poit ceo auer de cesser en <temps son> pier &c. *Natura Breuium*, 138, 141; /P. 6 E. 6, Plowden, 110. Bromley./

Vide Staunf[orde, *Plees del Coron*,] 57b: statutum de finibus anno 27 E. 1, [ca. 3], *de prisonibus quibu<scunque>*.

Lestatut Prerogatiua Regis voit ca. 1 que *rex habebit custodiam omnium te<rrarum eorum> qui de ipso tenant in capite per seruicium militare, de quibus ipsi t<enentes> fuerunt seisiti in dominico suo vt de feodo die quo obliierunt <de quocunque> tenuerunt per huiusmodi seruicium &c.* ore si home ad terre de <part sa> pier teigne del roy in capite & auter terre de part sa m<ere teigne del> auter seignior &c. & deuie seisie de tout sans issue per que le te<rre teigne del> roy descende a son heyre de part son pier, qui est deins age, <& auter terre> descende a le heyre de part sa mere, le roy nauera le <garde>.[2]

/Lestatut anno 2 H. 5, [st. 2], ca. 3, est que nul sera iure en enquestez &c. *sil neyet terres ou t<enementz de> 40 s. per an.* Vncore cestui a que vse serra iure &c. M. 15 H. 7, 13, [pl. 1], per Frowycke./

Lestatut Prerogatiua Regis voit ca. 3: *Rex habebit primam sei<sinam post> mortem eorum qui de eo tenent in capite de omnibus terris &c.* <Vncore de terre> teigne de roy in capite per socage tenure le roy nauera primer <seisin>. /De terre tenus dauter: P. 6 E. 6, Plowden, 109. Bromley./

Lestatut 25 E. 3, [st. 5], ca. 16, voit que *per lexcepcion de nontenure de parcel <nul> breue abatera forsque per la quantyty de le nontenure que est <alleage>.* Vncore en *praecipe quod reddat* de maner pur nontenure de parcell <tout le breue

---

[1]Fitzherbert, *Nouuelle Natura Breuium* (London, 1553; colophon, 1560), flyleaf.

[2]M. 12 E. 4, 18, pl. 24; Staunforde, *Exposicion*, 8v; Plowd. 204; Hatton, *op. cit.*, pp. 54-55.

abatera>. [P.] 21 E. 4, 25, [pl. 3], /*Cessauit*, 62. P. 6 E. 6, Plowden, 109. Bromley./

Lestatut De Religiosis voit que primer alienacion en mortmayne *pr*<*oximus*> *dominus intrabit & retinebit in feodo & hereditate*, ore si lese <est fait> pur vie, le remeynder pur vie a estrange, le remeynder en fee <a un auter> si le primer tenaunt pur vie alien en mortmayne, cesty en le re<meynder> pur vie poit enter & vncore non retinebit in feodo mes tan<que> pur terme de sa vie.

Lestatut Westminster 1, ca. 42 [43], voit que diuers joyntenauntes ou parceners en vn accion <ils ne> serroient essoyne *forsque al vn iour ne nient pluis que vn soule tenaun*<*t naueroit*>, sera entende apres que chescun ad estre vn foitz essoyne aperluy quar en a<pres ils ne> serront forsque come vn soule tenaunt quar clerement chescun auera vn <essoyne>. [M.] 2 E. 4, 21, [pl. 17].

Prerogatiua Regis, [ca. 1], recytant que le roy aura le garde de toutz <terres> queux son tenent in chief per seruice de chiualer morust seisie *de quoc*<*unque*> *tenuerit per huiusmodi seruicium* & vncore sil tient de<l roy per auter> seruice come socage ou franke burgage, le roy aura le g<arde> cybien si fuit teigne per seruice de chiualer. 9 H. 3; [P.] 24 E. 3, [24].

Westminster 2 [3], ca. 2, voit que si seigniour & tenaunt sont & le tenaunt fist feffement <dun> parcell de le tenauncy que le feffee tiendra del chief seigniour <*per particula*> *illa secundum quantitatem terre &c.* et ceo est de e<ste . . .> solonque la value del terre & nemy del quantytye pe<r . . .>. [P.] 12 E. 4, 11, [pl. 29]. Lytleton.

Prerogatiua Regis, ca. 1 *per huiusmodi seruicium* vncore tenure en so<cage . . .>.

APPENDIX II

Quant roy sera lye per statute[1]

<Le roy> sera lye per lestatut Westminster 2, ca. 1. Le seigniour Berclayes case.[2]

<Westminster 2,> ca. 5, ne lye le roy quar 6 moys nencurre vers le roy.

<Le roy nest lye> quant lestatut est generall & al temps de fesans de ceo le <roy aura> droit ou prerogatyue; il nest lye sil ne soit speciallment <nosme> come Magna Charta, ca. 11 [12], *communia placita non sequantur curiam nostram* <ne l>ye le roy. Issint lestatut de priorityes [Westminster 2, ca. 16]; issint Westminster 3 [ca. 1], de <ter>res; issint Marlebridge, ca. [4], de destresses hors de son fee. <Mes> ou le ley est speciall, & le roy naura droit ne prerogatiue a<pres> de fesans il serra lye, come Magna Charta, ca. 3, si tenant <in capite> en garde del roy soit fait chiualer durant son nonage il serra <hors de> garde & issint fuit aiudge en Sir H. [J.] Ratclyffe case.[3]

Issint si soit enacte que J. S. auera le manor de D. & tiendra <. . .> nulluy, pur ceo il enioyera le manor & ne tiendra del roy ne <. . .> nul auter. (en le conties de Oxford case).

<Et> fuit touche que le roy nest lye per lestatut de Westminster 3, mes il poit chaunger les seruices de son tenaunt. T. 10 H. 7, 23, [pl. 26].

Lestatut de anno 1 H. 5, [ca. 5], de addicions doit estre obserue cybien en enditementes <come en> accions per le roy ou proces dutlarye gist, come en case de commen <per>son; mes lestatut 15 H. 6, ca. 3, que voet *que en toutes saffeconductes les nosmes de les nieffes & de les maisters & le number des marynours ouesque le portage serront expressez*, ne lyera le roy, mes il poit graunter saffeconductes sans expresser ces matters, quar lestatut est en laffirmatyue & pur ceo le roy ad eleccion de ob-

[1]Fitzherbert, *Nouuelle Natura Breuium*, flyleaf.
[2]Plowd. 223 (3 Eliz.).
[3]Plowd. 267v (6 Eliz.).

seruer lun fourme ou lauter. Mes auterment serra si lestatut fuit en le negatyue. Et auxi cel estatut nextende forsque [a] le roy mesme & nul auter est preiudice per ceo, pur que il est a libertie de persuer lestatut ou auterment de persuer son prerogatiue, mes lestatut de addicions trenche al chescun commen person. [P.] 5 E. 4, Long Quinto, 33.[4]

Il est commen diuersitye quant statut est fait que restreyne le libertie de toutz gentz vncore le roy nest lye sil ne soit nosme per speciall nosme en lestatut come per lestatut Westminster 3 <toutz g>entes sont lyes forsque le roy, mes quant statut est beneficiall pur le roy <le roy poit> auaile de ceo coment que nest nosme en lestatut, quar auterment serra entendu que <le> roy ne voudroit auer assent a ceo, Mordaunt, T. 12 H. 7, 20, [pl. 1] & 21 <contra> per Frowycke. Et M. 13 H. 7, 7, [pl. 3], Wood: le roy nest nosme en lestatut de Merton, ca. 6, <que done> double value de mariage, ne en Marlebridge, ca. 6 de feffementes per collucion, <vncore> il aura benefyte de eux. Auxi le roy auera *quare impedit* apres <les 6> moyes, coment que nul mencion ne forprise soit fait de luy en lestatut <de> Westminster 2 (nota cest statut restreyne libertye de presentacions). *Ibidem*, fo. 8, Rede: <ont> plusiours statutes que done accions populer, & que le partie que sue aura lun moity <& le> roy lauter moitye, vncore le roy poit auer laccion luy mesme sil veut & donques il <auera> lentier forfette, come *decies tantum*, fourger de faux faitz, accion <de m>eintenaunce, &c. & vncore il nad ceo per les parollz de lestatut. Et fo. 11, [pl. 12] <. . .> de accions populer.

<Le roy> seisie dun reuercion ne serra resceiue sur defaut de tenaunt pur vie <Westminster 2, ca.> 3. [M.] 25 E. 3, 48 [91, pl. 1]. Nota parollz destatut *illi ad quos spectat &c.*

---

[4]Chrimes, *op. cit.*, pp. 261-62.

APPENDIX III

Vide quant statute donera remedye pur chose comensant en apres &c.[1]

Diuersity est pris per ascuns quant le premier statute vae per specyall parollz, que donques ne sera remedy &c., mes quant vae en generalty auterment. Come lestatut de Gloucester, [ca. 5], que done accion de wast vers lesse per ans, vncore ceo ne prouyde pur tenaunt per statute merchant ou staple que fueront dones apres per [Statutum de Mercatoribus etc.] pur ceo que ne forsque de lessee per ans per specyall parollz.

Mes quant vae en generalty auterment, come le dit statut de Gloucester, [ca. 11], que done que termor sera resceue a defender lour droit sur defaut cestui en le reuercion, & per lequity de ceo les tenauntz per statut merchant &c. serront auxi resceyues, quar termor est generall paroll & tenaunt per statut merchant est termor.

Vncore enconter cest diuersity nota lestatut 9 E. 3, [st. 1], ca. [3], done que en accion vers executours celui que primes vient respondera, & per lequytye de ceo issint est dadmynystratours queux fueront faitz per 31 E. 3, [st. 1], ca. [11]. Issint lestatut Gloucester, [ca. 3], done que si tenaunt per le curtesy alien oue garranty & assets descende a le heyre quil sera barre, & per lequytye de ceo si tenaunt en tayle que fuit create puis per lestatut Westminster 2, [ca. 1], vst alien oue garranty & assets descende a son heyre il sera auxi barre. [H.] 14 H. 4, 28, [pl. 37]; [M.] 21 E. 3, 28, [pl. 4]. Issint lestatut Westminster 2, ca. 4, done *quod ei deforciat* sur recouery per defaut, & per lequyty de ceo sur recouery per defaut en *cessauit* que fuit done puis per Westminster 2, ca. 21. Fitz[herbert, *Natura Breuium*], 156A, H. 5 E. 3; M. 6 E. 3, [35, pl. 27].

[1]Littleton, *Tenures* (London, 1557), flyleaf.

Indexes

INDEX STATUTORUM

185

INDEX

Account, 16, 17n, 25n, 111, 128n, 150n, 158
Actions popular, 180
Addition, 130, 131, 179-80
Adjudication, and legislation, 9n, 103n
Admeasurement of pasture, 18n
Administrators, 44, 55n, 143n, 148n, 140n, 159n, 181
Advowsons, 17n, 127
Age: see Infants
Aid par file marier, 145, 170, 172
Allegiance, 104
Allen, C. K., 9n, 50n, 68n, 92n
Amercement, 37, 120
Ancient demesne, not bound by some statutes, 13, 15-16, 18-27, 28; court of, 17, 18, 111n; King's courts and, 16-18, 18n, 31n; and acts of Parliament, 19-32, 39n, 40, 51-52, 110, 111n; taxation of, 111; not at common law, 21-22, 28; bound by express statutes, 19-20, 22, 25-26, 32, 111, 111n; bound by general statutes, 23-26, 28-30, 32, 32n, 40, 111; 'excepted out' of statutes, 13, 15, 22, 27-31, 31n, 35
Appeal, 37n, 135, 150n, 155
Aquinas, St. Thomas, 36n, 78n
Arbitration, 128n
Aristotle, 55, 78n, 118n, 141n
Ashe, Thomas, 79-80
Assizes, 16, 37, 70n, 106, 107, 108n, 112n, 114, 121, 132, 139n, 144, 150, 150n, 154, 157, 166; in K. B., 41n
Attaint, 112, 134, 152n
Austin, John, 59

Bereford, Sir Wm. (C. J., C. P.), 12n, 42, 45; and *De donis*, 9n, 42n
Bishop of Chichester's case, 106-108
Blackstone, Sir Wm., 67, 74n, 91
Blackwood, Adam, 98, 107n

Bonham's case, 71n, 79n, 85*ff*
Brooke, Sir Robt., 10, 23, 26, 30, 31, 39, 52n
Calvin's case, 97n, 98n, 166n
Canon law, statutes in, 36, 46n, 47n, 48n, 58n, 78, 129n
Capias, 52n, 118n, 149n
Castle guard, 118
Casus omissi, 9, 45, 58-59, 67; see also Statutes
Cessavit, 76n, 87n, 88n, 90n, 112n, 149n, 154n, 170n, 171, 177, 181
Chester, not bound by some statutes, 23n
Chrimes, S. B., 5n, 8n, 9n, 15n, 26n, 31n, 39n, 45n, 50n, 68n, 69n, 74n, 79n, 113n
Cinque Ports, not bound by some statutes, 23n; in Parliament, 109, 113
Coke, Sir Edw., 36, 39, 40, 45n, 51n, 64, 68n, 74n, 85*ff*., 99n, 105n-106n, 152n, 156n
Common law, rules of, and statutes, 9-10, 17, 21, 45, 47n, 52, 141-42, 143; technique of the, 4, 12-13, 36, 47-48n, 57, 58n, 61; supplemented by statute, 9, 143; 159n; superseded by statute, 40; equity of the, 48n; as inheritance of the subject, 49n; statutes bind all at, 20-21; statutes in derogation of: see Statutes; ancient demesne not at, 21-22, 28; London not at, 20n
Commons, 6, 90n, 105, 106, 106n, 113
Concio, Giacomo, 96
Conspiracy, 18n
Contemporanea expositio, 59, 139n, 152, 152n, 153n; see also Statutes, have been put in ure
Contempt, 104n
Convocation, 109, 110, 165
Copulatives and disjunctives, 136-40

189